'Lawrence and his bodyguard at Akaba. Summer, 1918.'

Images of
Lawrence

Images of Lawrence

Stephen E. Tabachnick

and

Christopher Matheson

JONATHAN CAPE
THIRTY-TWO BEDFORD SQUARE LONDON

Published by Jonathon Cape Limited,
32 Bedford Square, London WC1B 3EL.

First published 1988

A CIP Catalogue record for this book is available from the British Library.

ISBN 0-224-02556-2

Images of Lawrence was conceived by Thames Head Limited, a division of BLA Publishing Limited,
East Grinstead, Sussex, England.

A member of the **Ling Kee** Group

LONDON HONG KONG TAIPEI SINGAPORE NEW YORK

Design: *Helen Townson*
Editors: *Gill Davis*
        Dr. Wendy Madgwick

Phototypeset in Britain by BLA Publishing Limited/Composing Operations
Origination by Planway Limited
Printed and bound in Portugal

Contents

To Karla and Kim who were both there. C.A.M.

To Sharon, Daphne and Orrin. S.E.T.

Preface

One hundred years after his birth, T.E. Lawrence remains one of the most charismatic and ambiguous figures of our century. He has inspired over thirty biographies and countless radio, television and journal features in which he has been in turn idolized and exposed, and still the public fascination is undiminished. Lawrence owed his initial celebrity to probably the first, and certainly one of the most successful, of twentieth-century public relations campaigns, but the worldwide interest in Lawrence today cannot be attributed solely to Lowell Thomas's extraordinary touring slide show of the early twenties.

The first two parts of *Images of Lawrence* attempt to account for Lawrence's great and continuing popular appeal. Part I provides a straightforward factual history of his life as we now know it and reveals that he was indeed unique. Part II explores the development of the Lawrence myth (primarily in books, but also in theatre, film and television interpretations) from 1924 to the end of 1987. It shows how biographers have been influenced by their times as well as by the facts they have discovered, and what each generation has found most interesting about Lawrence.

Lawrence was not merely an intriguing personality. He was a brilliant polymath who did more things well than almost anyone else of his period. It is his work, rather than his life, that receives attention in Part III on the basis of documented evidence and expert opinion. During the past twenty years, researchers in many countries have come to realize that whatever Lawrence's personal quirks and vagaries, he has deeply influenced our view of the past, of warfare, and of the Middle East. Moreover, his mechanical work was extremely innovative; and in *Seven Pillars of Wisdom* he demonstrated just how good a literary self-portrait can be. This multi-faceted achievement is likely to prove a permanent aspect of his fame.

The photographs in *Images of Lawrence* (many of them published for the first time) are from a lifelong collection made by Christopher Matheson, who has captioned them with some revealing anecdotes about their origins and in some cases with notes on their misrepresentation in other publications.

For the reader's convenience, page references for quotations from the most frequently cited of Lawrence's works are given in parentheses in the text and are accompanied by the following abbreviations indicating editions used. Other sources are listed in the notes and bibliography at the end of the book.

CC Crusader Castles. London: Michael Haag, 1986.
HL M.R. Lawrence, ed. *The Home Letters of T.E. Lawrence and His Brothers*. Oxford: Basil Blackwell, 1954.

L David Garnett, ed. *The Letters of T.E. Lawrence.* London: Jonathan Cape, 1938.
M The Mint. London: Jonathan Cape, 1973.
SP Seven Pillars of Wisdom. London: Jonathan Cape, 1939–73; Harmondsworth: Penguin (in association with Cape), 1962–87. These editions have been chosen because they have had the largest circulation in the English-speaking world and are identical in page layout and extent (although there are some minor typographical differences and the 1973 Cape edition includes some amendments not found in the Penguin). Cape has a differently-paginated hardcover edition in print in England at present. The Penguin paperback edition of *Seven Pillars* is in circulation both in the United States and England today.

Unpublished written material is reproduced with the permission of the Harry Ransom Humanities Research Center of the University of Texas and the T.E. Lawrence Letters Trust. Sources are credited in the Chronological List of Photographs.

Christopher Matheson would like to acknowledge with grateful thanks assistance from Malcolm Brown, Julia Cave, Philip O'Brien, Jennie Rathbun, Betsy Roeth, the *Seven Pillars of Wisdom* Trust, Roger Sheppard, Donald Wilhelm and Jeremy Wilson. Stephen Tabachnick wishes to thank his wife Sharon of the Tennessee Technological University Library for advice and editing, and her colleagues, particularly Linda Mulder, for their selfless help with this book. He also acknowledges with many thanks information from Jillian Bryant, Andrew Carvely, Kevin Desmond, John McKinley, Edwards Metcalf, Philip O'Brien, C.C. Pearson, Jacob Rosen and Tom Watson.

February 1988　　　　　　　　　　　　　　　　　　　　　　　　　S.E.T. and C.M.

In 1920 Lawrence hazarded about this photograph: 'I think Goslett took it, outside his tent at Akaba one day when I hadn't got my cloak on.'

PART ONE

T.E. Lawrence:
The Man Behind the Mask

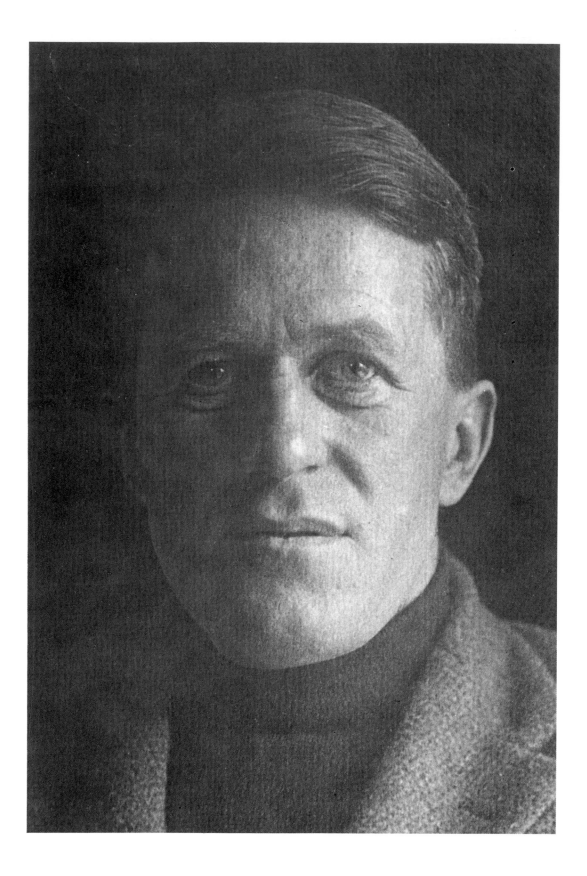

T.E. Lawrence:
The Man Behind the Mask

T.E. Lawrence was one of five sons of parents who never married. His father was an Anglo-Irish aristocrat named Thomas Chapman, once lord of a substantial house near Delvin in County Westmeath. Sarah 'Lawrence', his mother, was of English parentage, but had been brought up by an aunt in Scotland and then served as the governess to Thomas and Edith Chapman's four daughters. Thomas, who was unhappy with his wife, brightened up considerably when Sarah appeared and it was not long before she left the family's service and, with his support, took rooms in Dublin. Their first child, Montague Robert, was born there in 1885 while Thomas was still living with Edith. Their secret was disclosed when the Chapman family butler overheard the former governess call herself 'Sarah Chapman' in a Dublin grocery and followed her home.

Because Edith Chapman refused to grant her husband a divorce, Thomas and Sarah never married. They moved to the village of Tremadoc in North Wales and assumed the name of Lawrence. There, on 16 August 1888, Thomas Edward was born, but within a year they left for Kirkudbright in Scotland, where a third son, William, arrived in 1889. The search for a permanent home continued with spells at Dinard in northern France and at St Helier in Jersey. Meanwhile, their fourth child, Frank, was born in 1893. Finally they arrived in Oxford in 1896, where in 1900 Sarah gave birth to Arnold Walter. On her boys' birth certificates, Sarah sometimes used the maiden names of Maden or Junner for she herself had been illegitimate. The couple kept their unmarried status secret to avoid ostracism and decided to start a new life in Oxford.

Unquestionably the match weakened Thomas Lawrence's social standing. Formerly a sportsman, drinker and lord of a manor, he became a quiet teetotaler confined to an ordinary house in Polstead Road. Sarah, however, assumed a commanding role in the respectable middle-class household. Thomas continued to boat, bicycle, photograph and shoot, and taught his boys how to do these things well. He would visit his Irish estates once or twice a year to collect a small revenue. Although far less wealthy than he had been in Ireland, he was never forced to seek employment in England. He was a kind and shy man, so it was left to Sarah to assume the major role in disciplining the boys, sometimes with a birch. She insisted on regular, strict Evangelistic church attendance, but never revealed her guilty secret to anyone, taking refuge in the notion taught to her by her religious aunt that 'God hates the sin but loves the sinner'.

Portrait of Lawrence by Sims, 1935.

In the spring of 1894 the Lawrences returned to England and resided at Langley Lodge, Langley, Hampshire before moving to Oxford. This photograph, probably dating from 1895, shows the four Lawrence brothers with their mother in the doorway at Langley Lodge. Thomas Edward sits on the left.

It is possible to see in this unusual match the cause of Lawrence's fear of disruptive sexual passion and of all that could arise from it. He never married or felt fully at ease with women. Yet this may well be too easy an explanation of Lawrence's psychology; his youngest brother, Arnold, was happily married and pursued a more usual, if distinguished, life as a professor of archaeology.

From Lawrence's later letters, especially those to his close friend Mrs Charlotte Shaw, it is clear that he loved his mother but felt threatened by the strong will which had tamed his father and older brother; even close to the time of his death he was not eager to live near her. In adulthood he rejected her religious teaching (extreme enough to take her and his older brother Montague to China as missionaries in the 1920s and 1930s). But his knowledge of the Holy Land originally derived from Sunday school lessons. He preferred his easygoing father, but never respected him as much as he later did his mentors David George Hogarth, General Edmund Allenby and Air Marshal Hugh Trenchard. However, the marksmanship he learned from his father was useful in his career as a soldier; early photographic knowledge proved valuable during the Carchemish and Arabian episodes; and boating was something to which he returned toward the end of his years in the RAF. Most of all, his father bequeathed to him a casual attitude toward money which probably caused in him a certain vagueness about figures as well as an unusual generosity.

The knowledge of his illegitimacy (which he may have gained at the age of ten but more likely at seventeen when it appears he ran away to join the army and was bought out by his father) made him doubt authority and established customs. This was to prove helpful intellectually. He remained curious about the Chapman family and somewhat resentful that they never wanted formally to recognize him and his brothers. It seems he never met any of his four half-sisters who (like him) died unmarried, but they were ready to acknowledge, at least in conversation, their connection with the famous 'Lawrence of Arabia'.

Lawrence's youth appears happy apart from the shadow of illegitimacy; for fear of its discovery his parents kept the boys isolated from friends. The Lawrence brothers were largely, if not completely, their own society. Thomas Edward scorned school sports at the Oxford High School for Boys, which he attended from 1896 to 1907. School bored him, but he spent many hours exploring the archaeological remains around Oxford and rubbing brasses in nearby churches. He enjoyed various midnight pranks, firing a pistol with blanks into relatively quiet Oxford streets, searching out the underground drain system's passageways, and taking long bicycle trips with his father. Like many boys, he had his share of school fights, in one of which he broke his leg. Above all, he loved reading the medieval fantasies of Sir Thomas Malory and William Morris as well as the lyrics of the French Provençal poets, Shelley and the pre-Raphaelites. He also enjoyed accounts of military campaigns and Layard's Nineveh discoveries.

In 1908 Lawrence's volunteer work tidying up display cases at Oxford's Ashmolean Museum brought him to the attention of D.G. Hogarth, who was not only keeper of the museum and a highly esteemed archaeologist, but also an associate of the British Intelligence establishment. During Lawrence's years at Jesus College, Oxford, which

The Lawrence brothers photographed in Oxford by Gillman & Company in about 1898, T.E.L. on the left with his brothers Frank, Bob and Will. By this time Lawrence was attending the High School and a friend later wrote, 'His eccentricity seemed too pronounced. Or was it that he always wore a mask, the outer covering of which was at school irreverently termed by us his "grin"?'

lasted from 1907 until 1910, Hogarth directed him to the study of Arabic and the Middle East and took a special interest in him. In a small cottage of his own behind the family home, Lawrence indulged in the dreams and studies that were to result in a finely-tuned and aspiring intellect.

Lawrence soon combined his Middle-Eastern interests with his specialization in the history of the Middle Ages. In the summers of 1906, 1907 and 1908 he bicycled through France in order to study the medieval art of castle building. In 1909 Lawrence spent his summer walking a total of eleven hundred miles to the sites of thirty-six Crusader castles in what are now Lebanon, Syria and Israel in order to discover whether the Crusaders had been influenced by Eastern building styles or if they had brought their designs with them from the West, particularly France.

This photograph was taken by Lawrence in July 1907 before he left the High School in Oxford for a place at Jesus College. He worked the shutter with a length of rubber tubing and a bicycle pump which he had up his jacket sleeve. In the back row behind the Headmaster, A.W. Cave, is Lawrence's younger brother Will, then C.F.C. Beeson (Lawrence's friend), and (far right) Lawrence.

It was scarcely a conventional approach to thesis research, for the Middle East then, as now, was a dangerous place to venture alone, and the summer heat was devastating. The Arabian traveller Charles Doughty, with whom Hogarth had put Lawrence in touch several months before the trip, had warned the young man against the journey and had not exaggerated the hardships, but Lawrence, as always, was keen to test himself physically. He wrote to his mother on 22 September 1909, just before he left Aleppo in Syria for home, that his feet were 'all over cuts & chafes and blisters', that he had contracted malaria for a fourth time, that the temperature was 106 degrees in the shade and that his camera had been stolen (*HL*, p.108). Almost as if he were looking forward to his future position between the two cultures, he wrote: 'I will have such difficulties becoming English again: here I am Arab in habits, and slip in talking from English to French and Arabic unnoticing ...' (*L*, p.77).

Lawrence returned to Oxford confident of his physical stamina, intrigued by the Middle East and enormously enriched intellectually. The result was a BA thesis, 'The Influence of the Crusades on European Military Architecture to the End of the Twelfth Century', that won him first-class honours. Published in 1936 and again in 1986 under the title *Crusader Castles*, this account, although now outdated in some respects, proved a remarkably astute pioneering work in what was then a new field and it continues to be cited respectfully by architectural scholars.

On the grounds of this strong academic performance, Lawrence was given a 'demyship' (or small postgraduate scholarship) for the dig that Hogarth was conducting at Jerablus, the site of the ancient Hittite Viceregal city of Carchemish, on the Euphrates in Syria. Lawrence later described his Carchemish period, lasting from 1911 until 1914, as the

In October 1908 Lawrence joined the Oxford University Officers' Training Corps. He was a member of the signal detachment which operated on bicycles and he camped with them in the spring of 1909 and 1910. This photograph probably dates from one of those camps at Tidworth Pinnings, Wiltshire. Lawrence is in the front row (left) while the future Oxford publisher, Basil Blackwell, is in the back row (left). The semaphore signal reads 'O.U.V.' which undoubtedly stands for 'Oxford University Volunteers'.

best of his life. Under the guidance of Hogarth and C. Leonard Woolley, Lawrence performed odd jobs including photographing finds, rigging up simple machines, and caring for delicate pieces. He helped supervise the native workers (learning colloquial Arabic in the process) and enjoyed a somewhat antagonistic relationship with the German engineers building a bridge for the Berlin-to-Baghdad railway nearby. In high spirits he wrote to his brothers on 28 July 1912 that he had caught 'such a glorious spider; he is about four inches long in the body, hairy to the point of ugliness, with teeth and horns like a rhinoceros ... a beauty if ever there was one ...' (*HL*, p.226).

In this letter, he also mentions an Arab youth nicknamed Dahoum, with whom he was studying Arabic, 'who is cheaper than local labour, and who can cook and wait very well'. In the company of Dahoum, who is widely thought to be the 'S.A.' or Salim Achmed of the dedicatory poem in *Seven Pillars of Wisdom*, he made long journeys. In July 1913 he brought Dahoum and the workers' foreman, Hamoudi, home to Oxford with him. He delighted in the attention they drew as they bicycled in their skirts, while they rejoiced in the English abundance of trees and water. The very fact that this visit occurred proves not only Lawrence's friendship for both men, but an openness to cross-cultural experience unusual for his period.

In January 1914 Lawrence and Woolley met Captain Stewart Newcombe of the Royal Engineers at Beersheba for a survey of the northern Sinai desert. This expedition, which was ostensibly supported by the Palestine Exploration Fund as a study of the Israelite, Nabataean and Byzantine ruins in the area, was in reality a spying mission. In the course of it, the team mapped and studied the Turkish military infrastructure on the border of Ottoman Palestine and British Egypt only one hundred miles from the Suez Canal. The information gathered would prove useful later for the British assaults on Palestine during the First World War; Beersheba itself was to be the first town captured by General Allenby. During the course of this trip Lawrence and Dahoum evaded the Turkish police and improvised a raft on which they visited Jezirat Faroun, sometimes known as Coral Island, seven miles south of Akaba in the Red Sea.

Despite the military requirements of the survey and the speed with which it was conducted, it resulted in a serious archaeological study co-authored by Lawrence and Woolley which was published in 1915. Archaeologists today accept many of their findings in *The Wilderness of Zin*, including their plan of the city of Subeita (or Shivta) and their location of the Biblical Kadesh Barnea (where the Hebrews sojourned before entering Canaan).

When the war broke out in August 1914, Lawrence was in Oxford. With Hogarth's recommendation, he quickly found a job in the Geographical Section of the General Staff at the War Office, where he made maps of Sinai from the sketches of his Zin survey and worked feverishly to finish *The Wilderness of Zin*. Lord Kitchener himself wanted the book published as a cover to mislead the Turks about the team's spying activity. Lawrence performed so well that by December 1914 he had been transferred to the map section of Military Intelligence in Cairo. At first it was like old times: he served with Woolley and reported to Stewart Newcombe.

Until October 1916, Lawrence produced maps of the Middle East, interrogated Turkish and Arab prisoners and helped compile a handbook on the Turkish army. He was also sent on missions to the Western Desert where a rebellion of the Senussi tribes was giving the British considerable trouble, and to Kut in Mesopotamia (now Iraq) where an entire British army under General Townshend was surrounded and being slowly strangled by the Turks. The role of Lawrence and Aubrey Herbert (a member of Parliament who was also an expert on the Ottomans) was to offer Khalil Pasha, the Turkish commander, at first one and then two million pounds sterling to let Townshend's force go. The mission failed, but Lawrence reported the bungling and inefficiency of the Mesopotamian operations and was never forgiven for this by those responsible. He also saw at first hand that the Turkish commander did not trust the Arabs serving in his army, an observation that lent support to the idea of an Arab revolt against the Turks.

To many orthodox officers, Lawrence must have seemed a strange choice for this difficult mission. In April 1916 he was only 27 years old and a captain; furthermore, he was extremely sloppy in his dress, loved to go out of his way to irritate those military superiors whom he thought pompous or foolish, and did not hesitate to flaunt regulations.

However, his ability was apparent to his highly capable companions in the Arab Bureau, the special section that had been set up within Cairo Intelligence under Hogarth to monitor and co-ordinate covert activities in the Arab sphere. Lawrence managed to manoeuvre an unofficial transfer here from the map section in June 1916. Among those in the Bureau were Aubrey Herbert, Philip Graves, Kinnahan Cornwallis, George Lloyd and, for a time, the archaeologist and traveller Gertrude Bell, who had recognized Lawrence's potential when she had visited him at Carchemish.

Lawrence was immediately assigned the task of editing the *Arab Bulletin*, the Bureau's confidential intelligence newsletter to which he contributed a piece supporting the idea of a revolt by Sherif Hussein of Mecca against the Turks. Early in 1914, the Sherif's son, Abdulla, had sounded out Kitchener, then Consul-General of Egypt, and Ronald Storrs, his Oriental Secretary, about the possibilities of British support for a revolt and had received a negative reply. Britain and Turkey were not then at war. By 10 June 1916, however, when the Sherif publicly declared a revolution against the Turks and seized the holy city of Mecca, the British, although taken somewhat by surprise, were more than ready to offer aid against the Turkish enemy. The primary consideration was that the Sherif's revolt would defuse any possible call to holy war that the Turks could proclaim, since the Sherif was the guardian of the most important sites in Islam and was siding with the British. Muslim opinion in India and elsewhere would be placated.

When Frank and Will Lawrence were killed in France in 1915, T.E. wrote to a friend that 'it doesn't seem right, somehow, that I should go on living peacefully in Cairo'. Lawrence's chance for active service came on 13 October 1916 when he joined Ronald Storrs for a trip to Jidda to assess the needs and prospects of the Sherif's revolt. He decided that of the Sherif's four sons — Feisal, Abdulla, Zeid and Ali — only Feisal appeared to have the necessary energy and charisma to lead the uprising. Lawrence also concluded that no British or French assistance would be needed except for a small force of advisors and naval supply aid. The report, made upon his return to Cairo, angered the French representative Colonel Édouard Brémond, who wanted the operation to come under the control of the Allies, thus leaving France ultimately in charge of Syria after the war. On the other hand, it pleased Lawrence's superiors, including the Chief of Staff, Sir Archibald Murray, who was reluctant to spare troops for this distant and seemingly unimportant theatre. Suddenly the irritating Lawrence had become popular around headquarters, and just as suddenly, he was told by Colonel Gilbert Clayton, the Director of Military Intelligence, that he must return to advise Feisal himself.

At this point, the adventures for which Lawrence remains famous began to take place. Living and riding like a bedouin and assisted by a good deal of British gold, the supply ships of the Royal Navy and a support team of British and French advisors, he developed appropriate guerrilla tactics for the military situation in the Hejaz. Using the bedouin for quick strikes against the Hejaz Railway line and its protective Turkish outposts, he perfected a strategy that would render useless the large Turkish force ensconced in Medina and allow control of the countryside itself to fall into the hands of Arab forces. Later, military strategists around the world would acknowledge that Lawrence's guerrilla theory was innovative and influential.

The triumph of what Liddell Hart would one day call Lawrence's 'indirect' method came in the capture of Akaba in June 1917. Although the British Navy had in the past captured this seaport at the northern end of the Red Sea, the Turks continued to control the heights above the town, making a prolonged British presence there impossible. The Turks soon returned. Lawrence developed a plan in concert with Sherif Nasir and Auda abu Tayi, the Arab leaders of the expedition, which involved a long desert march to the east and north of Akaba and resulted in the capture of all Turkish outposts in the surrounding mountains. Thus they secured permanent Anglo-Arab control of the port.

In June 1917 during this march, Lawrence made a secret sortie behind Turkish lines as far north as Baalbek and Damascus with one or two bedouin companions. Although the exact details of the expedition remain unclear, it appears that he assessed Syrian support for Feisal and the Revolt's military prospects for success, and prepared the ground for

An undated photograph which probably shows Lawrence at the base camp at Akaba between July 1917 and August 1918. He wrote home on 8 March 1918 that 'They have now given me a D.S.O. It's a pity that all this good stuff is not sent to someone who could use it!'

Colonel Lawrence at the Paris Peace Conference, 1919, photographed by Harris & Ewing of Washington, D.C. James T. Shotwell of the American Delegation wrote: 'Colonel Lawrence ... with his boyish face and almost constant smile — the most winning figure, so every one says, at the whole Peace Conference.'

Feisal's eventual government in Damascus. Throughout the Revolt Lawrence was involved in numerous undercover activities and continued to suppply confidential reports to his superiors in the Arab Bureau. Much of this material has yet to come to light. Lawrence gave little away publicly about his intelligence activities but he was awarded the Companion of the Bath for the Syrian journey, and even received praise for it from the War Cabinet in London.

After Akaba, the Arab forces became the right wing of General Edmund Allenby's army in Palestine. To mislead the Turks, Allenby employed a clever stratagem devised by Colonel Richard Meinertzhagen, who had formerly been intelligence chief in the war against the German guerrilla leader Paul E. von Lettow-Vorbeck in East Africa. Meinertzhagen 'lost' a false set of plans indicating that Allenby's first attack would come at Gaza instead of at Beersheba. The Turks moved their main force to Gaza and the Australian Light Horse broke through the Turkish line at Beersheba on 31 October 1917 in one of history's last great cavalry charges. Lawrence may have learned something about devious guerrilla tactics from Meinertzhagen himself and from his accounts of von Lettow-Vorbeck, who remained undefeated at the end of the war. Lawrence now became the chief liaison officer between Feisal and Allenby. He concentrated on distributing propaganda among the bedouin tribes and co-ordinating Arab harassment of the Turks with British military strikes. The small regular Arab army (as opposed to bedouin raiding parties) extended its reach and came to the forefront when Allenby provided one thousand extra camels.

As the Revolt gained momentum in parallel with Allenby's victories in Palestine, Lawrence was captured by the Turks in the town of Deraa, where he had gone in Arab disguise for a reconnaissance. What happened to him there has never been satisfactorily established. The account he gives in *Seven Pillars of Wisdom* is deliberately vague; important details are glossed over and his statements contradicted or modified by other documents he wrote. According to *Seven Pillars* he resisted the Bey; as a result he was brutally whipped and sexually assaulted by the Bey's soldiers. He managed to escape later, keeping his real identity intact (he told the Bey he was a Circassian). Whatever the precise details, Lawrence became harder and darker in mood as a result of his treatment at the hands of his captors, but this did not prevent him from celebrating the supreme moment of the war, standing beside Allenby in a conquered Jerusalem only a few weeks later.

In addition to the Deraa tortures, the hardships of bedouin life, the wounds of battle and the mental strain resulting from the exigencies of war, Lawrence became troubled by his political role. In 1916, while still in Cairo Intelligence, he had been a fairly straightforward advocate of British control of the Middle East without much regard for the rights of the Arabs. During the Revolt, however, he found himself espousing the Arab cause more strongly, sometimes favouring its needs rather than those of the British. He wanted the Sherifian cause to triumph and Feisal to rule a semi-independent Syria with British advisory aid. None of this was in accord with the terms of a treaty that had been signed in 1916 by Sir Mark Sykes of the Foreign Office and M. Georges Picot, representing the Quai d'Orsay. Although unable to offer much military aid in the Middle East, France wanted control of Syria. In order to retain French support during the war and to legitimize her own political objectives in the area, Britain agreed to French control of Syria and Lebanon in exchange for recognition of Britain's right to control Palestine, Transjordan and Mesopotamia, with its huge oil deposits.

So, while Lawrence was leading a national Arab liberation movement against the Turks, he also became the spearhead of French imperial control of the Arab movement. His intended solution to this dilemma was to help the Arabs take Damascus and set up a government there before anyone else arrived, so that they and not the French would succeed in laying claim to rule in Syria. The Sherif's forces reached Damascus on 1 October 1918 and, with Lawrence's aid, Sherifian sympathizers (including the former Turkish military governor of Damascus, Ali Riza Pasha al-Rikabi) set up an Arab government there before the British generals arrived.

It seemed as if Lawrence's plan had worked. His efforts to persuade the Arabs to fight together, to overcome Arab suspicions of the British, to win British support for the Arabs and to stop Feisal from treating with the Turks (which he had been doing as recently as the last summer of the war) had resulted in straightforward victory. When Allenby arrived, however, he informed Feisal that a French advisor would soon be assigned to him. For this and other reasons, Feisal's government immediately fell under the shadow of dissension and uncertainty. Lawrence asked for leave to go to Europe, where he realized that the real battle for control of Syria would be fought.

The Oxford home to which Lawrence returned at the end of 1918 was sadly changed since two of his brothers had been killed in France. There was little time for sentiment, however. Lawrence had briefed Lord Curzon's Eastern Committee upon his return, advocating the Sherifian cause. As a protest against the Sykes-Picot treaty he refused to accept from King George V his official investiture with the Distinguished Service Order (for the Battle of Tafileh) and the Companion of the Bath. In an unpublished letter to

E.L. Greenhill (an armoured car company commander during the Revolt), he later wrote 'as for decorations: I resigned 'em all into H.M.'s own hands: he was nearly moved to tears'[1]. He also began an intense newspaper propaganda campaign for Feisal.

The Peace Conference at Versailles began on 18 January 1919, and Lawrence attended as a delegate for the Foreign Office and as Feisal's unofficial advisor. He made a lasting impression on Winston Churchill (beginning a lifelong association), gave speeches in French and English to several committees, and worked to reconcile Arab nationalists and Zionists (who had in the Balfour Declaration of 1917 been promised a 'national home' in Palestine). Even when his father died in April 1919 during the great influenza epidemic, Lawrence was absent from the Conference for only a few days. But it was all in vain. France was eventually awarded the mandate over Syria, and this position was confirmed by the San Remo Conference of 1920.

After Feisal despondently left the Paris Conference, Lawrence flew to Cairo in May 1919 in order to retrieve his wartime papers so that he could continue work, begun in Paris, on his poetic autobiography *Seven Pillars of Wisdom*. Other reasons for this trip have been suggested, such as advising Sherif Hussein on how to deal with his energetic and troublesome neighbour Ibn Saud, with whom he was in a state of constant war, but these remain speculative.

Lawrence was busy writing *Seven Pillars* during the trip and he claimed that the prose of the first chapter was influenced by the throb of the engines in his Handley-Page aircraft. The plane never reached Cairo. It crashed at Rome, and although Lawrence (now wearing a cast for a broken collarbone and with a section of rib poking into one lung) quickly continued his journey by air, he never quite recovered from this accident.

On 14 August 1919, about the time Lawrence returned to England after a short stay in Paris, Lowell Thomas opened his show *With Allenby in Palestine* at the Royal Opera House, Covent Garden. This performance was to make Lawrence the most celebrated soldier of the First World War. Lawrence had met Thomas and his cameraman Harry Chase twice during the two weeks they had spent in the Middle East and had posed for photographs. Although Lawrence never admitted it publicly, he helped Thomas by supplying him with information. He also quietly attended the show several times while stating his disdain for it to his friends. What at first had seemed like a lark and a good way to gain publicity for Feisal's cause, soon began to take on a life of its own, and Lawrence, like many subsequent 'celebrities', began to detest and hide from his own partially self-created public image. He was embarking on a fugitive and troubled bohemian existence just as the show started to gain momentum, and the contrast between his heroic public reputation and his increasing private awareness of political failure was devastating. At home in Oxford he was silent and thoughtful. By November 1919, following an agreement between Lloyd George and Clemenceau, all British troops were out of Syria and Feisal was forced to deal with the French government as well as with the many Syrian factions.

Lawrence took up a small fellowship at All Souls College, Oxford, where he met Robert Graves, and continued working on *Seven Pillars*. He persuaded Jonathan Cape to launch his new publishing firm with a reissue of Doughty's *Arabia Deserta*, which he loved. Except for short periods, he no longer found college life congenial and preferred to work in the London garret provided for him by the architect Herbert Baker. In another unpublished letter to Greenhill (27 February 1920) Lawrence expressed his state of mind:

'When I got back I tried Oxford for a bit, but gave it up, and am now employed in just making my ends meet in London. Lowell Thomas has made me a sort of public mountebank, so I lie quiet in rooms.'

Three weeks later he wrote to the same correspondent, commenting too optimistically on Feisal's situation in Syria just four months before the French evicted him by force:

'He's keeping his end up well, with the proper mean of force and reasonableness: and I have good hope he will pull through. What hinders him is rather the bad example we set in Mesopotamia than any particular power for evil of the French....I'm out of affairs, by request of the Foreign Office, which paid me the compliment of calling me the main obstacle to an Arab surrender. Now they're sorry, because Feisal alone is more difficult than Feisal & L.'

He commented with great insight 'I never went back to Syria after that October 4 [1918] — and I don't suppose I ever will. To have succeeded in the rebellion was a great crime: it was meant to be useful only! I'm sorry because digging up Hittites was good sport, and the Euphrates was a grand river for bathing in.' Lawrence referred to himself as 'a sort of hermit', and went on to say that 'I'm not in the City, except at night, when I walk round & round, and am gravely suspected by the police of loitering. I tell them they loiter themselves, but they are narrow-minded people, & think themselves specially privileged. It must be a golden life, a policeman's: no licence to meditate on final causes.' He hoped to build a house in Epping Forest and to settle down to print books and study the history of the Crusades.

Despite the fairly cheerful tone of this letter, Lawrence was often troubled during this period as he worked on his book. He relived the painful experiences of the victorious Revolt that was to result in failure when Feisal was expelled from Syria. He also began to commission illustrations by some of the finest painters of the period, such as Eric Kennington, Augustus John, Blair Hughes-Stanton and William Roberts, for the limited 1926 Subscribers' edition of *Seven Pillars of Wisdom*[2].

By July 1920 he was out of semi-retirement once again and writing letters to the press in support of the expelled Feisal and against British colonial control of Mesopotamia, where riots had erupted. When, in February 1921, Winston Churchill took over the newly-created Colonial Office and asked Lawrence to join it at a salary of £1200 a year, Lawrence readily agreed. The money would help finance his private edition of *Seven Pillars*. He also saw an opportunity to remedy his political failure by having Feisal placed on the throne of Iraq. This would at once placate the country and satisfy Lawrence's nagging conscience about what he saw (correctly or incorrectly, since all sides in the conflict were extremely treacherous) as Britain's betrayal of the Arab Revolt.

Lawrence attended the Cairo Conference in March 1921 as an official member of the Colonial Office. During the conference it was decided that Feisal should be offered the Iraqi throne and that his brother Abdulla, who had suddenly appeared in Transjordan at the head of an army threatening to attack the French in Syria, should be given the permanent rulership of Transjordan. During the months of July and August 1921, Lawrence attempted to negotiate a treaty with Sherif Hussein which would give Hussein protection from his neighbour Ibn Saud in exchange for recognition of the British Palestine and Iraqi mandates, but he was unsuccessful. Lawrence then became instrumental in the separation of Transjordan from Palestine, and in helping Abdulla stabilize his government. H. St John Philby, who succeeded Lawrence as British Resident in Amman, praised the work which he had carried out there during October and November 1921 under very difficult conditions. Then, in July 1922, Lawrence left the Colonial Office convinced that he had done all he could to fulfil his war-time promises.

A month later, a nervous Lawrence enlisted in the RAF under the alias John Hume Ross. He wanted to avoid publicity and his illegitimacy made attachment to the name 'Lawrence' arbitrary. His reasons for enlisting in the ranks are unclear but he undoubtedly needed a steady occupation and income. He also had a love of mechanical things and a desire to shut off his self-critical faculty in the action and fatigue of hard work; perhaps, too, he simply needed companionship.

In April 1921 Sir Herbert Samuel, the High Commissioner of Palestine, visited Amman to assist in setting up Abdulla's administration in Transjordan. Lawrence is seated next to the driver and Samuel can be seen wearing his white helmet.

Early in March 1923 Lawrence joined the Royal Tank Corps as Private T.E. Shaw. In June he wrote to D.G. Hogarth: 'A commission is out of the question. My prejudice against exercising authority would prevent my becoming even an N.C.O.!' For some unknown reason Lawrence borrowed a non-commissioned officer's jacket for this snapshot dating from his Royal Tank Corps enlistment.

Although recruit training in the RAF depot at Uxbridge was difficult, as Lawrence tells us in *The Mint* (the autobiography of service life that he began to write at this time), he survived its rigours and learned to fit in with his barracks mates. He bought himself a motorcycle and enjoyed fast riding as an escape from camp routine. He also continued his work on *Seven Pillars* as time permitted, and maintained friendly relations with some of the finest minds in England. He had been introduced to George Bernard Shaw, who became a valued literary consultant, while Shaw's wife, Charlotte, developed into a lifelong friend to whom he was to confide things untold to others, including the revelation — otherwise unconfirmed — that he had given in to homosexual rape by the Turks at Deraa when he could no longer stand the pain of the beatings.

In January 1923 Lawrence was discharged from the RAF photography school at Farnborough when the newspapers discovered his identity. At this time a hidden current, vaguely glimpsed in the Deraa chapter of *Seven Pillars*, began to surface. Lawrence had a young Scotsman, John Bruce, administer the first of a series of beatings which were to continue over the next twelve years. The beatings occurred at least ten times and indicate the lingering trauma of the war period when Lawrence's experiences had unleashed latent desires that might otherwise have remained only fantasies. The loss of self-control manifested in the flagellation sessions appears to be one meaning behind the statement in *Seven Pillars* that 'in Deraa that night the citadel of my integrity had been irrevocably lost.'

An undated photograph showing Lawrence during his second RAF enlistment. On 19 August 1925 he reported to RAF West Drayton and became 338171 A/C T.E. Shaw. There a flight-sergeant approached him saying him saying "'Hullo Ross!' … and a dynamo-switch-board attendant behind him said "Garn … that ain't Ross. I was at Bovington when he came up, and he's Colonel Lawrence.'"

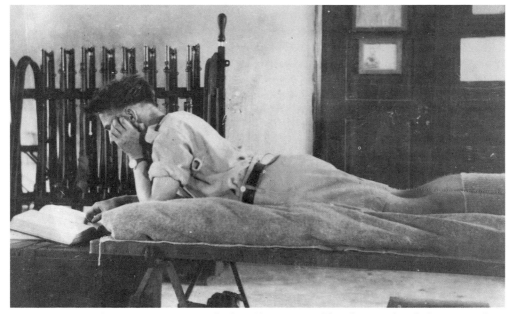

Lawrence at Karachi, 1927. He sent Mrs Charlotte Shaw a print of this photograph with this note on the back: 'This is now my kingdom: my bed. A constitutional kingdom: for I may not change it nor arrange it except after sealed pattern. The book is Ulysses ... Joyce's one. I heard the laughing little man preparing to snap me, & changed from my left elbow to the right. The portrait is unrecognisable, I think, but rather fun. The park-paling effect behind my head is a rack of rifles. Under the book is my box of clothes. Over the top of the bed the edge of a mosquito net. Under the bed me boots! I hope you'll laugh.'

Lawrence joined the Tank Corps in March 1923 as a private under the name T.E. Shaw, again in the hope of hiding his identity. He brought Bruce into the army with him and remained greatly displeased with his life in the barracks at Bovington. The men were of a lower calibre than those in the RAF, who filled a professional role in an exciting new branch of the armed forces. During these years Lawrence lived his most tortured existence, sometimes teetering (especially in his letters to Lionel Curtis) on the edge of a complete breakdown. His friendship with Curtis (an important political intellectual and editor of the *Round Table*), the Shaws and Mr and Mrs Thomas Hardy helped him at this time; so did ownership of his new cottage Clouds Hill, a mile from the camp, which he furnished in austere good taste and to which he could retreat to contemplate, write and listen to music by Elgar and Mozart.

Finally, after constant entreaties to his friends in high places, he was allowed back into the RAF in August 1925 and was soon posted to RAF Cranwell. His letters and *The Mint* confirm that he now became more satisfied with his life as a gifted and inventive mechanic.

He also completed work on the lavish private edition of *Seven Pillars of Wisdom*, having rewritten the manuscript several times over a period of seven years. The best printers and binders were retained, and by December 1926 the edition was in great demand. In a few months, the price rose from the original 30 guineas paid by some two hundred subscribers to £570; in 1980 it fetched more than £2000 on the rare book market[3], and its value has reached £9000 since then. *Seven Pillars of Wisdom*'s literary reputation, too, has steadily grown and the work is now regarded as a classic.

To help pay the costs of producing the private 1926 edition of *Seven Pillars*, Lawrence permitted the publication by Cape in 1927 of a shortened and expurgated version of his book under the title *Revolt in the Desert*. He allowed his publisher to sell only sufficient of this shortened version to pay his debts. And to avoid the publicity that he knew *Revolt in the Desert* would arouse, he had himself transferred to India in December 1926.

A series of shots taken at RAF Miranshah by Lawrence's C.O., Fl/Lt. S.J. Smetham, December 1928. Smetham wrote to Lionel Curtis on 8 August 1929: 'I took the trouble to study "Shaws" various poses and I consider the results very satisfactory.'

His life in India was quiet and devoted largely to literary pursuits: writing *The Mint* and translating Homer's *Odyssey* from the Greek for the American typographer Bruce Rogers. He looked on the *Odyssey* as a way of resting from his labours on *The Mint* while maintaining his literary skill. The RAF authorities did not welcome revelations about life in the ranks, so *The Mint*, although completed by 1928, was not published until 1955 (twenty years after his death), when some critics found it disappointing. Others called it a worthy contribution to twentieth century realism. His *Odyssey*, however, appeared in 1932 and immediately won scholarly appreciation.

Despite Lawrence's attempt to keep out of the public eye, the newspapers soon began printing sensational stories about his alleged exploits along the Northwest Frontier in India and on 8 January 1929 he was quickly shipped home from Miranshah. His arrival in Plymouth Sound was supposed to be secret but newspapermen photographed him trying to leave the P & O liner SS *Rajputana* unobserved and exploited their material.

From 1929 to 1931, Lawrence served under Wing Commander Sydney Smith at RAF Mount Batten, Plymouth. He took part in preparations for the Schneider Cup seaplane race and worked on improving air-sea rescue operations by devising a new class of speedboat specially for this purpose. He also learned to pilot a small plane.

Towards the end of his RAF career he enjoyed travelling around contractors' shipyards and taking part in discussions on future boat design. In fact, his technical expertise was sufficient to allow him to write a boat maintenance manual, and to suggest motorcycle improvements to the manufacturer George Brough. When the time came to retire, on 23 February 1935, he left RAF Bridlington with genuine sadness, as this fragment from a projected, but never completed, sequel to *The Mint* makes clear:

'The wrench is this: I shall feel like a lost dog when I leave — or, when it leaves me, rather, for the R.A.F. goes on. The strange attraction in the feel of the clothes, the work, the companionship. A direct touch with men, obtained no other way in life' (*L*, p.854).

Towards the end of 1928, to the embarrassment of the Indian Government, articles started to appear in British newspapers claiming that Lawrence was spying in Afghanistan. The RAF was asked to remove him and on 8 January 1929 Lawrence left Miranshah. Asked in Karachi where he would like to be posted, he said he wanted to return to England. He left Bombay on 12 January on board the S.S. Rajputana, and on 22 January wrote to Aircraftman Hayter, of Miranshah: 'At Karachi an irk lent me a civvy suit: so I sort of pass muster in the crowd. They stare at me too much for comfort. However, there it is. I shall be stared at, goodness knows, a lot more in England.' This photograph probably shows Lawrence in the suit on the voyage home to England.

Outside the commanding officer's residence at Mount Batten. Clare Sydney Smith (left), Lawrence, Squadron Leader Lloyd, the Smiths' daughter Maureen, unidentified woman, and Clare's sister Lily (right). The Smiths' Golden Retrievers Leo and Banner are also shown.

On 20 November 1934 Lawrence wrote to ex-Aircraftman Arthur Hall: 'Can we get snapped on a Saturday afternoon?' On 1 February he wrote 'Back again, and the photos here. Thank you very much for them. I call them pretty good: we are as regimental as two button sticks. I look like an S[pecial] P[oliceman] who has just caught you in the Bricklayers' Arms. Anyhow there can't be any row hereafter if I call you shortarse, can there? I had no idea I was so tall and thin and hard looking. If you see the damsel who took them, please thank her from me for painting my face so smooth.'

At the British Power Boat Company, Hythe with Harry Vane, Chairman and Managing Director of the engineers D. Napier & Son. Vane held this position from April 1931 until March 1932, and the photograph probably dates from that period.

Lawrence astride his last Brough Superior. He owned this machine from about August 1934 and was riding it the day of his fatal crash, 13 May 1935.

He retired to his Dorset cottage Clouds Hill, where he was content to potter and read, but in collaboration with engineer Edward Spurr he continued the work they had begun some three years earlier on the prototype of a ram-wing craft combining some features of a hovercraft and a hydrofoil. A working model of this revolutionary craft named *Empire Day* was produced by Spurr in 1938, with a dedication to 'L. of A.' written on the prow.

Lawrence also continued his correspondence with authors such as James Hanley and E.M. Forster. On his way back home from sending a telegram to the writer Henry Williamson, he swerved on his Brough Superior motorcycle to avoid two delivery boys and was fatally injured. The day of the accident was 13 May 1935 but he did not actually die until 19 May. Even this fatal accident was attended by mystery when one witness claimed to have seen a black car pass by at the time but no one else could remember or trace it.

These bare facts of Lawrence's life are not seriously questioned today, but it will be said that even this brief account has been influenced by the political, intellectual and cultural atmosphere of the 1980s and the author's personal point of view. Certainly, the many portraits of Lawrence created by biographers have reflected their particular times and personalities as well as the facts they have discovered. While biographers have steadily advanced our factual knowledge of Lawrence's life, their interpretations have also, of necessity, distorted it. Whether Lawrence has been depicted as a hero or a fraud has depended almost as much upon who was writing about him, and when, as upon which facts were available at the time; the history of Lawrence biography is to a large degree the history of changing attitudes in the twentieth century. In the pages that follow, the most significant and influential images of Lawrence projected by biographers in all media will be explored and set against the record of his actual, proven achievements.

PART TWO

Looking for Lawrence

After the First World War, the British public needed a hero whose very existence would lend that cruel conflict some sort of integrity; Lawrence's early biographers provided one. As Ronald Blythe comments:

> 'During the twenties and early thirties he was England's answer to Lindbergh, except that ... he was bigger, better and richer in human complexities than Lindbergh. ... The twenties liked his indifference to fame at a time when war honours and peerages were being snatched up like bargains. They liked his looks, which were the real McCoy after the pinchbeck sheik stuff of Valentino and the burnoused Lotharios of Miss M.E. Clamp. They also liked his amateurism, his "modesty" and his make-your-own kingdoms kit. He reappeared on the scene when patriotism had become rather smudgy and before empire worship had been safely channeled off into royalty worship, which left quite a lot of emotion going begging'[4].

In the 1930s, hero-worship of Lawrence even took on dangerous Fascist overtones before a second great war eventually caused a questioning of the psychology of over-powerful military and political leaders. A general rebelliousness against established heroes and a new preoccupation with psychological (and in particular sexual) explicitness began in the late 1950s. On the one hand, Lawrence was seen rather positively by Colin Wilson in 1956 as an example of 'the outsider' using pain to search for the outer limits of his 'moral freedom'. On the other, the new atmosphere of aggressive psychological investigation led many Lawrence biographers to charge him with sado-masochism. Biographers were also influenced by the atmosphere surrounding the final European retreat from empire, including the Suez crisis of 1956, and Lawrence was sometimes blamed in retrospect for having allegedly favoured the Arabs rather than the British and French.

In our post-imperial era, Lawrence has sometimes been accused of having preferred empire too much, at the expense of the Arabs. There is also a preoccupation with the theory that he was murdered, which is perhaps not surprising at a time when a man can be struck down in the centre of London by a terrorist bomb or the thrust of an umbrella spike. At the same time a more sophisticated understanding of sexuality has led to a calmer discussion of Lawrence's private life.

Seen as a whole, the history of Lawrence biography begins with uncritical super-glorification after the First World War which gives way to a period of debunking after the Second. Then, after 1968 when new archival and interview material became available, a less speculative and more balanced picture emerged to show how Lawrence's life could help us to understand our own dilemmas, particularly in relation to guerrilla warfare, the Third World and cross-cultural conflicts. The debate now turned on whether Lawrence had a positive or negative influence on Middle-Eastern and indeed world conflicts.

Just as Lawrence enjoyed seeing a different side of himself in each of the painted portraits or sculptures for which he sat, so he might be amused by the scope of the differing impressions offered by his many biographers across the century.

The caption for this photograph in Thomas's book reads 'The dreamer whose dreams came true'.

Chapter one

The Superhero

The first generation of significant biographers — Lowell Thomas, Robert Graves, Liddell Hart and Edward Robinson — who published books on Lawrence between 1924 and 1946, are unanimous in presenting him enthusiastically and positively. Despite inevitable distortions and omissions, their works exhibit the virtue of having been written by people who knew him personally and so they have a certain authenticity lacking in later views. At the same time, these biographers were heavily influenced by this personal contact and by the public view of Lawrence as a hero (which they helped to create); moreover, they were not privy to information that has appeared only in later years. Their opinions, though impossible to ignore, should therefore be seen as one extreme end of the spectrum of Lawrence assessments.

Lowell Thomas

In 1919 Lowell Thomas produced a slide show which was to be seen by millions in the major cities of the world. By exaggeration of Lawrence's deeds and character, it introduced a myth which has taken years to separate from the reality.

Thomas, a Princeton University lecturer who had given up his post to take part in Lord Beaverbrook's campaign to glorify Britain's role in the war, became one of the leading publicists of the century, largely on the basis of his successful Lawrence presentation. Yet even Thomas, who at the age of eighty-nine continued to believe Lawrence to be the most outstanding individual he had met in a lifetime of travels, at first underestimated his story's appeal. He thought that Percy Burton, the English impresario, was pulling his leg when he invited him in 1919 to present his New York show in London. But Burton knew what he was doing; after a long, grinding, largely immobile war fought for reasons that became ever more obscure, the British public wanted a hero in whom they could believe. In Lowell Thomas's version of Lawrence, they found a man who was modest yet unquestioningly brave, totally dedicated to the unambiguous and worthy goals of English victory and Arab independence, and who was intellectually brilliant. Thomas's Lawrence reaffirmed British courage and integrity and justified the sacrifice of the war years.

'The "uncrowned king" of the Arabs on the Governor's balcony in Jerusalem' is the caption that accompanies Lowell Thomas's reproduction of this photograph by Harry Chase. It was taken when Thomas and Lawrence first met in January 1918.

'Colonel Lawrence and the Author' reads the caption used in Thomas's book, although at the time of his visit Lawrence's rank was Lieutenant-Colonel. In January 1920 Lawrence wrote, 'I am painfully aware of what Mr. Thomas is doing. He came out to Egypt on behalf of the American Government, spent a fortnight in Arabia (I saw him twice in that time) and there he seems to have realised my "star" value on the film. Anyway since he has been in America and London, & has written a series of six articles about me, for American & English publication. They are as rank as possible, and are making life very difficult for me, as I have neither the money nor the wish to maintain my constant character as the mountebank he makes me.' But it is obvious from the photographs in Thomas's book and his later statements that Lawrence helped create the 'Lawrence legend'.

This image of Lawrence was, in fact, a little too good and simple to be altogether true. In his final comment on the subject in 1981, just four days before he died, Thomas attacked the David Lean/Robert Bolt film of 1962 for showing nothing authentic but 'the camels and the sand'. Unfortunately his own book deserves similar criticism.

In *With Lawrence in Arabia* (1924), Thomas tells not the history of a modern military campaign with its brutalities, political treacheries and other complexities, but rather 'the story of Lawrence and the war in the Land of the Arabian Nights' (p.viii) and that of 'Allenby, Britain's modern Coeur de Lion', who 'was leading his army in the most brilliant cavalry campaign of all time' (pp. viii–ix). Lawrence, whose own attitude toward religion was at best ambivalent (largely due to his mother's guilt-driven religious obsessions), appears as a Christian Crusader *par excellence* and a knight *sans peur et sans reproche*. Even had he known about them, Thomas undoubtedly would have said nothing of Lawrence's illegitimate birth, or of his suspected homosexual relationship with Dahoum.

Thomas's book also contains several unconfirmed and improbable (but not impossible) tales of Lawrence as a young archaeology student, running down to Egypt in 1912 to demand why Kitchener, then Consul-General, had allowed the Germans to gain control of the Syrian port of Alexandretta; of Lawrence threatening the Germans working on a railway bridge near Carchemish with drainage pipes that resembled cannons; and of Lawrence personally summoned to Cairo by Colonel Gilbert Clayton, Director of Military Intelligence there, instead of first having wangled an appointment through Hogarth's influence. Lawrence's expedition to the north in June 1917 becomes a truly Arabian Nights adventure, in which he dines with Ali Riza Pasha, the Turkish military governor and a secret Arab sympathizer, in his palace in Damascus. There is nothing about the Deraa incident, which was a crucial event in Lawrence's life. Only the Arabs kill at Tafas, and no mention is made of Lawrence giving orders not to take any prisoners. According to Thomas, Lawrence is the stereotype 'dashing Colonel' (p.390). He has an 'uncanny insight into the minds of Orientals' (p.190). Instead of a military liaison and

The caption for this photograph in Lowell Thomas's book reads 'The dreamer whose dreams came true'. Lawrence wrote in 1920 that Thomas was a 'wild American' who 'came to Akaba and took us all, and he never gave me copies. However as I look a perfect idiot in most he published, there probably isn't much lost.'

Akaba staff, 1918. Another photograph dating from Thomas's visit. Standing left to right, Langheim, Captain H.C. Hornby, the doctor Major William E. Marshall; seated Major P.G.W. Maynard, Lawrence, recently-appointed base commander Major T.H. Scott, and supply officer Captain Raymond Goslett.

intelligence officer acting on orders and in parallel with Allenby's major campaign, he becomes the 'Uncrowned King of the Arabs, who had achieved what no sultan and no calif had been able to do in more than five hundred years' (p.349). Auda abu Tayi — despite his greed, treachery and double-dealing with Turks and British (as recorded in *Seven Pillars*) — is referred to as 'the Bedouin Robin Hood' (p.155). Feisal — a king rather than a president, and a weak one at that — becomes 'the George Washington of Arabia' (p.337).

Thomas was certainly in a position to illuminate Lawrence's foibles but he never did so in his show or in his biography. Only after Lawrence's death did he admit that Lawrence was all too ready to supply him with information and showmanlike photo sessions, and came to see his show five times! In many cases Thomas was clearly repeating tall tales and propaganda, sometimes in garbled form, that Lawrence himself had told him in a spirit of mischief and mockery or in order to garner political support for Feisal.

Nonetheless, the basic stories of Lawrence's leadership of the Arabs and his secret intelligence work are true and Thomas certainly grasped the fact that here was a man who would continue to interest future generations. Thomas's final estimate of Lawrence as the equal of Achilles, Marco Polo and El Cid shows the extreme extent of his admiration, yet his book was reissued as late as 1967 and seems sure of remaining a popular classic.

While Graves was working on Lawrence and the Arabs, he had a lengthy correspondence with Lawrence who warned him on 1 October 1927 to ''Ware photographs, old thing. They are more dangerous, to-day, than portraits: for by the great extension of the habit of cinema-going, people have learnt the camera-technique, and are able to recognise a man easily by his photograph, as you or I would by his portrait. So I hope that if you decide to publish any photographs of me they will be of small scale and not characteristic. If necessary have the face changed a little by retouching. People believe that the camera cannot lie, and so they will credit your false photograph.' This was the first photograph Graves used in the body of his book, where it was captioned "'Aircraftman Shaw" in "Scruff Order"'. It shows Lawrence at RAF Karachi in 1927.

Thomas's Foreword to the 1967 edition is useful not only for his admission that his book was 'the rather hurried effort of a young reporter', but also for his explanation of the later attacks on Lawrence, which he attributes to the rivalry of the British administration in Mesopotamia, the hostility of the French, and the fact that 'he was a remarkable man, a great man' (p.x).

Whatever Thomas may have been, he was not a fool; and his summary of the main components of Lawrence's positive appeal seems permanently valid:

'At any rate, the Lawrence story is the stuff of which great legends are made: a rather shy archaeologist; a little man with a wild sense of humor who takes delight in cutting stuffy superiors down to size; an outsider who goes into so-called forbidden country ...; player of the key role in creating unity among fighting desert tribesmen who for centuries had been separated by bitter blood feuds; a wanted man with a large reward on his head, dead or alive, by the Turks; leader of forces that occupied the attention of almost as large a part of the Turkish army as was in combat against Allenby and his army. Plus the fact that he wore striking Arab costumes and was reputed to be able to outdo the Arabs at those things they could do better than other people do them.' (p.xii)

Robert Graves

The literary side of Lawrence's life gave him access to many of the outstanding writers and painters of his time. He met Robert Graves at a guest-night in All Souls College, Oxford, on 16 November 1919. Lawrence was discussing the Syrian-Greek philosophers and poets with the Regius Professor of Divinity and 'made an immediate hit with Robert by praising his [Robert's] poetry, which he said he had read while he was in Egypt'[5]. Thus the seed of the second biography, *Lawrence and the Arabs*, was planted. Contributing to the friendship of the two men was Graves's own sense of having been, like Lawrence, spiritually wounded in the First World War; and his soldierly delight in Lawrence's apparent success in challenging military authority.

On 4 April 1927 Graves broadcast a review of Lawrence's *Seven Pillars* abridgement *Revolt in the Desert* on the BBC, and in June of that year the publisher Jonathan Cape commissioned Graves to write a boys' book on Lawrence. Graves contacted Lawrence, then serving in Karachi, and upon receiving a very positive response, decided to turn the exercise into a full-scale biography. Unfortunately he had only six weeks in which to gather the material and write the book so that it could be published in time for Christmas. The result of this deadline pressure was, as Graves himself wrote in *T.E. Lawrence to His Biographers Robert Graves and Liddell Hart* (1938), 'a journalistic job' in which 'Two-thirds of the book was a mere condensation of *Seven Pillars* material' that Lawrence supplied to Graves in its 1922 and 1926 versions. Since the full *Seven Pillars* (at Lawrence's own request) would not be made available to the public until after Lawrence's death, Graves felt that his summarizing was justified. Lawrence also wrote Graves a lengthy letter explaining his intentions and motives during the Arab Revolt and supplied a detailed commentary on the first eleven chapters of Graves's text.

In return for this help, Graves had to agree not to comment in depth on the Deraa incident, or on certain other ambiguous elements in the Lawrence story; nor was he allowed to reveal Lawrence's contribution to the book. Lack of time meant he could not probe the 'S.A.' identity or research his theory that Lawrence could not come to terms with the existence of women.

Lawrence's own view of the outcome, expressed in a letter of 7 December 1927 to Graves, is one of the better things that has been written about this second biography and gives us some indication of Lawrence's own self-image at this time. Although he notes that the middle of Graves's book is only a 'more fluent repeat' of his own writings, and that Graves did not understand the political complexities of the Revolt, Lawrence comments that Graves's 'beginning is first class. You draw a portrait of the mind and manner of a living person. I do not know if I am like that: you know my blindness towards my own shape: but I do know that your reconstruction can stand up and walk on its own feet ... it is astonishingly life-like'[6].

The first two chapters of Graves's biography — along with the literary chapter 30, in which he calls *Seven Pillars* 'beyond dispute, a great book' — are undoubtedly the best, since they constitute the biographer's firsthand portrait of a man whom he knew over a period of seven years, rather than a mere précis of Lawrence's own material.

In these chapters, Graves initiates the idea that Lawrence kept himself compartmented among his many friends, showing each of them only a certain side of himself and never allowing the various facets to mix. He also attributes to Lawrence two essential natures — the bare, even fanatical, self that could blow up trains and hold to an ideal, and the over-civilized European self, which produced and enjoyed art and allowed him to criticize himself in action. Graves notes that the 'upper part of Lawrence's face is kindly, almost maternal; the lower part is severe, almost cruel' (p.41) — thus perhaps unintentionally encouraging the view taken by many of the next generation of biographers of Lawrence as a sado-masochist. Graves also noticed Lawrence's dislike of being touched, his desire to eat alone and his claim that the passion of love is 'unnecessary'. He further remarks that Lawrence's 'secret' is his 'extraordinary detachment' from others and that 'Lawrence's chief curse is that he cannot stop thinking'.

Anyone familiar with highly-motivated and self-critical people who feel that only criticism is truthful and praise is flattery will appreciate Graves's comment that 'the one thing that he [Lawrence] likes is to find someone who knows more than himself or can do something better than himself' (p.45).

Writing to Graves on 1 October 1927, Lawrence mentioned 'I got your letter with the prints of me on my "bike" last Sunday. They shall be returned to Sergt. Pugh.' This is one of the prints Lawrence was referring to and which Graves used in his book with the caption 'T.E. Lawrence on "Boanerges," The Motor-Bicycle.' Sergeant Pugh, of Lawrence's flight at Cranwell, was the photographer. On 10 December 1925 Lawrence wrote to a Tank Corps friend 'Crashed off the Brough last Monday: knee: ankle: elbow: being repaired. Tunic and breeches being replaced. Front mudguard, name-plate, handlebars, footrest, renewed. Skid on ice at 55 m.p.h. Dark: wet most miserable. Hobble like a cripple now.'

Essentially, Graves's biography, without discrimination, frequently shows a strong Oxford taste for tales of 'genius'. He is quite uncritical of Lawrence's story that he had read 'the best part' of the fifty thousand volumes in the Oxford Union Library in three years. Even at the rate of the six volumes a day which Lawrence claimed to have skimmed, the total comes to 6570 books, which is not even a fifth of those available, as Richard Aldington was later to point out. Graves writes that Lawrence 'could sit or stand for hours at a stretch without moving a muscle'. Certainly nothing in Lawrence's own account of himself leads us to believe that. Could it have been true that Lawrence 'never recognizes a face. ... He would not recognize his mother or brothers, even if he met them without warning'? Or was it simply that shyness kept Lawrence from looking people in the face? Did Graves, himself knowing a writer's thirst for publication, really believe Lawrence's claim that *Seven Pillars of Wisdom* 'was never intended for publication'? Graves sometimes introduces more mysteries into a Lowell Thomas story. He writes that during his northern ride Lawrence did not dine with Ali Riza Pasha in Damascus, as Thomas had said, but only that Lawrence made arrangements with prominent Arab Revolt sympathizers for action to be taken after the Turks were expelled.

In Graves's favour, it must be said that he gives indications that he understood the difficulty of separating fact from fiction in the stories Lawrence shared with him. He writes openly that 'In reviewing Lawrence's life, one has to accept casually ... immoderate feats; they are part of his nature and the large number of them that can be verified excuses one's credulity for others of the same remarkable character that are pure fiction' (p.25). This is the difficulty that all Lawrence biographers have faced as stories were retold by Lawrence himself and others, each time in a somewhat different form, yet, as Lowell Thomas originally pointed out, and Graves repeats, no one who was present during the Arab Revolt came forward to question Lawrence's account, although he sent copies of *Seven Pillars* to many participants early on. Graves's private view may well have gone deeper than he cared to state in the biography. In letters to Lawrence, and in later writings, Graves makes it clear that he regarded Lawrence's RAF service as a betrayal of his intellectuality, but in the biography itself no such criticism appears.

Despite all this, Graves's book does contain many events and impressions that are convincing. Graves points out that Lawrence confirmed what has been accepted as the correct site of the Biblical Kadesh Barnea in the Sinai desert. The Red Sea is known to be shark-infested at times, so Lawrence's trip to Jezirat Faroun or the Coral Island on an improvised raft during the Zin survey was certainly quite daring. The testimony of Sergeant Pugh of the RAF (that Graves includes in a separate section of his book) is some confirmation of the Deraa tortures, since Pugh saw the scars that Lawrence says were the result of the Bey passing a bayonet through his ribs. Pugh also saw Lawrence ignore a broken arm, a documented instance of his ability to bear pain. Above all, every observation by Graves about Lawrence's character and actions during the time they knew one another is valuable eyewitness testimony.

If Lawrence is portrayed larger than life in this book, nevertheless Graves introduced a psychological complexity to his subject — an aspect that is lacking in Lowell Thomas's hagiography. His portrait of a most erudite, intellectual, yet 'foxy', self-critical and divided Lawrence would reappear again and again in later biographies.

B.H. Liddell Hart

Lawrence had wanted his story to be treated by a military expert and in B.H. Liddell Hart, author of many books of military history, he found his man. As if to confirm Graves's statement that Lawrence never told one friend about another, Graves was completely unaware of Liddell Hart's book until it was published in 1934.

Liddell Hart's caption reads 'Lawrence amid the results of a raid'. On 29 March 1917 Lawrence laid his first mine on the Hejaz railway, near Aba el Naam Station. His report on the attack notes that 'The locomotive was behind the northern building and got steam up, and went off (reversed) toward Medina. When it passed over the mine it exploded it, under the front bogies (i.e. too late). It was, however, derailed, and I hoped to see the machine-gun come into action against it, but it turned out that the gunners had left their position to join our attack on the station, and so the seven men on the engine were able to "jack" it on the line again in about half an hour (only the front wheels were derailed) and it went off towards Istabl Antar, at foot pace, clanking horribly.' His second raid on the railway took place a few days later.

While Liddell Hart clarifies much of Lawrence's military activity, like Graves and Thomas he does not include precise sources in his book *'T.E. Lawrence': In Arabia and After*[7]. Some accounts of certain incidents (based, again, on Lawrence's own testimony) also contradict stories in the two earlier biographies. For instance, Lawrence told Thomas that he had dined with Ali Riza Pasha in Damascus, but to Graves he confided that he 'neither dined, lunched nor breakfasted with Ali Riza Pasha' in Damascus. He then told Liddell Hart that Ali Riza did meet him, but outside Damascus. Which of the accounts is true? From his report to Clayton, first made available in Garnett's edition of the letters in 1938, it appears that the version Lawrence told Liddell Hart is the correct one: Lawrence did meet Ali Riza Pasha three miles outside Damascus. Lawrence told Graves that he preferred to maintain an incorrect account of this incident and, as Knightley and Simpson were to point out much later, his war diary contains details not in the report. Perhaps the idea of giving three different versions to his early biographers was Lawrence's way of receiving justified credit for his great feat while at the same time muddying details for political and intelligence reasons. The result, however, was to throw suspicion on Lawrence's truthfulness, especially before his report became available in 1938. At all events, the full story of this northern ride remains unfathomed.

Liddell Hart also repeats Thomas's story about Lawrence using drain-pipes resembling cannons to scare the Germans building the Baghdad railroad; yet to Graves Lawrence had denied even the existence of drain-pipes at Carchemish. A story of the Carchemish period which Lawrence added to Liddell Hart's typescript, reads:

'The Armenian revolutionaries had come to him for help and advice, and he had dipped far into their councils. The opposition party of the Kurdish reactionaries against the Young Turks had encouraged him to ride in their ranks and seek opportunity in the Balkan crisis.'

This account seems wildly exaggerated — would these people appeal to a young archaeologist with limited experience of the Near East? Or was Lawrence in fact already involved deeply in intelligence work during the 1911–14 period? Liddell Hart does not mention Lawrence's illegitimate birth, and the Deraa incident is given scant coverage in one brief paragraph.

During the writing of his biography from 1929-34, Liddell Hart became Lawrence's valued friend. The book was published in March 1934 and on 2 June the biographer and his wife visited Lawrence at the British Power Boat Company at Hythe. Lawrence wrote to Hart on 14 June that 'The photographs are, as you say, excellent beyond the wont of such things.... You and I get off about par. Very good.'

It would seem that through the contradictions and omissions of these three early biographies Lawrence intended to leave behind a trail of mystery that has lasted in many respects to the present day. While true in its general outlines, Lawrence's story as told in the 1919–46 period leaves many gaps and is vulnerable to criticism. Only when British archives were opened to the public in 1968 and new people came forward to testify about Lawrence would there be any real factual detail to balance the earlier uncritical praise or sceptical speculation.

Liddell Hart's military assessment of Lawrence's career is on firmer ground than his general biographical details.

'Military history cannot dismiss him as merely a successful leader of irregulars. He is seen to be more than a guerrilla genius — rather does he appear a strategist of genius who had the vision to anticipate the guerrilla trend of civilized warfare that arises from the growing dependence of nations on industrial resources.'

This view has been upheld by later writers, most notably Douglas Orgill, Robert Asprey and Konrad Morsey. Liddell Hart was also the first biographer to grasp the truth about Feisal — that he was dealing with the Turks as late as the summer of 1918, and that only Lawrence's intimation that he knew of this correspondence stopped it. In *Seven Pillars*, which was not to be available to a broad public until 1935, Lawrence treats this incident half-humourously, masking its seriousness. The treachery of both British and Arabs that now emerges certainly modifies Thomas's Crusader-Saladin picture.

Despite its balanced and careful consideration of the military and political questions, Liddell Hart's book is in many ways even more image-making than the Lowell Thomas biography. He too begins by referring to Lawrence as a 'Crusader' and in his last chapter raises Lawrence to a level of deification by comparing him to Napoleon and Marlborough, even proposing him as a political saviour:

'I am told that the young men are talking, the young poets writing, of him in a Messianic strain — as the man who could, if he would, be a light to lead stumbling humanity out of its troubles — he seems to come nearer than any man to fitness for such power — in a state that I would care to live in....He is the Spirit of Freedom come incarnate to a world in fetters.'

Here is a clear expression of the dangerous desire (typical of the 1930s, which saw the advent of the Mosley marches) for an overwhelmingly powerful leader. Lawrence, who displayed no interest in leading a political movement, wrote to Robert Graves that Liddell Hart 'seems to have no critical sense in my regard'. Liddell Hart's image of Lawrence as a potential dictator was bound to result in a backlash against him from a later generation that had fought a second world war against dictators. Even in this early period of hero-worship, there were those who took a more critical viewpoint. D.H. Lawrence wrote in *Lady Chatterley's Lover* of a Colonel C.E. Florence who seemed to love fame too much; and Herbert Read in 1928 expressed the opinion that, compared to the great Arabian explorer Charles Doughty, Lawrence was too self-advertising.

Edward Robinson

In his *Lawrence the Rebel* (1946) Edward Robinson presents some interesting ideas, but his book has been neglected. Robinson claims to have been with Lawrence in Arabia and to have kept notes about his activities, although he had no contact with Lawrence after that. Robinson had previously published a simplified boys' book called *Lawrence: The Story of His Life* in 1935 which, along with R.H. Kiernan's similar effort, *Lawrence of Arabia*, was one of the first biographies to appear after Lawrence's death.

The reception of *Lawrence the Rebel* has been clouded by two unfortunate events: in 1929 Robinson was convicted of forgery, and in 1937 he was again charged, this time with selling papers loaned to him by A.W. Lawrence in order to pay a blackmailer. Robinson served three months in prison as a result[8]. Furthermore, in *Seven Pillars* Lawrence lists the roll of servicemen participating in the campaign but there is no mention of an Edward Robinson — only a T.R. Robinson. A check by the Ministry of Defence as to whether Edward Henry Tyler Robinson did in fact serve in Arabia has so far proven inconclusive. Nevertheless his book purports to be an eyewitness account, and although his sources are vague or unnamed, Robinson does provide intriguing, if unverified, new details of the secret northern trip:

'He then slipped into Damascus. At this stage of the revolt, his influence with the Arabs … put a price on his head … in the bazaars of the towns and the gossip centres of the villages it was common knowledge that the capture of the Englishman, dead or alive, would secure a reward of five thousand golden sovereigns.

… Intelligence reports received later in the year confirmed that he had managed to get into the inner councils of the Turco-German commands. (He referred once to a "meal in the Town Hall at Damascus, a gilded room with tables and carpets"!) It was learned from the sources that, as a merchant of obvious wealth but unknown origin, he sold non-existent grain, crops, camels, stores, etc. on terms which were so favourable to the Turks that they actually cultivated his friendship.' (p.80–1)

Although Robinson modified the story given in his boys' book of Lawrence having actually 'discussed future plans with German head-quarters staff', he stands by the claim that Lawrence penetrated the 'inner councils' of the enemy during this Syrian spying mission. He says nothing about Ali Riza Pasha but tells us for the first time that Lawrence was disguised as a merchant and that 'It was reported that he had even dined with the military staff at Turkish headquarters' in Damascus (p.83).

Robinson claims to have had knowledge of dispatches and access to official intelligence documents but his reluctance to name sources renders his story speculative. His personal view of Lawrence is also intriguing. At about the time of the capture of Jerusalem (which took place just after the Deraa incident in which Lawrence was caught and tortured by the Turks), he reports:

'Lawrence was summoned to headquarters, where they were worried about his health. He'd had some sort of shock, for something had happened to change him. He ate more sparingly than ever, and rarely in company. Where he might mark a day with two or three words of greeting, the minimum was reduced to absolute silence. Of his gentleness, none was left. His humour turned to bitterness, and in his fighting from this time onward he spared neither himself nor his fellows nor his enemy.'

Robinson goes on to say:

'The puzzle was solved for us years later when we read in the *Seven Pillars of Wisdom* of his arrest and torture in Deraa. It was then easy to understand the Lawrence of the last year of his campaigning. But we were without that tale of horror, and merely knew that we were dealing with a changed man' (p.122).

It might be suspected that Robinson is making these comments after the fact, reading into Lawrence things that were not there at the time but which he deduced from later reading. On the other hand, he gives many verifiable and original details of the campaign that could easily have been contradicted by others who were there. No one has yet done so.

Having possibly confirmed that the Deraa incident did take place and affected Lawrence's personality, Robinson concludes:

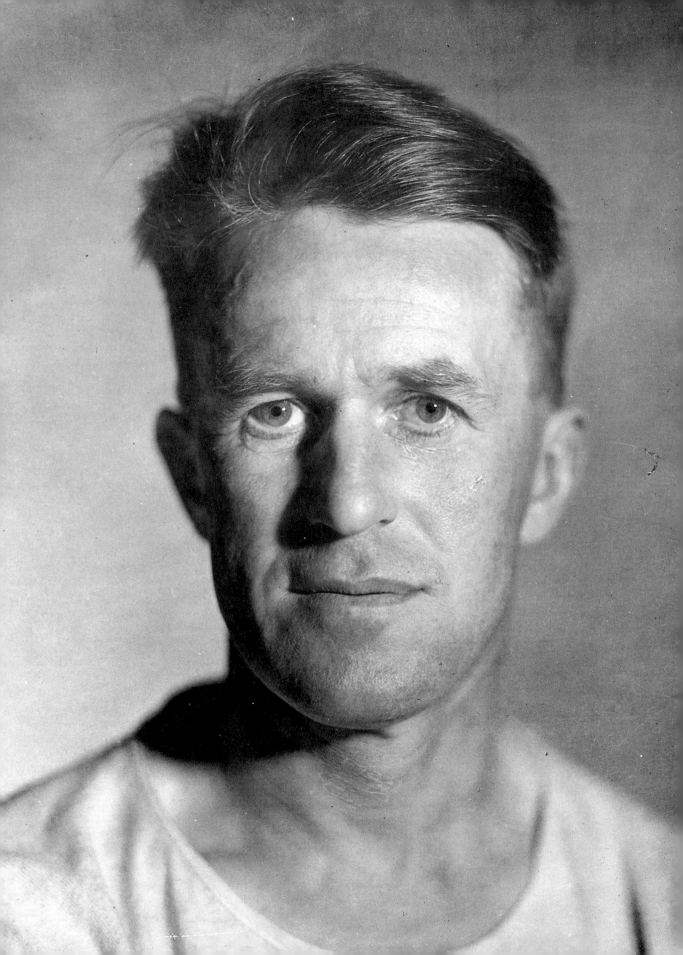

'But from what I have seen of Lawrence and any sort of human agony, he hates anything which causes it, and hates more to be the cause of it himself. What he will do when he is angered is another proposition. He hates the Turks now' (p.141).

In his account of the Tafas massacre, his notes show that Lawrence gave the order 'No prisoners' (p.182) and confirm the terrible picture Lawrence gives of the torture of the villagers by the Turks. Robinson thus becomes the first biographer to connect Lawrence's torture at Deraa with a possible desire for revenge.

On the question of Lawrence's death, Robinson exhibits a healthy scepticism about sensational newspaper accounts that Britain was in peril because Lawrence had died with 'his brain still holding the secrets of the country's war "planes"'; that it was not really Lawrence who had died but someone else; and that foreign agents had been trying to destroy secret documents found on Lawrence. Even so he does remark that 'the inquest was an unsatisfactory affair, and despite the verdict of "accidental death" everyone present was left with a funny little doubt' (p.225). In part this was due to the unconfirmed sighting of a black car but to his credit, Robinson declined to speculate further on this matter.

Like Thomas, Graves and Liddell Hart, Robinson thought of Lawrence as a great man. So too did Charles Edmonds [Professor C.E. Carrington], who published a brief and largely uncritical biography in 1935, and Victoria Ocampo, an Argentinian literary critic, whose almost mystical characterization of Lawrence (based only on his own writing) appeared in 1942 under the title *338171 T.E.*. The heroic view was also predominant among most British memoir writers of the period, including Vyvyan Richards, who wrote two portraits of Lawrence, the contributors to A.W. Lawrence's collection *T.E. Lawrence by His Friends*, and Clare Sydney Smith, who described her contact with Lawrence during his last years in the RAF in her book *The Golden Reign*. A new generation of biographers was to react against this early appraisal by questioning the contradictions in the early works and by bringing previously submerged doubts to the surface in an era that revelled in psychological analysis and re-evaluation of all heroes.

Robinson's 1935 book was the first to feature any of Howard Coster's portraits of 1931 although he did not use the pose shown here. Lawrence wrote his mother on 30 October 1931 in praise of the photographer's work: 'that photograph given me by Coster, the London photographer who asked me to sit for him a month ago. Pity it is so large for I think it a very good [likeness?] as a photograph.'

Chapter two

The Age of Aldington

Not everyone in the period before the Second World War subscribed to the view of Lawrence as a superhero. In addition to D.H. Lawrence's and Herbert Read's criticisms, Sir Andrew Macphail in his *Three Persons* (1929) praised Lawrence's writing ability, but sought to deromanticize his military role. Lawrence was also attacked by General Édouard Brémond in *Le Hedjaz dans la guerre mondiale* (1931). Brémond, who was responsible for representing French interests during the Arab Revolt, found Lawrence obstructive and devious, and even considered him to be a psychiatric case. Since Lawrence made no secret of his opposition to French control of Syria as outlined in the Sykes-Picot agreement of 1916, Brémond's exasperation is certainly understandable.

Another French writer, Léon Boussard, was the first to reveal (although without malice) the illegitimacy of Lawrence's birth in his *Le Secret du colonel Lawrence*, published in 1941. In addition, Major N.N.E. Bray's laudatory 1939 biography of Colonel G.E. Leachman (Lawrence's counterpart in Mesopotamia), accuses Lawrence of posturing and of achieving really very little. Moreover, in 1938 the Arab nationalist writer George Antonius credited Auda abu Tayi rather than Lawrence with the planning and leadership of the expedition that captured Akaba. However, these were minority voices that went largely unheard in the general approval that greeted the biographies of Thomas, Graves and B.H. Liddell Hart.

Then in 1955 Richard Aldington published his *Lawrence of Arabia: A Biographical Enquiry*. The book was a vitriolic condemnation of every aspect of Lawrence's life and career. Whatever else may be said about Aldington's biography (and he was almost hysterically attacked for wanting to destroy a national hero) it must be perceived even today as the kind of work that changes attitudes forever. Aldington's influence can be seen in every other portrait of the period, including Terence Rattigan's play and Robert Bolt's film. Now Lawrence's alleged sado-masochism and dishonesty came to the forefront and replaced the heroic themes.

Aldington treated his subject with an extraordinary obsessiveness which manifested itself in more thorough research than anyone else had done to date, and he overlaid this detailed study with shrewd sarcasm worthy of an eighteenth-century polemicist. The impact of his work was increased by several factors.

This undated photograph probably shows Lawrence at Akaba some time in 1917–18. Richard Aldington said 'Lawrence usually dressed in robes of spotless white'.

The 1950s marked the culmination of British and French withdrawal from empire, including painful defeats in the Suez crisis of 1956 and in Indochina. The end of the decade was also the time of an incipient sexual openness and rebellion against authority evident in the writing of the 'Angry Young Men' such as John Osborne, John Braine and Alan Sillitoe. Combining politics and the new psychological emphasis, almost all Lawrence biographies of the period following Aldington dwelt on his alleged self-glorification, homosexuality and sado-masochism as well as his unpatriotic favouring of the Arabs over the British. This was a complete change from the earlier image of Lawrence as a man idealistically serving both British and Arab peoples simultaneously.

Richard Aldington

Born in about 1892, Richard Aldington took part in the First World War on the Western front, where he was both gassed and shell-shocked. His biting fictional criticism of the war, *Death of a Hero*, attained some celebrity when it appeared in 1929 but then dropped from sight, as did the author. He was never forgiven in Britain for having sat out the Second World War in the United States, and his death in 1962 was ignored by several English newspapers[9]. Lawrence himself did not think Aldington a very good novelist (as Aldington no doubt knew), although he wrote a blurb for Aldington's translation of Pierre Custot's *Sturly*. In 1980, Stephen Spender commented that Aldington was a 'man of no talent'[10].

Essentially Aldington's quarrel arose from his feeling that Lawrence had received enormous credit for having done little or nothing in an easy theatre of the war (and for writing about it) while his own and other soldiers' military and literary contributions were relatively neglected. In the conclusion to his 'biographical enquiry', Aldington comments sarcastically on an English society that he regarded as thoroughly corrupt and hypocritical: 'Lawrence was the appropriate hero for his class and epoch.' But Aldington's desire to make Lawrence the scapegoat for the many ills of English society blinded him to the fact that Lawrence had been no less wounded mentally and physically by the war than he had himself.

Aldington subjects the pre-war period of Lawrence's life to especially close scrutiny. He was the first English writer to mention Lawrence's illegitimacy and to attribute much of Lawrence's evasiveness to it. He catches Lawrence out on a number of stories that he told about his experiences before the war: besides the exaggerated claim for the amount of his reading in the Oxford Union Library, there was the pistol mentioned in an anecdote about how he was attacked during his 1909 Middle Eastern walking tour which Lawrence described variously as a Webley, a Colt and a Mauser. Aldington suggests that Lawrence ran away to join the Artillery at the age of seventeen because of his recent discovery of his illegitimacy, and he questions Lawrence's relationship with his mother, whom he sees as smotheringly powerful. According to Aldington, Lawrence's cavalier attitude toward precise figures and routine labour and his prowess with revolvers and boats owed much to the example of his aristocratic father, who was proficient in sport but refused to work to raise his family's standard of living. He attributes Lawrence's extraordinary will-power to his need to resist the demands of his wilful mother, while his lifelong aloofness and loneliness arose from the family's self-enforced isolation because of its guilty secret. He sees Lawrence's tendency to exaggerate his cycling and other exploits as compensation for the feelings of inferiority caused by his illegitimacy. Aldington also emphasizes the mother's segregation of Lawrence and his brothers from women, and Lawrence's later abnormal attitude toward sex.

Whether this approach was right or wrong, no one had subjected Lawrence's personality or stories about his youth to such careful analysis before or pointed out the lack of concrete evidence that the researcher still frequently confronts.

On the basis of this doubt as to the truthfulness of Lawrence with regard to minor matters, Aldington then moves on to question larger issues: Lawrence's claim of meeting Kitchener before the war when he was a young archaeologist and Kitchener was running Egypt; his knowledge of all the strategic writers he claims to have read, which Aldington attributes to his tutor's membership in an Oxford 'Kriegspiel' or war games club; and the nature of Lawrence's relationship with the Arab named Dahoum or Salim Achmed, whom Aldington names (this is now generally accepted) as the 'S.A.' of the *Seven Pillars of Wisdom* dedication.

He challenges many of Lawrence's assertions about the Arab Revolt, in particular that the Arabs did not *want* to take Medina, which Aldington claims merely hides the fact that they *could not* take Medina. He believes that far fewer than twenty-five trains were blown up and asserts that the Battle of Tafileh, which Lawrence won, was of little value because shortly afterwards, when Lawrence was at British headquarters, the town was recaptured by the Turks.

Aldington supports the suggestion that Auda abu Tayi may have been the real planner of the Akaba expedition, and says that the idea of taking the city had been discussed before Lawrence arrived on the scene. While he accepts that Lawrence made his northern ride behind Turkish lines in June 1917 he suggests that Lawrence went on the Akaba expedition merely as Feisal's envoy to Arab leaders in Damascus rather than in any military capacity.

Since neither Jemal Pasha nor Liman von Sanders (the Turkish army commanders) mention Lawrence in their books, Aldington decides that the offer of any reward for his capture was unlikely. He stresses Feisal's weakness and his attempt to betray the British during the last summer of the war as undermining the importance of any of the Arab Revolt's military operations. Aldington says that Lawrence was not the first to discover the value of propaganda and guerrilla tactics, and that the Arab Revolt was a political sideshow while the British were doing the real work of fighting in Palestine. Finally, in a charge to be repeated many times by other writers, he accuses Lawrence of sadism because he allowed no Turkish prisoners to be taken at Tafas.

Having disposed of Lawrence as a military commander and of the Arab Revolt as simple banditry without practical significance, Aldington proceeds to attack Lawrence's post-war diplomatic record. He points out that Lawrence's support of the Hussein family ended in failure, since the French expelled Feisal from Syria and Ibn Saud triumphed over Sherif Hussein. Moreover, Aldington suspects that Lawrence's return trip to Egypt in 1919, allegedly to collect papers for his book, was actually an attempt to help the Sherif's son Abdulla lead his army against Ibn Saud, and concludes that it was lucky Lawrence's plane crashed in Rome because he was spared Ibn Saud's complete triumph over Abdulla. While admitting that Lawrence was able to influence Churchill in the Colonial Office, Aldington dismisses the story that Lawrence made Lord Curzon cry during a Cabinet session, as well as the statement that he was offered the High Commission of Egypt. For Aldington, Lawrence's political legacy is nil.

He thinks little more of Lawrence as a writer, finding *Seven Pillars* over-written and the 1926 Subscribers' edition of the book a monstrosity of design. He congratulates Lawrence ironically for the clever strategy of making the book well known by refusing to allow wide publication of its full edition during his lifetime; and stresses the fact that Lawrence helped both Lowell Thomas and Robert Graves with their biographies, and then made them deny that he had contributed in any way to the books in order to denigrate their apparent hero-worship.

Lawrence's entry into the RAF he sees as part of a severe mental disorder but points out Lawrence's continuous contacts with friends in high places and his private sources of income which, Aldington claims, made Lawrence's life somewhat easier than that of the average recruit while he complained of harsh treatment. Finally, he denies Lawrence any important role in boat design and accuses him of overt homosexuality while in the service and at Carchemish.

Aldington concludes with a psychological attack on Lawrence's personality, the key to which was 'an abnormal vanity' and its 'identical opposite — abnormal self-depreciation. ...' Because of the knowledge of his illegitimacy, Lawrence wished only to prove himself to the world. His was a nature perpetually at war with itself, reflecting the clash between his father's easy going, effortlessly superior aristocracy and his mother's guilt and strong will. According to Aldington, Lawrence serves largely as an example of how a neurotic misfit can perform an arch imposture on his period by devoting all his talents to self-glorification rather than actual achievement.

This is not a pretty portrait, and many writers give us glimpses of it even today. Not until the 1970s would this view be effectively challenged and some balance brought convincingly into the picture. Yet even if one takes Aldington's evaluation at its worst and subtracts all the negative qualities that he saw in Lawrence, very many positive points remain in Aldington's own account, a fact that has hitherto escaped notice.

Thus, Aldington is forced to admit that Lawrence was a precocious child, reading Macaulay at the age of seven. Furthermore, Lawrence did have a remarkable will and forced himself to perform extraordinary physical feats (even if he exaggerated them somewhat) such as going for dips in the Cherwell at night during the winter. The lasting impression at Oxford, Aldington concedes, is that Lawrence was one of the most brilliant students of his year and had the ability to absorb and excel in a subject quickly. His thesis, later published under the title *Crusader Castles*, is inaccurate according to Aldington but he cannot deny that it won Lawrence first-class honours and is based upon a strenuous Middle East walking trip in which Lawrence inspected thirty-six, if not the fifty, castles that he casually claimed. Although Lawrence's contributions to *The Wilderness of Zin* (1915), which he wrote with C. Leonard Woolley, are 'topographical' rather than 'archaeological', nonetheless he made them; and he did investigate the alleged site of Kadesh Barnea. Furthermore, Lawrence was a superb pistol shot, early bettering Hubert Young, a professional army officer, and he helped to arm the British Consulate in Aleppo under threat of a Kurdish uprising in the pre-war period.

Although Aldington recognizes such incidents which point to Lawrence's involvement in intelligence work from an early date, he never takes into account the possibility that Lawrence had done even more than he claimed, not less, but could not speak about it. He says that Lawrence had no official mission when he accompanied Ronald Storrs to Jidda to speak to the leaders of the incipient Arab Revolt, but never seems to have considered that Lawrence might have had a secret intelligence mission which he screened in *Seven Pillars* with tales of being on holiday. While he blames Lawrence for being indiscreet in writing to Hogarth about a possible Gallipoli attack, he is insufficiently appreciative of the fact that Lawrence did have access to privileged information. He criticizes Lawrence for reporting a remark about dead Armenians, supposedly made by Aubrey Herbert to Khalil Pasha during the negotiations for the ransom of General Townshend's army at Kut, but does not see how unusual it was that Lawrence, then a young staff officer in Cairo, was chosen for this delicate negotiation.

Aldington stresses Lawrence's alleged 'Francophobia' while aknowledging that it was not limited to Lawrence alone; he omits to say that Lawrence liked France and the French very much despite his opposition to their Middle-Eastern policies.

As for the Revolt itself, Aldington is forced to confess that 'few professional officers could have done ... as successfully' as Lawrence in leading the bedouin. He must also admit that Lawrence *did* destroy trains, if not so many as he said. He *did* go on his northern ride, although his report is more optimistic than Aldington thinks it should have been. The Deraa incident definitely occurred in Aldington's view, except that Lawrence admitted to Mrs Shaw (in a letter Aldington discovered in the British Museum) that he surrendered to the Bey's pederasty (instead of having resisted it) when he could no longer take the pain of the beating. If this account of the Deraa episode is true, we may well ask if Lawrence deserves to be blamed for his behaviour, or praised because he did not give away his real identity to the Turks?

Finally, Aldington admits that 'Where he differed entirely from the pukka sahib or Blimp type was that he did not share their Wog and Gippo attitude to Arabs.' This is an important point against those who would later charge that Lawrence was a racialist. However, having praised Lawrence for this sympathy, Aldington perversely accuses him of favouring Arab rather than British interests. To an Aldington writing in the 1950s, when the feeling of the end of empire was very much in the air, Lawrence's pro-Arab activity and sympathies were reprehensible. In the 1980s it may seem that Lawrence's hope for Arab semi-independence rather than complete submission to Great Power rule was positive and far-sighted.

Self-contradiction infects much of Aldington's view. Although he charges that Lawrence is not a writer of great fiction, 'Only a man widely conversant with literature, and in possession of a genuine gift for fitting words to thought and experience could have worked out a style so high-flown and exacting and maintained it through so long a book' as *Seven Pillars of Wisdom*. He is forced to add that Lawrence had 'gifts [and] remarkable strength of will' and that he 'certainly was free from the love of money either as power or pleasure' although he 'lacked common sense in handling it'. According to Aldington, Lawrence was not as happy in the service as he sometimes claimed, although he did become so in his last years in the RAF. Lawrence thought Lenin a great man but, Aldington says, Lawrence did not want to lead a political movement and there was no sign that he approved of Fascism.

He died swerving to avoid harming two boys on bicycles; yet Aldington cannot refrain from criticizing Lawrence's driving record in a final gratuitous shot. To his credit, he does refrain from speculating on the mystery of the black car.

Aldington was undoubtedly Lawrence's harshest critic, yet throughout his condemnation he was compelled to pay due respect to the unusual qualities that Lawrence exhibited and even to praise them. On the basis of what is contained in his book, Aldington could be charged with always choosing the worst explanation rather than the best, and with rendering negative judgements where positive ones were just as plausible. Above all, Aldington himself more than once laments that all the evidence was not available to him. In fact, there is not a single reference to archival material in his book; the Public Record Office archives were not opened until 1968. Moreover, with the sole exception of Antonius, he did not consult Arab opinion.

If Aldington displayed less humility than is proper when conducting a difficult incomplete investigation, still, as Christopher Sykes points out in his preface to the second English edition of Aldington's book, he succeeded in clearing 'the ground of rubbish, efficiently and thoroughly '.

Flora Armitage

The first attempt to respond to Aldington was made by Flora Armitage in *The Desert and the Stars* (1955). This romantic interpretation of Lawrence's career would undoubtedly have been rather more so had it preceded Aldington's publication, six months earlier.

Flora Armitage was a British government representative resident in New York and clearly an admirer of Lawrence, calling him 'a great man for all his foibles and fallibilities.' She devotes special attention to Lawrence's early years and concludes that his parents'

disparities created self-distrust and a rift between his intellect and emotions on the one hand and his fallible body on the other. She agrees with Aldington that Lawrence probably joined the Royal Artillery at the age of seventeen when he discovered his illegitimacy.

Armitage gives a very colourful account of Carchemish but her view of Lawrence's relation with Dahoum is that this was not homosexual; she believes that Lawrence simply enjoyed scandalizing people with unorthodox behaviour. She readily admits, however, that Lawrence was biased against women.

In dealing with the Arab Revolt, Armitage had no access to archival material or to Arabic, French and German sources, and she lacks a critical historical sense, largely accepting Lawrence's letters at face value. Her account of the Revolt must be considered as just a sympathetic interpretation of *Seven Pillars* material and she makes no stand about Lawrence's part in the plans to attack Akaba. She accepts his northern ride behind Turkish lines in June 1917 but contributes nothing to its description and is unconvincing about the political aspects of the Revolt. Claiming, for instance, that Auda's 'loyalty was steadfast and enduring, as was his irascibility', she neglects to discuss his treacherous dealings with the Turks, which are documented in *Seven Pillars* itself. She makes no mention of the massacre of the Turks at Tafas by Lawrence's own order, although in the epilogue to the English edition she says that Lawrence would have been unable to restrain the Arabs, and that immoral acts are sometimes perpetrated in the heat of battle.

In her commentary on the Deraa incident, however, Flora Armitage notes what Aldington had missed — that in *Seven Pillars* Lawrence wrote openly that 'a third man rode me astride' while two others pulled his legs apart, and that this 'was momentarily better than more flogging'. She thus disputes Aldington's interpretation, writing that 'He yielded certainly, or felt that he had yielded, to the assault of one or more of his punishers' rather than to the Bey himself. This emphasis on the correctness of the Deraa account as written, and on Lawrence's self-blame for human weakness, whether or not such blame was deserved, are likely to be cited in any debate on the incident. Even Aldington believed that it had happened because of the flogging scars noted on Lawrence's body by the RAF recruiting examiner and the letter to Mrs Shaw. For Armitage, Deraa's importance lay in 'the discovery that physical punishment could arouse in him that ecstasy of nerve and blood which his mind so violently rejected' and she claims that 'For men of Lawrence's temperament there is an almost irresistible desire for submission.'

Armitage believes that 'S.A.' of the *Seven Pillars* dedicatory poem was neither Dahoum nor the Palestinian Jewish spy for the British, Sarah Aaronsohn, as has sometimes been suggested but, improbably, Lawrence's own personality.

She wonders if Lawrence might even have married had there been opportunities to meet women before the war. According to her, afterwards it was too late because of the Lowell Thomas publicity and the personal problems he had suffered. He did not hate women, but hated sex. Lawrence certainly had a fatal tendency to self-denigration. Thus, Armitage writes (reflecting the new permissiveness in sexual discussion beginning in the 1950s) that in the RAF there was pain which he 'willingly endured' but also 'illicitly enjoyed'. Essentially, Lawrence could be fascinated by pain but still recoil from it 'in guilty horror'. In a hint of what would be, in 1968/69, sensational revelations of self-imposed flagellation, Armitage says, 'His body was brought into subjection by classic means' —

Flora Armitage used this photograph in the American edition of her biography with the caption 'Aircraftman Ross on one of the family of "Boanerges"'. It actually shows Lawrence when he was Aircraftman Shaw, and was probably taken at RAF Cranwell by Sergeant Pugh. Lawrence wrote a message on the back to an unknown person: '...here is a photograph of Boa.... These were taken for the maker of the machine, to show technical details of its build. The rider is an accident.'

undoubtedly prompted by A.W. Lawrence's oblique reference to this in his collection *T.E. Lawrence by His Friends*.

So — even the staunchest proponents of Lawrence were now obliged to yield some ground to Aldington, especially with regard to Lawrence's alleged dishonesty and abnormal psychology. In the epilogue to the English edition of her book, Armitage directly answers some of Aldington's points, claiming that Churchill thought it 'very likely' he had discussed the High Commission of Egypt with Lawrence. She points out that Liman von Sanders took over the Turkish command in 1918 and therefore may have been unaware of Lawrence, but that Jemal Pasha's aide-de-camp told Colonel Newcombe that there was a price of £3000 on Lawrence's head. Armitage is nevertheless forced to admit that Aldington's is an 'important book' which will have to be 'reckoned with in the conclusions of any future biographer of T.E. Lawrence'.

Psychological interpretations stressing possible sado-masochism (seen in muted form in Armitage's book) and homosexuality began to take precedence over all others in the first two postwar decades. The next English-language biography, Anthony Nutting's *Lawrence of Arabia: The Man and the Motive* (1961), clearly exemplifies this trend, as does Terence Rattigan's play *Ross* (1960) and the David Lean/Robert Bolt film *Lawrence of Arabia*, which appeared in 1962.

Terence Rattigan

The play *Ross* is a fictionalized account, and so free from documentation. Rattigan seizes on two points — the statement attributed to the Bey 'You must understand that I know:

This photograph of Lawrence at Bridlington on 26 February 1935, the day he retired from the RAF, appeared as the frontispiece in the English edition of Flora Armitage's book. Lawrence's C.O. later wrote 'A few of us saw him off from the harbourside at Bridlington, including Ian Deheer who took a snapshot of him just before he pedalled off. He was in his familiar rig — scarf, sports jacket, flannel trousers, sitting on his bicycle, and leaning against the harbour wall .... He gave a half smile, and a half wave of the hand and he was on his way. We never saw him again.'

and it will be easier if you do as I wish' (*SP*, p.453) and the fact that Lawrence was able to escape easily the next morning — in order to create his theory of the Deraa incident. He proposes that the Bey identified Lawrence and wanted to destroy him psychologically by having him raped and forced to recognize that he was a homosexual before allowing him to return to the field broken in spirit.

This seems to be an extremely improbable interpretation of the Deraa incident. It assumes that the Turks knew they were holding T.E. Lawrence instead of the Circassian that he claimed to be and, moreover, that they understood his personal psychology in depth. In both the earlier and final manuscript versions of this incident in *Seven Pillars* Lawrence had made it clear that the Bey did not know his identity. Rattigan's interpretation also asks us to believe that the Bey, having identified Lawrence, would actually let his opponent escape and make no claim to the honour of his capture. Small wonder that when the play was staged at the Haymarket Theatre in 1960 several critics thought it brilliantly written, but too imaginative, and perhaps the product of Rattigan's vicarious need to discuss his own sexual life.

In the late 1960s the biographers Phillip Knightley and Colin Simpson discovered in the Humanities Research Center at the University of Texas a letter about this incident. Written by Lawrence to W.F. Stirling in 1919, this letter amazingly supports at least part of Rattigan's imaginative reading. It contradicts what Lawrence wrote in *Seven Pillars* about the Bey's failure to recognize him and gives a hitherto unknown version of the incident:

'I went into Deraa in disguise to spy out the defences, was caught, and identified by Hajim Bey, the governor, by virtue of Abd el Kadir's description of me. (I learned all about his treachery from Hajim's conversation, and from my guards.) Hajim was an ardent paederast and took a fancy to me ... I was unwilling, and prevailed after some difficulty. Hajim sent me to the hospital, and I escaped before dawn, being not as hurt as he thought. He was so ashamed of the muddle he had made that he hushed the whole thing up, and never reported my capture and escape.'[11]

Even though this letter shows the Bey letting Lawrence go because of a 'muddle' rather than for the psychological reason of releasing a broken enemy commander, it reveals that the Deraa incident is susceptible to almost any interpretation including Rattigan's. *Ross*, always notable for the wit with which it is written, now seems a much more valid and plausible play than when it first appeared in 1960.

Anthony Nutting

Nutting was the first biographer to comment on Rattigan's play, finding it altogether too fanciful, but Nutting himself offers interpretation rather than concrete new evidence about Lawrence, and clearly shows the sexual and political emphasis of the Aldington period. Although Nutting often sees Lawrence in a positive light, he states that Lawrence favoured the Arabs above all, and implies that he was influenced in this by his sexual psychology.

Much of Nutting's account of the Arab Revolt is largely a retelling of *Seven Pillars of Wisdom* filled in with dialogue and atmosphere often imaginatively created. The discussion about Lawrence's principles of war and his northern trip are weak, having no basis in documentary evidence, and he speculates rather unconvincingly:

'It is difficult to see what this hazardous exploit could have accomplished that could not have been achieved by messages relayed by one or several of the secret agents who plied continuously between Damascus and the Arab armies ... it was as likely as not one of those compulsive acts of bravado by which he sought constantly to prove himself to himself and to his Arab comrades.'

A different pose from the one Anthony Nutting used, probably showing Lawrence at the motorcycle factory in Haydn Road, Nottingham, taking delivery of his sixth Brough Superior SS100 in October 1930; he had written that 'Brough cannot promise me the bike till the morning of October 2'. Brough supports himself on sticks because he had recently been involved in a crash.

Surely Lawrence's presence on the long and difficult trip to Akaba through the Sirhan desert was enough of a public demonstration of his bravado? Lawrence must have had a better reason for adding the Syrian journey than merely showing off.

Moreover, like Lowell Thomas, Nutting inserts gratuitous Crusader and religious references into his speculative recreation of Lawrence's thoughts:

'... and now on the threshold of the Holy Land this new missionary for men's freedom found himself walking in the footsteps of the greatest of all saviours. How had he [Lawrence] got there, unless by some divine ordinance?'

Nutting also makes the mistake of saying that Lawrence's letter to Mrs Shaw about the Deraa incident, quoted by Aldington, 'cannot today be traced'. In fact, the letter was and is available in the British Library to any serious researcher.

The bias of his period shows when Nutting discusses political issues. Although the Arabs and British were both treacherous according to Nutting, in the clash between his Arab and British allegiances Lawrence 'cast his lot with the Emir and would put his interests before anyone else's.' Moreover, in *Seven Pillars* 'he made little mention of the British and even less of the French contribution to the winning of the war against Turkey and the success of the Arab revolt.' In October 1956, just before the Suez crisis reached its peak, Anthony Nutting delivered a speech to the Conservative Party Conference at Llandudno in which he spoke for Anthony Eden's government by stating 'we shall not flinch' in the confrontation with Nasser over his nationalization of the Canal. To Nutting, who as a member of government had attempted to reassert Britain's traditional power over the Arabs, it would seem apparent that Lawrence had favoured them over British interests. But to the generations of biographers preceding and following Nutting's, Lawrence's alleged tilt towards the Arabs was not so obvious.

aucracy sometimes gives him convincing
ting, Lawrence's political misgivings were
10m to trust nor whom to blame for the
stresses that Lawrence was often caught in
wanted to appease the French and the
, which wanted only to finish off the Turks
and everything, and the Government of

and Lawrence's personal life in particular
At Deraa Lawrence learned that he was a
pain disclosed a perversion of the flesh
himself and mocked by his tormentors he
s is an extreme and unsupported, though
1 in the Deraa chapter. Reminiscent of
ead, is his statement that after Deraa
r in his judgement of himself and others
ting's claim that at the Tafas massacre,
killer, no longer restraining himself and
tion of the blood feud. Indeed his
. almost suggested a suicidal intent.'
ado-masochist who uses the Arabs to

[handwritten marginal notes: "son of pain" = ...; of "Odysseus"; "Ulysses" = Latin form; (Odysseus, Greek); to pg 25; TRANS]

...Lawrence's part during his period in the
...suggests that 'S.A.' was an 'imaginary conception'. But Lawrence loved Syria because there 'he made deep and lasting friendships with men, such as Sheikh Hamoudi, and found a kindred spirit in the beautiful young Arab named Ahmed'. So Nutting does hint at homosexuality during the early period at Carchemish. His biography illustrates the high point of one prevalent interpretation of the time — Lawrence as a sado-masochist, and very possibly a homosexual who acted as he did for personal far more than for political reasons.

Robert Bolt

In his script for the David Lean film biography *Lawrence of Arabia*, Robert Bolt continued to explore the sado-masochistic theme. The film was a striking visual evocation of the desert and it introduced Lawrence to a wide audience but it suffered from the usual cinematic tendency to collapse, select and even invent incidents and characters.

Bolt's distortions are very obvious: Lawrence is shown burning his finger deliberately to symbolize his known proclivity to self-testing as well as to put the 'pain' theme clearly in place from the beginning. He is made responsible for leading the boys Daud and Ferraj on a trip through Sinai in which Daud dies in a sandstorm. This incident, too, never occurred. Bolt clearly means it to represent Lawrence's feeling for Dahoum (who in fact died of typhus before the Arab Revolt ended) but in so doing introduces an extraneous element of guilt. On the screen Lawrence overtly confesses to Allenby that he enjoyed executing Gasim but in *Seven Pillars* Hamed the Moor, not Gasim, was executed and Lawrence never confessed to anyone that he enjoyed killing, although he worried that he might grow to like power too much.

Auda abu Tayi enters only in the middle of the march on Akaba, although some credit him with the inception of the plan. The long road to Akaba is shortened because the intervening battle at Aba el Lissan is omitted. Lawrence's northern ride is also omitted as is much of the early progress of the Revolt. There is a hint of Auda's duplicity with the

Turks but Feisal's treachery is never discussed. Lawrence is shown to believe in Arab unity, when in fact he merely preached it to the Arabs as a matter of expediency while always remaining aware of how unlikely it was.

More serious and actually out of character is Lawrence's early criticism in the film of the Arabs as 'barbarians' and of their fatalistic beliefs. In his famous 'Twenty-seven Articles', a primer for British agents working with the Arabs, Lawrence makes it clear that such a course of overt criticism is never to be recommended. Rather, he preferred to work through the Sherifs. Even Aldington praises Lawrence for his lack of superiority to the Arabs. Sherif Ali is also shown out of character: he shoots Lawrence's guide in cold blood while the book records no such episode.

In the film the Deraa incident takes on a different relevance. There is no suggestion that Lawrence received sexual satisfaction from the beating, or yielded to the Bey's entreaties or to general sodomy. However, Lawrence wishes to leave the movement after this incident because he was ready to tell the Turks anything and simply realizes that he was not as tough as he should have been. So Bolt's version simplifies the incident considerably, especially in view of Lawrence's own accounts.

D.G. Hogarth, Lawrence's lifelong mentor and the man who brought him into intelligence work, is drawn completely out of character as the refined and sinister 'Dryden'. Instead of supporting and aiding Lawrence, Dryden cynically goes along with the policy of turning Syria over to the French, and does not display undue concern for Lawrence's mental or physical health. Perhaps Dryden is intended to be the more distant Ronald Storrs? If so, Hogarth has been eliminated. Lawrence's subsequent career at the 1919 and 1921 political conferences, as well as his life in the RAF, are not shown at all.

So the film made many changes: it was not a documentary, nor subject to the truth. Nonetheless, Bolt deserves praise for having remained faithful to a reasonable interpretation that makes sense of, without too greatly exaggerating, the conflicts and character of Lawrence during the period of the Revolt — according to the information known in the early 1960s. He is especially good on the conflict Lawrence felt between his British and Arab loyalties.

As Bolt portrays him, Lawrence begins his involvement in the Revolt as an unconventional, civilized and idealistic soldier. He has no patience with army routine, deplores the waste of human life, and treats the Arabs as an oppressed people who can become great again. He proves himself the equal of the bedouin when he rescues the lost Gasim and participates in long camel marches. He tells the Arabs that they can become powerful if their separate warring tribes are unified. Subtly, Bolt shows Lawrence both amused at his own adoption of Arab clothes and also genuinely sympathetic to the Arab cause; and Peter O'Toole's fine acting makes this ambiguity of Lawrence's — his shifting from self-consciousness to genuine absorption in his Arab role — convincing.

After the Deraa incident, persuaded to return to the Arabs, Lawrence does so in a spirit of revenge against the Turks. So Lawrence (who had opposed unnecessary bloodshed at the beginning of the Revolt) is shown to enjoy participating in the massacre of the Turks at Tafas. In this scene, as in the finger-burning incident and Lawrence's confession of enjoyment in killing, Bolt's film fits the sado-masochistic emphasis of its period.

Perhaps best of all is Bolt's imaginative portrayal of a cynical conversation between Feisal and Allenby in which both men (as well as Dryden) are shown to be eager to get rid of Lawrence, who has received too much publicity and perhaps too much power to suit them. Lawrence is taken from Damascus by an English driver, and tries to wave to bedouin who do not recognize him in his British uniform. He reacts with an ambiguous facial expression when the driver happily tells him that he's 'going home'. His dilemma of not knowing who he is and what the future will hold is suitably underlined. Lawrence is seen enjoying the publicity put out about him by Lowell Thomas (called Jackson Bentley in the film), who is wrongly shown accompanying the Revolt all the way to Damascus; we also see Lawrence repelled by this publicity when he remembers all the bloodshed in which he had to be involved to be considered a 'hero'.

Despite the discrepancies, in many ways Bolt actually achieved a fairly legitimate and powerful interpretation of Lawrence's own writings. Since the continuing international fame of Lawrence was partly due to this film in the 1960s and even after, it is fortunate Robert Bolt and David Lean together created an image that is still relevant today, and that Peter O'Toole's sensitive portrayal gave the general public an uncannily compelling Lawrence.

Foreign Biographies

Although the film continued to make Lawrence accessible to a wide audience from the 1960s onwards, he had already proved a subject of great interest in many foreign countries and inspired there some of the finest work in the field.

Erik Lönnroth

An academic historian from Sweden (a country that had not been touched by Lawrence's activities at all), Lönnroth produced a notably neutral and careful assessment of Lawrence in 1943 but only in 1956 did a revised edition (under the simple title *Lawrence of Arabia*) become available in English. This was perhaps due to the controversy that developed immediately after the publication of Aldington's 'biographical enquiry'. Lönnroth's view of this is stated in his introductory chapter:

'Aldington was able to tear many legends to pieces, and his work undoubtedly represents a necessary reaction against the previous one-sided idealisation of Lawrence in the literature written in English. But that is not to say that Aldington's picture can be accepted as "the truth". ... Aldington's ability critically to evaluate the data in the sources which he had collected is not on a par with his industry in collecting them. His interpretation of the material is one-sidedly unfavourable to Lawrence, and he seems to be primarily interested in branding him as a liar. ... The distinction between deliberate lying and involuntary distortion, between mythomania and the usual imaginativeness of memoir writers, does not seem to be quite clear to Aldington. Still less does he make any systematic distinction between actual records of events and subjective testimony, or between primary and secondary evidence.'

Lönnroth bases himself upon direct source material, including the *Secret Despatches from Arabia* (1939), Lawrence's wartime reports to the Arab Bureau. Whatever was available to researchers at that time he examined closely and without prejudice. He found that the documents 'often give astonishingly copious and precise information, if they are used in the right way'. Lönnroth concludes that *Seven Pillars* is a subjective memoir, not an objective history and so is not entirely factual on some essential points:

'What is clear is that Lawrence bore the main burden of responsibility for the operation of the Arab army, but his actions no longer appear as the result of a carefully thought out and revolutionary strategy, as has generally been assumed. The burden of his military undertakings gravitated between *ad hoc* planning from event to event and leading raids and skirmishes on the one hand, and the maintenance of communications with British headquarters on the other. That he could achieve just this is no less of a miracle, if one considers his meagre military training. ... He experimented and theorised unceasingly on the basis of those realities with which he had to deal on the Arab front. Many of his actions and opinions give a remarkable impression of far-sightedness.'

In keeping with his view of how *Seven Pillars* smoothed out the actual history of the Revolt, Lönnroth finds that Lawrence did not choose Feisal as the Revolt's leader at the beginning; rather that Feisal assumed a primary role in Lawrence's thinking later on. Lönnroth also thinks that Lawrence was acting only as a 'private person' during his first trip to Arabia, not an intelligence agent, and he remarks that Ronald Storrs makes no particular notations about Lawrence's presence during this trip, indicating Lawrence's then relative unimportance in the planning for the Revolt. Rather than choosing to leave Medina alone (as Lawrence claims in *Seven Pillars*), it appears Lawrence 'was concerned to make a virtue of...[his]...one major failure', namely 'the successful resistance of Medina against the Arabs' (p.31).

With regard to the expedition against Akaba, 'it is not quite clear who thought out the plan' but the likeliest version 'seems to be that Auda worked out the details for the march through the desert ... but that Lawrence's was the strategic will behind the expedition. This is confirmed by the fact that the march against Akaba was combined with a reconnaissance which Lawrence undertook alone far into Syria.' According to Lönnroth, who uses Lawrence's own report, the northern journey was made for the purpose of drawing up 'a plan for the grouping of Arab forces in Palestine and Syria in order to support a British offensive from Sinai' (pp.34-35). During this trip, Lawrence spoke to Ali Riza Pasha (the Turkish military governor of Damascus) a few kilometres outside the city; he also met with Nuri Shaalan, an important Arab leader.

At Deraa Lawrence received 'a frightful beating...[which]...gave him a shock with lasting after-effects' (p.46). Lönnroth believes that Lawrence's *Seven Pillars of Wisdom* 'polemic against the strategy of annihilation and the military theorising associated with it belongs to the pacific nineteen-twenties, as do also the self-accusations and the morbid emotional state'. In fact, according to Lönnroth, at Tafas in September 1918 Lawrence was in complete agreement with the Arabs' indiscriminate killing of the Turks, and he was not an exemplar of pacifism although he did sometimes regret bloodshed during the war.

'S.A.' is a person who died before Lawrence reached Damascus, but Lönnroth does not confirm or deny Aldington's statement that 'S.A.' was Dahoum; this question, like Aldington's claim that Lawrence was a homosexual, Lönnroth leaves open for want of facts: 'Lawrence's emotional life was terribly inhibited, above all on the erotic plane, but also in everything connected with bodily satisfactions' (p.97).

For Lönnroth, the biggest crises in Lawrence's life were his plane crash *en route* to Cairo in 1919, and his political defeat when France received the Syrian mandate at the Paris Peace Conference. 'It was as though the mainspring in his taut mechanism of will was now broken. It was never to recover its former power' (p.88). So Lawrence acquiesced in the settlement of the Cairo Conference of 1921 at which Feisal received the throne of Iraq and Abdulla the throne of Transjordan; he simply wished to end his Arab involvement and escape from politics. He did, however, remain loyal to the Hussein family, and never revealed that Feisal had actually betrayed to the Turks that a major British offensive was imminent in Palestine in the summer of 1918. (Feisal's betrayal is mentioned in the memoirs of the German General Liman von Sanders.)

Lönnroth was also the first to point out that although the Nazi foreign affairs representative, Kurt von Ludecke, tried to establish contact with him in the early 1930s, Lawrence rejected these advances.

Ultimately, the academic Lönnroth sees Lawrence as a disappointed romantic who carried out important and praiseworthy spontaneous actions. Lawrence's problem was that he 'found it difficult to accept reality as it was.' He 'was a stranger to simple and unselfconscious pleasures, and tore apart all everyday illusions with merciless analytical criticism' (p.97).

Jean Béraud-Villars

Inevitably the French press reaction to T.E. Lawrence in the 1920s was rather negative after his opposition to French control of Syria. Nonetheless *Revolt in the Desert* appeared in a Payot edition in 1928 and sold well. By 1929 there were rumours that André Malraux wanted to write a book about Lawrence; and in 1942–44 he produced a lengthy but incomplete work which has been rescued and edited by Maurice Larès, but not yet published.

Malraux's work was not the first sign of French interest in Lawrence: Victor Meulenijzer's *Le colonel Lawrence, agent de l'Intelligence Service* appeared in 1939, Roger Stéphane's *Portrait de l'Aventurier* in 1940 and Léon Boussard's *Le Secret du colonel Lawrence* in 1941. Other signs of French interest included Malraux's novel *The Walnut Trees of Altenburg* (1943), in which the hero is based on Lawrence, and many early articles. Aldington's book was published in French in 1954 before it appeared in English. A strong continuing fascination is indicated by the more recent works of Jacques Benoist-Méchin, Maurice Larès and Vincent Mansour Monteil.

As Maurice Larès has commented, the French (wrongly) believe that Lawrence hated them but that he had a right to do so; and they have remained fascinated by the enigma of Lawrence. Jean Béraud-Villars's *T.E. Lawrence or the Search for the Absolute* (French 1955; English 1958) remains one of the best Lawrence biographies. Essentially, Béraud-Villars — writing at a time when ideas of European unity were new and very current — charges Lawrence with exacerbating Anglo-French tensions and thus having weakened rather than strengthened Europe, but he still sees Lawrence as a 'great man' who was 'at once a war leader and an artist' (p.xi).

Most importantly, Béraud-Villars understands that Lawrence's role as secret agent precluded his full disclosure of information and that the record would remain murky for some time to come. Thus, Lawrence's journey to Jidda with Storrs was an intelligence trip, not a holiday as claimed in *Seven Pillars* and in Lönnroth's biography.

Working without archival material or knowledge of Aldington's book, Béraud-Villars throws doubt on many of Lawrence's claims. Lawrence's strategic chapter 33, for instance, 'is full of special pleading, obviously written after the event, and in the light of facts which he could not have known at the time'.

According to Béraud-Villars, it would have been wise from the Allied point of view to land European troops in Arabia, just as Colonel Brémond (the French liaison officer and Lawrence's bitter opponent) had wanted: Lawrence scuttled the plan, not because he thought it bad but solely because it would have ended his own unique role with the Arabs and their Revolt.

For Béraud-Villars, a colonel in the French army, the bedouins' military value was virtually nil and Lawrence was fighting a one-man war. He is convinced that much of *Seven Pillars* is devoted to disguising this, to making it seem as if the Arabs were good fighters, and dedicated to the cause of nationalism, when in fact Lawrence was forced to push the movement forward himself. Auda and the Emir Feisal dealt treacherously with the Turks while the British Imperial Camel Corps accomplished far more than Feisal's army. Even the Arabs' entrance into Damascus was achieved not because they arrived there first but because the British allowed them to enter first. In fact, according to Béraud-Villars, only the non-Arab portions of the army fought well — the British and French elements, the Gurkhas and the Egyptian units. Feisal and Lawrence were never really compatible, and after the war, when he became King of Iraq, Feisal treated Lawrence coldly.

Despite Lawrence's praise for the Sherifian forces in *Seven Pillars*, the fact that he had to do everything himself 'only increases Lawrence's stature as a fighter and leader, and reveals his extreme ability as a politician' although 'it seriously weakens the legend he had striven to create of the Sherif's army'. In making these negative assessments of the Arabs, Béraud-Villars was no doubt influenced to some degree by the passions surrounding the growing French troubles in Algeria, the loss of French Indochina, and the death of his son in French Guinea. The French retreat from empire occurred at the same time as British withdrawal, and was no less traumatic for France. Writing his biography in an atmosphere of Arab nationalism, just a year before the joint Anglo-French invasion of Egypt, Béraud-Villars (like Aldington) perhaps predictably charged Lawrence with irrational actions against British-French unity.

According to Béraud-Villars, after the war Lawrence was bound to his aim of a Sherifian Syria under English tutelage; but in fact he 'certainly was not the anti-colonialist of principle which people have wished to make of him' (p.250): he helped the British keep control of Egypt, and had no concern for Ireland or India. He was simply anti-French, a feeling he shared with many of his countrymen.

By contrast, Maurice Larès has recently claimed in his *T.E. Lawrence, la France et les Français* that Lawrence did not in fact 'hate' the French, although he did strongly oppose their Middle-East policy; he enjoyed his early times in France and was influenced by French literary and archaeological interests. According to Larès, although Lawrence did not get on with Brémond, and resented the French attempt to control Syria, he did mention the French contingents in the war very favourably, and he opposed English colonization of Iraq with far more vigour than he displayed against the French in Syria. So perhaps Lawrence's 'inexplicable' dislike of France is inexplicable simply because it never existed. Indeed perhaps Lawrence had very rational reasons for opposing French rule in Syria, as will become clear when his diplomatic activity is examined.

With regard to Lawrence's sexual experience, Béraud-Villars says that Lawrence was a latent if not a practising homosexual and his relationship with Dahoum was not 'natural'. Lawrence was raped at Deraa and his willingness to write about this 'Gestapo scene' fairly openly, made him the forerunner of the modern writers of political brutality.

Béraud-Villars believes that Lawrence's depleted state after the war might have been the result of disappointment and poor physical health; it also possibly owed something to a disagreement Lawrence had with British Intelligence, which began to swing in favour of Ibn Saud and against the Hussein family. But essentially Béraud-Villars believes that the root of Lawrence's problems was that he housed within himself two personalities — one a wilful, conscience-stricken and puritanical fanatic, the other 'an hysterical woman, perfidious, lying, unstable, with a taste for travesty and treason, and a love of causing quarrels' (p.314).

The Mint, his RAF memoir, reveals a 'persecution mania, his morbid need to suffer, and above all his unhealthy desire to humiliate himself morally and physically' (p.336). Towards the end of his life, 'his enormous vanity increased ... and drove him off and on to a sort of mythomania' in which 'He exaggerated the role which he had played at different times in his life' (p.345).

Yet despite this severe judgement of Lawrence's character and his apparent favouring of the Arabs in the war, Béraud-Villars realizes that he is dealing with a brilliant commander, an important innovative writer and, above all, with an intelligence agent whose very weaknesses, such as a talent for petty quarrels and intrigue, were the sources of his success.

No one else could have fulfilled Lawrence's role among the Arabs; no one else could have written *Seven Pillars*. Béraud-Villars's Lawrence emerges as productive in spite of his pronounced pathological qualities. This analysis of Lawrence's character, however objective, owes much to the atmosphere of the age of Aldington, in which Lawrence's personal, particularly sexual, psychology rather than his reason was said to have determined his political actions.

Suleiman Mousa

Suleiman Mousa set out to write *T.E. Lawrence: An Arab View* (Arabic 1962; English 1966) because, as he says, none of the previous biographers 'took the trouble to come to this part of the world and investigate the Arab viewpoint' and, apart from Antonius' brief treatment, 'the Arabs themselves have not attempted to put forward their side of the argument'. Moreover, just as Aldington and Béraud-Villars may have been subconsciously impelled by the threat of rising Arab nationalism in the 1950s to denigrate the Arab role in the First World War, so Mousa may have been encouraged in his re-examination of Lawrence's career by the Arabs' growing confidence and their nationalistic consciousness.

Besides adding Arabic works to the Lawrence bibliography, he expressed a point of view hitherto practically unheard in the West, namely that the Arab Revolt was far more important to Allenby than Aldington had claimed, and owed more to Arab needs, inspiration and execution than to Lawrence, who remained in the last analysis a 'British citizen with a great regard for his country's interest' and 'a real desire to see the Arabs win, simply because they were British allies' (p.265). Although Mousa readily admits that Lawrence was a very unusual and gifted personality, he outstrips Aldington in claiming that Lawrence completely fabricated many incidents in order to call attention to himself in *Seven Pillars*. Lawrence had 'the advantage of his pen, while the bedouin and Arab regulars enjoyed no such gift ... the secret of his magnified stature' (p.263).

Mousa's first point, about the value of the Arab Revolt to Allenby, is one of those issues involving British and Arab national pride that can never be decisively proved either way. It is clear that without British supplies and money, the Arab Revolt could not have progressed as it did; and also that the British and Australians did the large bulk of the fighting in the Palestine campaign and broke the back of the Turkish army. It is equally clear that the Arab guerrilla movement had great propaganda and psychological value. Moreover, it tied up large numbers of the enemy and many supplies that might otherwise have been diverted to the main front; so the movement definitely saved British lives besides serving Arab objectives.

Mousa's most important charges against Lawrence should be examined against the testimony of a secretive personality who in his 'Twenty-seven Articles' advises working only through native rulers and keeping oneself in the background. Mousa states that Lawrence entirely fabricated the story of his having taken a northern journey behind Turkish lines in June 1917 and that he completely invented the Deraa incident.

Mousa's evidence on the first point is one man's remembrance (forty years after the event) that Lawrence never left the Arab group during its ride toward Akaba and could not therefore have been away in the north for two or three weeks. Not only is this negative evidence weak, but there is now very strong positive evidence for the journey, some of which was not available when Mousa wrote his book.

As Gideon Gera has recently commented:

'Today, with many British archives — public and private — open, there can be no doubt that this outstanding feat was actually performed. Even before that, however, sufficient evidence to counter the Mousa thesis was available. The "trip" was mentioned in the official history and Lawrence was commended by Wingate for a high award for his "magnificent achievement", appointed a Companion of the Bath, and congratulated by the War Cabinet.'[12]

Unless we assume that the British had no means whatsoever of checking on their agents and simply awarded honours on the basis of the agents' own claims, and unless we are prepared to forget Lawrence's own pencilled war diary report on the trip and solid archival evidence, we must today accept the fact of this journey.

With regard to the Deraa incident, the case is somewhat more ambiguous since there are no available witnesses and little documentation. Mousa's claim that it never happened rests on his view of Hajim Bey's character, which is said to have been honourable. Mousa also questions how a man as exhausted as Lawrence after his beating could have ridden four hundred miles to Akaba on a camel. Yet even Aldington accepted the basic truth of Lawrence's story because of the scars seen on his body by the RAF recruitment doctor, and the letter to Mrs G.B. Shaw he discovered in the British Museum. Colonel Richard Meinertzhagen, Sergeant Pugh and Private Arthur Russell reported seeing scars on Lawrence's ribs and back. Edward Robinson claims to testify on the basis of his diary that Lawrence was severely shaken after returning from Deraa to Akaba. Finally, as noticed in the discussion of Rattigan's play, in 1919 Lawrence wrote a letter to Stirling in Cairo GHQ in which he mentioned the Deraa incident. Mousa did not have this piece of information available when he wrote his book, since Knightley and Simpson discovered it only later.

In addition, A.W. Lawrence, in his reply to Mousa, points out that barbarities were attributed to Hajim Bey by at least one witness. Concerning his journey to Akaba after the beating, in his 1919 letter to Stirling, Lawrence avers that the beating did not hurt him quite so badly as Hajim Bey thought, so he may well have been more capable of the journey than Mousa says.

Also, Mousa's view that no massacre by either Turks or Arabs took place at Tafas except in Lawrence's imagination, must be set against affirmative evidence from Brémond, Young, Robinson, Kirkbride and Peake.

Mousa strongly contests Lawrence's view of Feisal as weak. He denies that Feisal would have treated with the Turks — simply on the basis that Feisal was known to be level-headed and prudent. Yet the evidence for Feisal's actions comes not only from Lawrence but also from the memoirs of General Liman von Sanders.

In view of their post-war military and political disasters, were Sherif Hussein's family members as capable as Mousa largely presents them, or is Lawrence's more critical view of them correct? As Mousa was a Jordanian government employee when he wrote his book, he may have been committed to upholding the reputation of the Hussein family, who in his account can virtually do no wrong. He even admits without disapproval that Sherif Hussein gave financial support to a Mesopotamian uprising against the British in 1920, when he was receiving British subsidies. In fact, the Husseins' reign in Jordan is the only lasting, stable political achievement to their credit.

Mousa's final charge against Lawrence is that he favoured Zionism as well as Arab nationalism. This is indeed the case, but surely it is to Lawrence's credit that he tried to bring both sides together, and could sympathize with the aspirations of both Arabs and Jews?

Although they can readily be challenged, Mousa's criticisms were to prove important for the next period of Lawrence biographies, when political questions, made current by the oil crisis and Third World issues, continued to affect perceptions of Lawrence. Meanwhile, Aldington's book (which undoubtedly influenced Mousa's view that Lawrence was a liar) exerted a hold into the 1970s and beyond. Despite the positive biographies of the 1950s and 1960s (to which can be added Stanley Weintraub's study of Lawrence's relationship with George Bernard Shaw, *Private Shaw and Public Shaw* (1968)), it would take from 1969 to the present day to achieve some balance between the idealistic superhero and the sado-masochistic anti-hero — for a more convincing Lawrence to emerge from these conflicting images.

Chapter three

A Prince of Our Disorder?

The best biographies of the contemporary period, beginning in 1969, are notable for their reliance on new material not available to previous biographers. The psychiatrist John Mack uses such evidence to present Lawrence as a 'prince of our disorder', who transformed his personal neuroses into public accomplishments and attempted to solve many of the problems of his period. This positive view has been disputed by contemporary followers of Aldington, who have charged that whatever Lawrence's intentions, his personal vagaries resulted only in political failures. Yet the tone of the debate is less extreme than in previous periods, with both sides more prepared to see mixed positive and negative features in Lawrence's personality and career.

In the current controversy about the connnection between Lawrence's personality and his politics, probably the most frequently-debated questions are whether or not he was an imperialist or a Fascist. Attention to these issues has been fueled by public interest in oil politics, Third World ideology and the Vietnam War, and the related thrust and counter-thrust of intelligence agencies and terrorists. More writers than ever before have dwelt on the highly speculative spy-thriller issue of whether or not Lawrence was murdered.

Despite all this, the new biographies do not solve such genuine mysteries as what he did on his secret northern ride, who was responsible for planning the Akaba attack, what exactly happened at Deraa, and why Lawrence joined the RAF. The many gaps in our knowledge of Lawrence's life and continuing disagreement over his attitudes and roles guarantee that more will be written on Lawrence in the years to come. The authorized biography by J.M. Wilson, scheduled for publication in the second half of 1988, will perhaps throw light on some of the riddles.

Knightley and Simpson

Phillip Knightley and Colin Simpson, two investigative reporters at *The Sunday Times* in London, set in motion the new approach to Lawrence by making use of then recently-opened files of the Public Record Office, hitherto embargoed Bodleian Library letters, and interviews with as yet 'untapped' witnesses. Their well-publicized *Secret Lives of Lawrence of Arabia* (1969), commanded widespread attention from academics as well as general readers.

Lawrence arrives in Damascus in his Rolls Royce in October 1918.

Some of Knightley and Simpson's new evidence was exciting and provocative: Boutagy, a Christian Arab who had worked as a spy for Lawrence, revealed details about the extent of Lawrence's network and his methods of dealing with spies. His role as a 'tough, hard working' intelligence officer is thus enormously enhanced. Knightley and Simpson also provide new documentation about Lawrence and Arab-Jewish relations.

On the personal side, they produce the letter about the Deraa incident written in 1919 to W.F. Stirling at General Headquarters in Cairo. In this, Lawrence states that he was betrayed by Abd el-Kadir's description of him, was recognized as a British officer, resisted the Bey's attempt to sleep with him and so was beaten. He then managed to escape, being less hurt than the Bey thought. This document is interesting in that it contradicts both *Seven Pillars* and the Charlotte Shaw letter in which Lawrence says he 'gave away' his bodily integrity, implying that in some way he acquiesced in a rape.

Knightley and Simpson were also able to contribute evidence from Tom Beaumont, who served with Lawrence; he helped identify 'S.A.' as Dahoum by remembering that Lawrence broke down and wept at Umtaiye when he learned that Dahoum had died of typhus. This would explain the 'S.A.' poem's elegiac mood, although Beaumont's memories (like any other remembrance of an event long past) must be treated with appropriate caution.

The most interesting new personal revelation in the Knightley and Simpson book arose from their interviews with John Bruce, a Scotsman. Bruce said that he had administered to Lawrence (at Lawrence's own, but indirectly expressed, request) some ten beatings with birch rods over a period of twelve years, starting in 1923.

Knightley and Simpson's book includes new visual research, such as this previously unpublished photo of Lawrence. The caption reads 'Lawrence arrives in Damascus in his Rolls Royce'. But either the caption or Lawrence's memory is incorrect because Lawrence wrote to his friend Walter Stirling in October 1924 that 'My memory of the entry into Damascus was of a quietness and emptiness of street, and of myself crying like a baby with eventual thankfulness, in the Blue Mist by your side.' Stirling, Chief Staff Officer with the Arab forces, is not at Lawrence's side, nor does the picture show empty streets, although it clearly dates from the period of Lawrence's stay in Damascus at the beginning of October 1918.

'Lawrence and Feisal on a visit to HMS Orion before the Paris Peace Conference' is the caption for this photograph in the British edition of Knightley and Simpson's book. In the American edition a slightly larger group is shown along with a note (dated 15 December 1918) by Feisal in Arabic, which translates as 'I present my respect to the glorified British fleet'. Nuri al-Said and Tassim Bey Qadri stand behind Feisal with the ship's captain, Rear-Admiral A.C. Leveson, at left.

Although Knightley and Simpson can be credited with bringing a new depth of evidence to the study of Lawrence, the use they make of their fresh material frequently raises doubts that invalidate their overall portrait of his life. One of their most prominent researchers was Suleiman Mousa, who agreed to share his Public Record Office discoveries with them. In fact, their book follows what can be described as the Mousa line, that Lawrence was a cold-blooded imperialist agent who cared nothing for the Arabs and sought only to advance British interests.

The problem with this interpretation is that the very documentation Knightley and Simpson quote contradicts this one-sided view of Lawrence. In 1919, Lawrence listed his motives for pursuing the Arab Revolt as follows: Personal — regard for an individual Arab; Patriotic — a desire to help win the war for the British; Intellectual curiosity — the desire to feel what it was like 'to be the mainspring of a national movement'; Ambition — to create an Arab Dominion of the British Empire that would be run as 'an independent ally of Great Britain'. Far from showing Lawrence as a British imperialist, this document neatly balances his Arab sympathies against his British side. His fourth ambition, to create an independent Arab ally of Great Britain would, in his opinion, serve both Arab and English interests.

Knightley and Simpson, following Mousa, accuse Lawrence of wanting to keep the Arabs divided instead of united. They simply ignore the opinion Lawrence rendered again and again, and which seems to be justified by many of today's events, that the Arabs themselves were unable to unite. So even if the British had wanted to help them achieve unity (which they patently did not) this would have been an impossible Utopian goal. The two authors conveniently ignore the many proven incidents of internal Arab disunity such as the revolt of Abd el-Kadir and the constant opposition to Feisal by the Damascene urban notables, which would have supported Lawrence's view. Moreover they quote Lawrence as saying in his diary 'We are calling them [the Arabs] to fight for us on a lie and I can't stand it.' Surely that was not the uncaring, one-sided declaration of an imperialist agent?

Knightley and Simpson's book smacks rather too much of the hindsight of the radical 1960s, according to which Lawrence was not sufficiently in favour of total Third World independence. They seem to be demanding more foresight than is possible for any human

Lawrence is in the back row third from right, his brother Will is in the third row from the front to the right, and his friend C.F.C. Beeson is seventh to the left from Lawrence in the back row, at the Oxford High School for Boys in 1906. John Mack was the first to make use of this photograph but only the detail showing Lawrence is included in his biography.

being. Significantly they neglect to mention that Feisal was engaged in a double game involving the possible betrayal of his British allies to the Turks and that after the war he was even financing revolt against the British in Iraq.

Knightley and Simpson show that Lawrence hoped to win Jewish intellectual and financial support for Feisal's kingdom in exchange for Jewish settlement rights in Palestine. In saying that Lawrence could not therefore be a real friend of the Arabs they follow Mousa, but they differ with Mousa's denial that Feisal signed an agreement with Chaim Weizmann. Knightley and Simpson show that this did occur, and at Lawrence's instigation. From this agreement it becomes obvious that both Feisal and Weizmann thought more of the intended co-operation than do Knightley, Simpson, or Mousa. The important point is that Lawrence was the only person in history (apart from President Jimmy Carter) able to bring Arab and Jewish nationalists together to sign an agreement. This indicates that he was a friend of both peoples, just as his letters and *Seven Pillars* demonstrate.

Although their historical judgement is suspect, Knightley and Simpson did contribute greater insight into the prevailing view of Lawrence's secret activities. The idea that Lawrence was an intelligence agent at Carchemish before the war has been denied by several biographers but, by tracing his actions and motives, the authors make a shrewd case for his unofficial involvement and his possible training by Hogarth. They show that, a very short time after his arrival in Cairo, Lawrence was running agents like Boutagy who were part of a larger network that he may well have begun before the war. Here, as in their revelations about 'S.A.' and Lawrence's flagellation, Knightley and Simpson have produced interesting information. They also conjecture that Lawrence might have been keeping his eye on IRA activities while in the RAF, and say that he actually warned Trenchard about what he felt were the suspect loyalties of H. St. John Philby.

While Knightley and Simpson do not make their case for Lawrence's alleged obsessive British imperialism, they do present genuinely new evidence in many areas; future biographies would have to do the same or seem weak by comparison with theirs.

John Mack

While not without faults, John Mack's *A Prince of Our Disorder* (1976) is a balanced answer to the Aldington-inspired line of criticism; it was the most serious and solid of all the Lawrence biographies ever to appear up to the end of 1987. Carefully weighing earlier criticisms of Lawrence against copious new documentary material and interviews — particularly with bedouin who remembered him — Mack, a psychiatrist, is especially well-equipped to provide an unsensational perspective on Lawrence's states of mind.

Mack sees Lawrence as a genuinely precocious child. Lawrence's knowledge that his parents were deceivers made him exaggerate the degree of his own deception of the Arabs. His illegitimacy caused him problems of self-esteem; he created an idealized medieval self and suffered greatly when he failed to measure up to impossible standards. In *Seven Pillars of Wisdom*, he tried to create such an ideal self-image but could not sustain it and relapsed into frequent self-deprecation, sometimes exaggerating his deeds when his awareness of failure was greatest. Thus, Lawrence's claims to the original conception of a British landing in Alexandretta are false; and the description of his meeting with Feisal is romanticized in *Seven Pillars*.

Mack says that Janet Laurie rejected Lawrence's proposal of marriage and that this, coupled with his mother's domination of the home, alienated him from women. He 'was less uncomfortable with homosexual than with heterosexual concepts of behavior' (p.424) but was not an overt homosexual. The bouts of flagellation were intended to destroy the body's sexuality and act as a punishment for Lawrence's guilty feelings about having been weaker than he should have been at Deraa and for having enjoyed sexually some aspects of the torture he experienced there. But what actually happened at Deraa remains unclear.

Despite these very real handicaps and a tendency to aggrandize unnecessarily a life that was already highly unusual and even heroic, Lawrence appears in a very positive light in Mack's biography. Precisely because Lawrence was torn 'between his actual view of

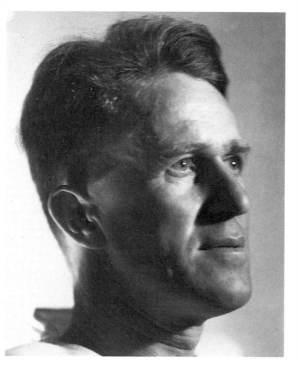

Mack wrote under this photograph: 'Portrait of Lawrence by Howard Costa, done around 1930'. It was probably taken late in 1931 and the photographer's correct name is Coster. Vyvyan Richards relates that Coster caught sight of Lawrence looking at portraits in his window, then went out and invited Lawrence to sit for him.

himself and his merciless ideal expectation', he was impelled to achieve extraordinary things. Lawrence becomes a new heroic type for the modern age — a hero who is concerned about the loss of human life resulting from his commands and who feels ambiguous about his very desire to rule others. Lawrence was born in an age that glorified war but he could not bring himself to do the same. He never forgave himself for losing control and ordering no prisoners to be taken at Tafas.

Furthermore, he was a progressive political voice in what was still an imperial age. Unlike Knightley and Simpson, who saw Lawrence as an almost Satanic imperialist under the control of Lionel Curtis's Round Table of Empire builders, Mack points out that Lawrence never even met Curtis until after the war, was actually beloved by the Arabs (as old bedouin sheikhs and British eyewitnesses remember) and was able to sympathize with British and Arab as well as Arab and Zionist aspirations. The attempt on the part of today's Arab nationalists to denigrate Lawrence is the result of their embarrassment at the large role he played in the beginning of their movement and their view of him as an imperialist. In fact, 'in the period after the Armistice, Lawrence's was one of the few voices of conscience ... urging Great Britain, France and the other Western powers to uphold certain of their commitments and to respect the right of the Arab peoples to self-determination. He retained a concept of the British Empire, but it was an empire of voluntary affiliation for mutual advantage, not one of conquest and control' (p.316). Exactly what he did on his famous northern ride and his role in the Akaba planning may remain unclear but his accomplishments in both episodes are undeniable. Driven by his own personal need to achieve an ideal, Lawrence channelled this compulsion into achieving the aims of others — whether Arabs or friends in the RAF. On occasions when such aims failed to be realized he was equally persistent in trying to accomplish the next best thing. Lawrence is a 'prince of our disorder' who directly confronted many of the dilemmas of his period.

As scrupulous and serious as Mack's biography is, his explanations of Lawrence's need to exaggerate sometimes appear to be apologies for lying. Lawrence's claim to have arranged the capture of Erzerum by the Russians is evidently false, as Aldington had

John Mack captions this 'RAF 200 leaving from Plymouth. On board were Fl/Lt. Beaufort-Greenwood, Wing Commander De Courcey, A/Lt. [sic — should be Fl/Lt.] Norrington, Corporal Bradbury and Aircraftsman Shaw.' The photograph probably dates from 1931 because on 10 June Lawrence wrote from Plymouth that 'Last week we ran down from Southampton here in 7 hrs. in one of the new R.A.F. boats.'

charged. Mack's explanation that this indicates Lawrence's lack of self-esteem is not likely to make an apparent lie any more palatable. Mack's failure to find any evidence of overt homosexuality may seem naïve to those who remember Lawrence's nude sculpting of Dahoum, or his sensuous 'S.A.' poem, his positive view of Farraj and Daud or his friendship with the handsome Airman R.A.M. Guy — whom he addressed as 'Poppet' or 'Rabbit'. Similarly, his judgement that Lawrence's flagellation was an attempt to destroy the body's sexuality is undermined by testimony that on one occasion he required the beating to be strong enough 'to produce a seminal emission'. Mack's labelling of Lawrence's arrangements for his flagellation sessions as 'creative psychopathology' comes close to praise for abnormal and harmful behaviour. His statement that Lawrence did not commit suicide on his motorcycle but 'was, however, less vigorous in preserving his own life than he might once have been' (p.411) seems highly speculative. Despite these shortcomings, *A Prince of Our Disorder* remains the best reply to extreme views of Lawrence's politics and states of mind.

Elie Kedourie

Elie Kedourie, a scholar of Middle-Eastern history at the London School of Economics, has questioned Mack's political judgement. In one very critical chapter in his collection of articles on various Middle-Eastern subjects, *Islam in the Modern World*, Kedourie shows that, despite Mack's strong defence, the Aldington point of view is far from vanquished, and that we can expect the positive and negative attitudes toward Lawrence to continue side by side indefinitely. Kedourie is unequivocal about Lawrence having lied in *Seven Pillars* where he claimed that Feisal was brave. Lawrence thought him weak and cowardly, as he told Liddell Hart. He lied again, according to Kedourie, when stating that the Arabs reached Damascus first, for he knew full well that the British had allowed them to enter the city first as a symbolic gesture. Furthermore, Kedourie says that Lawrence was not the inventor of guerrilla warfare, and that Mack's claims for the contribution the Arab Revolt made to the war effort are not well founded.

Above all, according to Kedourie, the American Mack suffers from contemporary Western political self-flagellation (caused especially by grave doubts about the validity of the Vietnam War) when he praises Lawrence's pro-Arab role and asserts that the wars of colonial powers are doomed to failure and are unworthy in any case. For Kedourie the truth is that the Sherif of Mecca was no more legitimate an aspirant to rule the distant Syrians than were the French or British; and Lawrence wrongly accused the British of having betrayed the Arabs.

Precisely why Lawrence, an outsider, should be interested in a variety of Arab nationalism, and what Arab nationalism has contributed to civilization 'are both quite obscure'. What Lawrence really did, according to Kedourie, was to confuse his personal needs, especially his love for a particular Arab, with political needs, and to demand that politics solve his personal problems. His example has served to encourage an overly romantic view of politics that leads to terrorism, coups and the cult of personality rather than to the positive heroic results that Mack sees. As an eccentric supporter of one Arab ruler's cause at the expense of his own country, no less than as an abnormal flagellant, Lawrence is a prince not of our disorder, but only of his own, therefore in Kedourie's eyes an example not to follow.

The Mack/Kedourie rift is an extension of the Superhero-Aldington debate, although the terms of the debate are now less extreme. Kedourie is ready to concede that Lawrence showed skill and bravery in warfare and talent as an author, while Mack is openly cognisant of Lawrence's tendency to exaggerate. The weight of research and balanced judgement begins to control the outer limits of Lawrence biography.

Desmond Stewart

Desmond Stewart's *T.E. Lawrence* (1977), a sceptical biography written by an acknowledged Middle-East expert, includes very little new evidence. Its many unsupported speculations appear particularly jarring after the well-documented presentations that preceded it. Probably Stewart's singular contribution to this debate is to demonstrate that unverified and wild assertions will no longer go unchallenged, no matter how clever they are.

Stewart shrewdly questions some of Mack's apparently naïve claims: he doubts, for instance, Janet Laurie's story that Lawrence proposed to her — not only on the basis that she was very old when she made this claim but because it resembles too many other literary proposal-rejection tales. He also follows Aldington and Béraud-Villars in thinking Lawrence a homosexual but purely on the basis of his reading and associations.

He concurs with Knightley and Simpson in believing that Lawrence was involved in British Intelligence prior to the First World War. He even goes so far as to claim that the third phase of Lawrence's 1909 Middle-East walking tour to explore castles was actually an intelligence assignment in which Lawrence was expected to learn as much as he could about the railway the Germans were constructing in northern Syria and to report on that to Hogarth — but he presents no real evidence to support this. He also offers the clever but undocumentable suggestion that Lawrence made up a story about having been robbed during this trip to conceal the fact that he had sold the camera bought for him by Hogarth in order to raise the money for his journey home. Essentially, Stewart supports Aldington's charges against Lawrence's truthfulness, stating that Lawrence early displayed a tendency to 'gild the lily' and to lie outright in order to avoid the consequences of his actions.

The problem is that Stewart offers far less proof in support of his sceptical interpretations than Lawrence might offer for his exploits. To prove his northern trip and his meeting with Ali Riza al-Rikabi (the governor of Damascus) Lawrence had his pencilled diary and an official report to headquarters which could be checked. To deny that Lawrence met al-Rikabi, Stewart has only the latter's word and that of his son, but in the period of Arab nationalism following the Second World War they may well have been loath to be associated, even in memory, with a Western agent. To explain Lawrence's dislike of Abd el-Kadir, Stewart can only speculate that el-Kadir denounced Dahoum, but we have Lawrence's own statement in *Seven Pillars* that el-Kadir betrayed Feisal's movement to the Turks. Besides, in his letter to Stirling in 1919, Lawrence makes it clear that el-Kadir had betrayed him personally at Deraa. Although Lawrence's account cannot be proved, it seems unnecessary to drag Dahoum into this matter when no evidence connects him to it in any way.

Stewart's most unfounded speculations concern the Deraa episode. On the basis of two casual remarks which Lawrence made about Azrak, the initials 'S.A.', and Lawrence's post-war interest in Kennington's portraits of Sherif Ali, Stewart decides that the Deraa incident did not take place at all. Instead he suggests that Lawrence allowed Sherif Ali to beat and sodomize him at Azrak and then made up the Deraa story. While there are legitimate questions about what happened at Deraa — deriving from Lawrence's conflicting testimonies — there is no real evidence to support Stewart's amazing counter-claim. It must be suspected that he was simply looking for a new twist with which to sell yet another biography of Lawrence. Since Lawrence obviously intended the initials 'S.A.' to mystify, Sherif Ali seems too obvious a solution; and the poem carries no suggestion of sado-masochism. Stewart's attempt to tease out a secret meaning by means of pure literary interpretation seems like an elaborately erected but unstable house of cards.

In any case, if the Azrak incident were true, as Stewart claims, why would Lawrence have invented the Deraa incident at all? Why not simply keep it secret instead of drawing attention to himself through a false account of a similar incident? Lawrence would have to be far more pathological for this charade than Aldington, or even Brémond, ever thought him. Moreover, Stewart seems strangely unaware of the letter to Stirling, although it appears in Knightley and Simpson's book. It is not mentioned in his analysis, perhaps because it is documented evidence that — counter to Stewart's suspicions — the incident at Deraa did occur. Nonetheless, Stewart's two pages of questions raise legitimate doubts about the form of this incident that we have in *Seven Pillars*.

Stewart's insinuation that Lawrence was murdered and Clouds Hill subsequently rifled by the security services is just as wild an invention as his Azrak theory. As might be expected, however, it prompted a flurry of speculations, such as Matthew Eden's novel *The Murder of Lawrence of Arabia* (1980).

Stewart, rather than Lawrence, seems to have confused fact and fiction. *T.E. Lawrence* provides no positive solutions and its only value lies in its raising of doubts. Ironically, Stewart's death, not Lawrence's, might be the subject of an investigation. He died some years after completing this book, claiming — according to rumour — to have been poisoned in Cairo.

H. Montgomery Hyde

One of the virtues of H. Montgomery Hyde's *Solitary in the Ranks* is that it clearly answers some of Stewart's wilder speculations. Hyde states that there is no evidence to show that Lawrence (as Stewart claims) ever attended flagellation parties given by one 'Bluebeard', an underworld German resident in London. Indeed if Lawrence had done so and had been recognized, then public exposure would have been inevitable. By the same token, Stewart's suggestion that Lawrence was interested in Fascism is disproved by an extract from Sir Oswald Mosley's own memoir in which he states that he never met or had any contact with Lawrence, despite rumours to the contrary. In any case, there exists at least one letter in which Lawrence categorically asks a Mosley aide not to make him 'any part of your club'. Hyde is also refreshing in his very thorough examination of the murder theory, concluding that it can be 'dismissed as fantasy. His death was the result of pure accident.' To gainsay Stewart's charge that the security services rifled Lawrence's belongings after his death, he cites A.W. Lawrence's testimony that he was living at Clouds Hill very soon after the fatal accident and found Lawrence's many letters and papers completely undisturbed.

Hyde's book also has the virtue of focusing attention on Lawrence's years in the ranks and his achievements during this period, without giving undue attention to his idiosyncrasies. Although he presents relatively little new material, Hyde makes good use of previously unpublished letters from Lawrence to the chief of the RAF, Air Marshal Sir Hugh Trenchard. He brings out some interesting details of Lawrence's service life, such as Lawrence's claim to a result of ninety-three per cent in the Rolls-Royce Tank Corps course test as the 'highest ever given'. He follows up the later careers of some of those in contact with Lawrence, such as Bertram Thomas (the first European to cross Arabia's Empty Quarter). Montgomery Hyde reveals that he himself fulfilled the work Lawrence had begun by persuading the British Government to release the Roger Casement diaries.

From Lawrence's letters to Trenchard, it can be seen that as late as 1927 he genuinely felt his work at the 1921 Cairo Conference and at the Colonial Office to have been most productive: 'my share in helping settle the Middle East atones for my misdeeds in the war. I think so anyway.' According to Hyde, he also believed that Arab nationality was as much his creation as the RAF was Trenchard's. With regard to Ibn Saud (and perhaps his own fanatically religious mother) Lawrence commented that 'Religious theories are the devil, when they are made too hard, and begin to dictate conduct.' Yet Leading Aircraftman B.V. Jones reports Lawrence in 1927 calling the Old Testament, *War and Peace, Don Quixote, Moby Dick* and *Arabia Deserta* the world's greatest books, in that order.

Montgomery Hyde's book fits a recent emphasis on Lawrence's English — as opposed to Arabian — period which stems perhaps from the loss of Empire. But while he successfully makes the case that Lawrence's years in the ranks were productive, he does not quite convince us that they were as 'rich' and 'exciting' as the war years.

Michael Yardley

The most recent British biography, Michael Yardley's *Backing into the Limelight* (1985), contains some new information and opinions, but not quite enough of either to merit a great deal of attention.

Yardley maintains that the stories denigrating Lawrence's father's first wife, Edith (who was apparently called 'the Vinegar queen' by locals) 'are not well supported and may have resulted from an attempt to justify her husband's behaviour by those sympathetic to him and his second family.' He supports the view that Lawrence's Calvinistic upbringing 'provides some ... explanation for the masochistic self-denial which became a feature of his life', and that Lawrence may have suffered from a fear of venereal disease as a result of the Deraa incident. We learn that 'During the Second World War ... *Seven Pillars of Wisdom* was to be sent by the British to some Resistance commanders as a text book on irregular warfare', that Dale Carnegie (the American author of *How to Win Friends and Influence People*) helped Lowell Thomas to write the script of his London show on Lawrence, and that the show itself, aided immeasurably by Harry Chase's photographic inventions, was a pioneering form of multi-media presentation. These are all interesting new ideas, and Yardley also supplies some new information about Lowell Thomas's career. Much to his credit, he rejects the theory that Lawrence was murdered, and accounts for the military security surrounding Lawrence's death by pointing out that a

Yardley's caption reads 'Group photograph at Carchemish (Lawrence and Woolley front row).' The front row, left to right, shows Abd es-Salaam, Gregori, Lawrence, Woolley, Fuad Bey, Hamoudi and Dahoum, who is brandishing a sword.

new air force expansion was soon revealed and that the authorities did not want this to be linked, in any way, with Lawrence. As Yardley points out, however, their overconcern with security may have resulted in more publicity about Lawrence's death than would otherwise have been the case.

For the rest Yardley presents largely either known material, errors, or superficial judgements unsupported by facts. Some of his errors are excusable; not so his consistent passing of judgements without analysis or proof to support them. For example, *Crusader Castles* 'though interesting ... is rather a disappointment when reread today'. A disappointment for whom? Surely not for the scholars who cite Lawrence's BA thesis even in the 1980s. He says that the reasons for Lawrence's northern trip were 'never satisfactorily explained' but with some depth of thought it is possible to explain them very well, as Gideon Gera did in 1984[13].

While Yardley refers to a 'large body of academic work' which he certainly should have known about when his book was published, he demonstrates a cursory or non-existent knowledge of that work. His bibliography lacks any reference to Morsey's historical book published in 1976. No reference is made to Larès book in the text and no academic articles whatsoever are listed either in the text or notes. Finally, he makes very superficial use of the Meyers and O'Donnell studies which he does include.

Yardley does make one undeniable point: 'One wonders what may happen next in the continuing saga of Lawrence of Arabia. After fifty years it shows no sign of abating.' For Yardley, this is at least partially due to Lawrence being involved in so many different fields of endeavour and having occupied official positions that brought him into contact with Arab and Jewish nationalism as well as with Germany, Turkey, France, Britain and America.

In addition to the French, Swedish, Arabic and Spanish works mentioned in these chapters, biographies have been written in Norwegian, German, Japanese, Italian and Hebrew, and no doubt writers in even more languages will offer their unique personal and national perspectives in the future. New evidence will probably be discovered and will modify our views. Later generations, too, will see Lawrence's ambiguous story in the light of their own world views.

The question of whether or not Lawrence was a prince of the disorder of our particular period continues to be debated, even as we learn more about the facts of his life. Half a century of Lawrence biographies suggests that in his many manifestations he has become a permanent fixture of worldwide mythology.

Chapter four

Lawrence in Motion: The Television Documentaries, 1962-86

The five British television documentaries on Lawrence are important adjuncts to the written biographies because they include almost all of the known motion picture footage of him in existence, contain interviews with important witnesses and researchers and constitute brief biographies in their own right. They prove visually that the main events in Lawrence's life did take place as they have been described in this book's biographical account, and that they were not merely the inventions of Lowell Thomas or the fantasy of some other biographer. We actually see Lawrence at Feisal's side, in Allenby's entourage in captured Jerusalem, picnicking with F.N. Doubleday and his wife, and working on his fast boats. By contrast, the recent Australian dramatization *The Master Illusionist* (shown in Australia and the United States but never in Britain) provides only another highly speculative interpretation of his life and is not redeemed even by Steven Vidler's excellent acting in the role of Lawrence.

The earliest BBC documentary, *T.E. Lawrence:1888–1935* (written and narrated by David Lytton and produced by Malcolm Brown, with Liddell Hart serving as adviser) remains one of the best explorations of Lawrence's life in any medium. Shown on 27 November 1962, it preceded the first presentation of the David Lean/Robert Bolt film *Lawrence of Arabia*, which opened in London only a fortnight later.

The documentary includes copious and authentic visual evidence of Lawrence's life. This is augmented by important interviews — with Dr C.F.C. Beeson, Lawrence's boyhood friend in Oxford; Fareeda el-Akle, who taught him Arabic in Syria; Alec Kirkbride and S.C. Rolls who participated in the Arab Revolt; Lowell Thomas who created the larger-than-life Lawrence; A.W. Lawrence, his youngest brother; Jock Chambers, his barracks orderly at Farnborough photographic school; Sydney Smith who was his commander in the RAF at Mount Batten; and Clare Sydney Smith, the author of *The Golden Reign*, her memoir of that period.

The documentary introduces us to Pat Knowles, an 'earwitness' of his fatal accident, and to Mrs Celandine Kennington, the wife of the artist who supervised the production of the 1926 edition of *Seven Pillars* and who sculpted Lawrence's effigy. Henry Williamson and David Garnett insist that while Lawrence was reserved and celibate, he was not homosexual. Clare Sydney Smith and Siegfried Sassoon speak of his enormous charisma

An undated photograph of Lawrence which was printed in the Daily Express on 28 May 1920.

From the footage shot prior to the reading of Allenby's proclamation following his official entry into Jerusalem on 11 December 1917. Lawrence stands to the right of the officer with his back to the camera.

and 'power over life'. Each of these witnesses offers authentic testimony to Lawrence's great abilities and unique personality. A.W. Lawrence speaks of his brother's sense of humour, which enabled him to come to terms with the severe disappointment of the Paris Peace Conference.

Although the film does not discuss Lawrence's flagellation problem, which came to light publicly only in 1968, it does not attempt to hide the troubles as well as the glories of Lawrence's early life and career. We are told, for instance, that he knew of his illegitimacy before he was ten but 'didn't care a straw' (this seems unlikely in view of his later attempts to conceal it). His intellectual prowess is also made clear: he is said to have been reading Macaulay when he was four, although seven now seems the more likely age. His *Crusader Castles* thesis is 'outdated today but did pioneer the field'.

For the war period, the documentary follows *Seven Pillars* very closely without critical analysis. Lawrence is shown to have had ideas above his station in the army in Cairo and to have occupied a unique position among British advisers to the Arabs. The film's narrator says that Lawrence liked the freedom of the desert life, and used his opportunities in the Revolt to take hundreds of superb photographs. He is regarded as the mind behind Akaba but his secret northern trip is not discussed. At Deraa, he refused the Bey's entreaties and as a result was tortured and 'used by the guards for their own pleasure', with the result that he felt irredeemably sullied and experienced an indefinable change in his personality. At Tafas, 'No power could restrain the massacre that followed' although Lawrence did participate. The narrator says that no one knows what were Lawrence's personal motives during the war but at Versailles he felt the Arabs had been betrayed and came to despise his own part in the Revolt. He wrote himself out of both politics and the war in *Seven Pillars of Wisdom* and felt that the 1921 Cairo Conference solved all outstanding problems of British commitment to the Arabs.

According to the narrator, six years of tension during and after hostilities had exhausted Lawrence, and the RAF training was almost tougher than he could bear. In the Tank Corps, he was on the verge of a mental breakdown. He could not solve the paradox between flesh and spirit, although he commented that he would destroy a beautiful cathedral to save a little girl's life. He was happier after he returned from Karachi and worked under Sydney Smith; Clare Smith described the situation on her husband's base as giving Lawrence 'a complete sense of family life' which he otherwise lacked. He worked on the Schneider Cup seaplane which later led to the Spitfire; he developed a fast boat for air-sea rescue work; and he also enjoyed picnics with literary figures. In his cottage, Clouds Hill, he led a very simple life with 'I don't care' inscribed over the door.

We are told that by the time he retired from the RAF he had grown almost mellow. Yet the legend still clung. Lawrence was neither saint nor charlatan, the film concludes, but a complex many-sided person, who has become the subject of both extreme adulation and extreme denigration. He impressed himself on his time, and impressed important men. In its straightforward account of Lawrence's life, this documentary avoids speculation and remains one of the most authentic biographies.

Seventeen years were to elapse before the BBC followed up this early documentary. In January 1979 *Lawrence of England*, the story of Lawrence's life after the Arab Revolt, was shown in two half-hour parts — 'Something Broken in the Works' and 'Leading from the Ranks'. Written and narrated by Alan Lomax, this documentary is not as coherent nor as detailed as the earlier production. It offers little new information, despite the presence of a new witness, C.H. Carr, a news editor who saw Lawrence in Damascus. W.E. Johns is mentioned as testifying that Lawrence's RAF application was rigged by his superiors even though he failed his medical.

This still from the film footage shot when Lowell Thomas and his cameraman Harry Chase visited Akaba around May 1918 shows Feisal facing Thomas with Lawrence standing to the right of Feisal. Thomas later used this film in his production With Allenby in Palestine and Lawrence in Arabia. Lawrence wrote to Thomas: 'I saw your show last night and thank God the lights were out.'

A photograph taken on the steps of Feisal's house in the Avenue du Bois, Paris on 22 January 1919, on the same occasion that a film was shot. Left to right are Rustum Haydar of Baalbek, Brigadier General Nuri as-Said, Captain Pisani (the commander of a French artillery detachment in the Arab Revolt), Feisal centre front, Lawrence, and Captain Tassim Bey Qadri.

The programme's chief interest lies in Lomax's extensive interviews with Jeremy Wilson, Lawrence's official biographer, who gives us a glimpse of his own position on several important questions. Contrary to Robert Bolt's script for the feature film which focused on Lawrence as a man ruined by war, Wilson sees him as affected by the war in a different way — forced to tell daily lies to the Arabs. In the ensuing peacetime negotiations Lawrence was depressed by the situation in the Middle East but thought, unrealistically, that the 1921 Cairo Conference had solved the Arab problem.

In response to a question about why Lawrence joined the ranks, Wilson says that Lawrence probably did not know the answer himself. During this period, however, he supported his late brother Will's fiancée financially (and this girl, Janet Laurie, was the one T.E. himself was said to have proposed to before the war).

According to Wilson, speed was a lust for Lawrence. On his motorcycle he enjoyed an animal release which was some compensation for his lack of personal life. Wilson sees the flogging ritual as a form of derangement with a masochistic basis and comments that the account we have of it may be wrong in its details. For Wilson, Lawrence was asexual rather than homosexual; before the war, he may even have proposed marriage, and there was no evidence then to suggest that he was homosexual. Afterwards his view of sex of any kind was totally negative. Lawrence's threat of suicide should he not be allowed back into the RAF from the Tank Corps may well have been genuine; it was repeated in several letters.

Two of the most important new pieces of visual information included in the programme are a news film of Lawrence arriving from his service in India aboard the S S *Rajputana* and a brief motion picture of the hovercraft prototype or ground effect vehicle that Lawrence developed with the engineer Edward Spurr. Clare Sydney Smith testifies that Lawrence had a 'terrific knowledge of boats' and was a perfectionist as a mechanic, while Bill Sheaff of the British Power Boat Company remarks that Lawrence developed a new form of hull design.

Jeremy Wilson rejects the theory that Lawrence committed suicide, believing that it would have been altogether the wrong moment for suicide, because Lawrence was just starting to adapt well to his retirement and had many plans; he also rejects the idea that Lawrence was murdered.

The RAF's quiet recall of Lawrence to England went awry, for he was filmed leaving the S.S. Rajputana on 2 February 1929 at Plymouth. This photograph was taken on the same occasion and appeared in the following day's Sunday Pictorial over the caption 'Colonel Lawrence, in his uniform as Aircraftman Shaw, leaving the liner Rajputana in a naval pinnace.' Lawrence wrote to E.M. Forster: 'I am being hunted, and do not like it. When the cry dies down I'll come out of my hole and see people — unless of course the cry doesn't die down, and the catchers get at my skin. I have a terrible fear of getting the sack from the R.A.F. and can't rest or sit still.'

On *BBC Newsnight*, 13 May 1985, the fiftieth anniversary of Lawrence's fatal accident, an interesting if incomplete examination of the various death theories was presented by John Witherow of *The Times*. The crux of his argument is that the inquest was badly handled and that the authorities themselves did not know what had happened. The biographer Phillip Knightley agrees that it had been a sloppy affair.

The programme all too briefly explored the evidence arousing suspicion. Lionel Chapman, a lorry driver who arrived at the scene of the accident soon after it occurred, said at the time that Lawrence was conscious for some moments; for some reason, he refused to repeat this statement at the inquest. Moreover, Lawrence's bike was jammed into second gear, indicating a speed of less than forty miles per hour. An experienced driver like Lawrence would be very unlikely to crash at so low a speed. Corporal Catchpole (who later committed suicide) insisted that a black car had passed Lawrence at the exact time of the accident, although the two boys he swerved to avoid saw no such car — as one of them, Frank Fletcher, repeated on the programme. Catchpole was supposedly told not to mention the black car, and various papers were removed from Lawrence's cottage.

Rodney Legg, a 'Lawrence researcher', mentions that in Dorset, where the accident occurred, local people felt strongly that Lawrence had been murdered. He also says that clothes had been found in a dustbin near Clouds Hill and had then disappeared. Ronald Clark, an expert on the Brough Superior (the motorcycle model on which Lawrence met his accident) claims that George Brough himself had told him that black paint was found on the inside of the handlebar of Lawrence's motorcycle. The position of the paint implied that a car had brushed the handlebar, causing Lawrence's accident.

An Australian television producer, Mal Read, had found a document showing that Lawrence approached the Nazi authorities about procuring a copy of the diary of Roger Casement, the Irish revolutionary executed for treason by Britain in the First World War. Phillip Knightley reflects that if Lawrence were toying with the idea of joining Mosley's party and becoming a Fascist, British Intelligence might have wanted to kill him.

What the programme failed to present are some of the reasons for dismissing the murder theory, as Jeremy Wilson had dismissed it, along with the suicide theory, during the Alan Lomax programme. To begin with, Corporal Catchpole, as his suicide indicates, may have been the victim of mental instability all his life. The boys saw no car; and one of them, Frank Fletcher, sticks to his testimony even today. If George Brough found black paint inside the handlebar, why did he not come forward with the information? Could it be because he did not think it either convincing or important? Even if the black paint were present, where is the proof that it was definitely linked to an event on that day and with that particular (or indeed any) vehicle? If a black car were present, and brushed against Lawrence on his motorcycle, is it not rather more likely that this was a genuine accident and that the driver kept going because he was afraid of the consequences or was simply unaware of what had happened? In any case, there is no reason to jump to the conclusion that murder was intended.

The accident itself may have jammed the motorcycle into second gear so Lawrence could have been travelling far faster than forty; and earwitness testimony about alleged gear changes would be extremely unreliable. As to the local inhabitants, their suspicions are worth no more than the unsupported belief of anyone not present at the accident. Who saw the clothes referred to by Rodney Legg, and how reliable was the unnamed witness? Might not the clothes have been discarded and retrieved by any casual passer-by?

The lorry driver, Lionel Chapman, was undoubtedly in a state of shock after witnessing the accident and may have realized later that he was mistaken about Lawrence having been conscious. In any case, he never alleged that Lawrence actually said anything, even if conscious for a few moments.

Finally, Lawrence was thinking about writing a life of Roger Casement and was most likely in contact with the Germans simply to procure the documents which they held. All indications are that he had no interest whatsoever in Fascism and rejected Mosley completely, as H. Montgomery Hyde has shown.

In 1931 Lawrence started his involvement with RAF marine craft by working on the 200 series seaplane tender. In this still from a strip of unidentified film, he is shown with men who are probably Air Ministry officials and staff from the British Power Boat Company at Hythe.

Above left: Lawrence probably met the American publisher F.N. Doubleday in late 1918 or early 1919, and they became firm friends who got together whenever Doubleday visited England. The lady in this undated still from movie footage of one of their meetings in 1932 or 1933 is probably Mrs Doubleday, who later wrote: 'As the years went on, my husband was not very well, and T.E.'s tenderness, kindness and attention to him were most beautiful. He had a way of sitting and looking at him that was most touching. It was rather like a small boy looking up at his father whom he dearly loved.'
Above right: Lawrence at a picnic with Mr and Mrs Doubleday. A still taken from the movie footage of 1932 or 1933.

In short, what the BBC programme did not make clear is that many people seem to want Lawrence to have died in as interesting and mysterious a manner as he had lived during the Arab Revolt, and that they would seize upon any detail to make an interesting death possible. Before we can believe that Lawrence was murdered or committed suicide, consciously or unconsciously, far more substantial evidence will be needed.

The main fault with *The Master Illusionist* (directed by Geoff Burton and Michael Caulfield and produced by Mal Read in Australia in 1983) is that it purports to be a dramatized but true version of Lawrence's life while presenting several pure speculations as visual fact. The murder theory, for instance, is accepted completely, and British agents are shown planning Lawrence's death because they are afraid that he will 'tell all'. What Lawrence could have known as an ex-RAF mechanic in 1935 that would merit his death is not, however, stated. Lawrence's alleged proposal of marriage to Janet Laurie is shown as fact. An actor playing Leonard Woolley says that Lawrence was not a homosexual at Carchemish but he is depicted in a very close, obviously homosexual, relationship with Dahoum. Lawrence is also shown being forcibly raped by soldiers at Deraa in graphic detail, but this image contradicts what Lawrence said to Charlotte Shaw in the letter that is actually read over this scene. Lawrence is depicted as enjoying the massacre at Tafas. There is no sign in the film that Feisal had been dealing with the Turks and the narrator goes on to say that Allenby could not have taken Damascus without the Arabs, which is unadulterated, and rather unsound, speculation.

When he is in the ranks after the war, Lawrence is seen deriving obvious sexual pleasure from the beatings rendered by Bruce, although his feelings during all ten sessions cannot be known and testimony is contradictory; here, as elsewhere, this film imposes the most sensational interpretation. Of his less sensational but very impressive mechanical skills and the satisfactions he latterly derived from the RAF we are told little or nothing.

There is no excuse today to pass off as even semi-documentary such a distorted focus and unqualified speculations. In this film Lawrence emerges as an even more rabid sado-masochist and homosexual than Nutting had evoked — and a murder victim to boot — but we learn very little of his actual achievements in archaeology, intelligence, strategy, diplomacy, engineering and literature.

From the footage shot on board the ship RAF Aquarius. Lawrence is second from right. On 5 April 1934 he wrote: 'I have been a fortnight in Cheshire, Liverpool, the Irish Sea and Plymouth, testing a new ship.' He was undoubtedly referring to the 33,900 ton vessel Aquarius because on 8 April he wrote to Paymaster-Captain Archibald Cooper, 'to say "Thank You" for the Aquarius ...'.

The cut version of this film (which was shown on American Public Broadcasting television on 13 February 1985) eliminates an interview with the real-life Tom Beaumont (who served in the desert with Lawrence) and an episode showing a dramatized George Bernard Shaw mocking Lawrence. It flows less smoothly than the original version but shares with it the virtue of Steven Vidler's fine acting. He is able to portray Lawrence as a sensitive romantic intellectual who is destroyed by self-sacrifices that prove to be worthless when France gains Syria. This fine portrayal, however, cannot compensate for the distortions of a script which is a throwback to the Aldington debunking era, with the murder story thrown in for good measure.

The half-hour 1985 film documentary *The Shadow of Failure* (directed by Jeff Goodman, produced by Ken Seymour, and narrated by David Rogers and Richard Worthy) offers a much less sensational view of Lawrence's life, emphasizing the productivity of his final years in the RAF. Historian Dick Benson-Gyles stresses Lawrence's many kindnesses to his friends during this period and Lawrence's own feeling that these last years, rather than his Arabian experience, constituted his real success. The murder theory is mentioned, but Frank Fletcher testifies that he saw no black car and goes into much more detail about the fatal accident than he does on any other programme. Archie Cheesman, a fellow serviceman at Mount Batten, says that he saw no trace of homosexuality in Lawrence's behaviour. There is, however, no mention whatsoever of Lawrence's flagellation, and so the film may err on the side of restraint. There is also no reference to Lawrence's innovative final work on ram-wing craft. But the technique of juxtaposing historical film clips of the Arab Revolt and Lawrence in his fast boats with clips of recent Arab-Israeli battles and of RAF air stations today makes Lawrence's own quoted statements very relevant. The viewer receives a well-documented yet concise account that fits the current emphasis on Lawrence's English years.

Another fine documentary, *Lawrence and Arabia*, was shown on BBC television in 1986 (produced by Julia Cave with Malcolm Brown as associate producer). This programme extends Malcolm Brown's earlier pioneering documentary, in particular with its exposition of A.W. Lawrence's reaction to the public discovery of the flagellation story. A.W. Lawrence admits that he had known of his brother's flagellation since shortly after his death but had made no direct comment because 'It's not something people can understand easily.' He insists, however, that T.E. hated the thought of sex, and was trying to exorcize it in a medieval fashion. Arthur Russell confirms the Deraa story to the extent that he actually saw the scars of the Deraa beating on Lawrence's back, as well as the bayonet scar on his ribs.

In his brother's view, Lawrence had too much to do in his life, and it half-killed him. In part his popularity owed much to his disdain for worldly success, for the prestige he achieved when very young and subsequently despised. His brother concludes that Lawrence answered some religious requirement in people, the need for an heroic figure.

The Arab view is here presented for the first time in a documentary. While Suleiman Mousa plays down Lawrence's role in the Arab Revolt he does not discount it completely, admitting that Lawrence was popular with the bedouin because he lived like them. Auda abu Tayi's son confirms this but maintains that the Akaba idea was his father's, and Mousa grants Lawrence only a share in the attack.

Edward Said, however, as a younger generation Arab nationalist, goes further, accusing Lawrence of outright racialism because he talked about 'the' Arabs as though stereotypes and thought white Europeans to be superior. James Lunt answers by saying that if Lawrence were a racialist he could not have achieved all he did during the Arab Revolt. Feisal would have thrown Lawrence out of the camp if he had shown the slightest sign of patronizing him.

Said also charges that Lawrence's conception of little states has done more harm than good in the Middle East yet he does not consider Lawrence's repeated opinion that the Arabs were incapable of unity in his time. Neither does he mention Lawrence's vigorous public campaign against the British colonization of Iraq. Ironically, the new element of Third World ideology, represented by Said, has given the Lawrence story its most recent application. No doubt it will prove equally adaptable — and equally impossible to judge decisively — in the conflicts of future generations.

This review of the major Lawrence book, theatre and film biographies must end, where it began, with Lowell Thomas. Interviewed toward the end of his life on Dick Cavett's programme in the USA, Thomas said that the only question he would have liked to ask Lawrence was why he did not continue his archaeological career after the war, instead of joining the ranks. (One answer might be that he would be suspect in any Middle Eastern country; another, that at All Souls after the war he seems finally to have come to the realization that a scholarly vocation was too inactive for him.)

Without giving any details, Thomas accused the film *Lawrence of Arabia* (and some biographies) of being unauthentic. He reminded the audience that he had actually known Lawrence in Arabia, and insisted that Lawrence was a phenomenon, exactly as he had portrayed him in his show and book. It must be added that, however flawed Thomas's own biographical work might be, his positive view of Lawrence's actual abilities and achievements is largely justified, as will be demonstrated in the next section of this book, when the results of diligent research based upon the study of recorded evidence will be examined.

PART THREE

Looking at Lawrence Today

Today, the many contrasting images of Lawrence have been supplemented by a new, less debatable one: that of Lawrence the brilliant polymath. By moving the focus from Lawrence's personality to his work, researchers during the last twenty years have laid the foundation for a permanent appreciation of his contributions to society. Knowledge of Lawrence's personal life, although interesting, is no more relevant to an assessment of his actual accomplishments than knowing whether or not Shakespeare was a homosexual contributes to an appreciation of his stature as a dramatist.

When Lawrence's achievements are seen in the light of expert opinion and solid documentary evidence there can be no doubt that he was not only extremely versatile but also very talented. He was a pioneering archaeologist, a superb intelligence agent, an important military thinker, a resourceful if failed diplomat, an excellent mechanic and a great writer. This is quite a list of accomplishments for someone who died at the age of forty-six, and few other people of his period can match it.

Lawrence and George Lloyd in late October 1917.

Chapter one
The Archaeologist

As an archaeologist, Lawrence wrote, co-authored, or participated in the production of three works: *Crusader Castles* (his 1910 BA honours thesis on medieval military architecture in Europe and the Middle East); *Carchemish Parts I* and *II*, on Hittite excavations, published by D.G. Hogarth (1914) and C. Leonard Woolley (1921) with Lawrence's participation; and *The Wilderness of Zin*, co-authored with C. Leonard Woolley and published in 1915, on the Biblical, Nabataean and Byzantine sites in the southern Negev and northern Sinai deserts. Despite Lawrence's impressive list of publications and professional work achieved at an early age, his accomplishments in the field of archaeology have been largely unappreciated by biographers.

Crusader Castles, 1906-10

Lawrence's BA thesis was written on the basis of extensive journeys by bicycle to study medieval French castles in the summers of 1906, 1907 and 1908 and an eleven-hundred mile walking tour of the Middle East in the summer of 1909, during which he visited thirty-six castles of the Crusader period. His tutor, Reginald Lane Poole, was so delighted with the work that he gave a dinner party in Lawrence's honour. His examiner, B.H. Hutton, described it as 'most excellent', and Lawrence was awarded a 'First' largely on the strength of this achievement.

Lawrence was always fascinated by the medieval period and had also memorized two books on Layard's discoveries at Nineveh. All the same, it is not customary for BA students in any country to do extensive primary research, even for an honours thesis, let alone venture great distances on foot in dangerous foreign terrain. The bibliography, notes and introduction reveal that Lawrence was working in a new field — pioneered by the Frenchman E.G. Rey only forty years earlier. The text flows well and exhibits a mature but refreshingly original attitude: he observes, cheekily, that 'Violently controversial points are usually settled by a plain assertion, for simplicity and peace. If they are of importance in my argument they will be discussed' (*CC*, p.23). In fact, everything Lawrence asserts is backed by argument and illustration.

Gertrude Bell and T.E. Lawrence at the Cairo Conference 1921.

Since Lawrence's main argument in *Crusader Castles* has often been over-simplified in a way that makes him seem uncompromising and therefore wrong, it may be fruitful to examine exactly what he was claiming. The authorities Rey, Diehl and Sir Charles Oman propounded the argument that the castles the Crusaders built in Syria and Palestine were influenced, almost exclusively, by Byzantine and Arab castle builders. On the basis of his rigorous field-work, Lawrence countered that 'examination of Crusading castles in Syria itself, and a comparison of them with contemporary castles in France appear to lead to conclusions wholly different.' Lawrence claims, 'It is obvious that in the early state of the Latin kingdom ... castles erected in Syria were of a purely Western pattern.' Later 'the two great orders' in Syria itself 'developed rival styles', the Hospitalers being influenced by Europe, and the Templars by the East. Lawrence concludes that, apart from the Eastern influence on the Templars, Crusader styles in Syria come from the West:'There is not a trace of anything Byzantine in the ordinary French castle, or in any English one: while there are evident signs that all that was good in Crusading architecture hailed from France or Italy.'

Lawrence's errors occur when he exaggerates to strengthen his case; for him, Athlit, or Chastel Pèlerin (a Templar castle based on the Eastern style) is a 'stupidity' (*CC*, p.87) but subsequent excavation by C.N. Johns and study by Robin Fedden and John Thomson show a complex powerful castle. Yet, even here Fedden and Thomson concede Lawrence a point: he had stated that the keeps of the castle were 'in true Byzantine style, of thin walls' and that this was a weakness. Fedden and Thomson agree[14].

Even though Lawrence's stress on the influence of the West represents one end of the scholarly spectrum, it is a legitimate position based upon both reason and examination and this view continues today to be cited in discussions of the problem. Fedden and Thomson write, 'There has been much dispute whether the Crusaders learnt initially from Byzantine models or whether, as T.E. Lawrence held, their inspiration came from the West. There is some truth in both these extremes, but each undervalues the Crusaders' ability and achievement'[15].

There are exceptions but many of Lawrence's specific conclusions are now accepted. Castle Saone or Sahyun provides an excellent example of Lawrence's analytical expertise. He states that this castle, 'probably the finest example of military architecture in Syria', was built by the Crusaders on Byzantine foundations. He especially notes the 'pinnacle to support the bridge' over the moat, '110 feet high with its cap of masonry'. He includes a drawing and a photo of this and is also fascinated by the square keep of Saone which 'bears a distinct resemblance to the keeps of North-west Europe, only modified to suit the local conditions' (*CC*, p.63). The result is a lower type of ceiling than was usual in Europe. He notes too that 'The straight staircases, and the drafted blocks of which the tower is built are of course not European features' and concludes on this basis that 'The Crusaders brought with them to Syria their architects, who also acted as chief masons: but the mass of the work must have been done by the natives of the country, the Syrians accustomed to build Greek fortresses. They naturally adopted their own technique in doorways and staricases, and ways of dressing stone, but their secondary position is evident. The keep form owes nothing to the Greeks' (*CC*, p.64).

Recent scholarly thought confirms Lawrence's views. R.C. Smail praises Lawrence for his pioneering work on Saone:

'The most valuable and original contribution made by T.E. Lawrence to the subject of crusader castles was to emphasize that the Franks continued to erect such buildings [with square tower keeps] in Syria. Lawrence's predecessors, as well as scholars who have written since ... wrote at length on Crac des Chevaliers, and other great castles; but the Syrian tower keeps they mentioned hardly at all.'

Smail, like Lawrence, concludes about Saone that 'The Franks used local materials and, presumably, some local craftsmen; Syrian influence is therefore to be expected in details of construction, if not in the general plan and form of the castle'[16].

Just like Lawrence, Fedden and Thomson single out the support pinnacle as especially impressive and state that the keep, 'from the first half of the twelfth century ... of the solid square type going up all over Europe', is of 'relatively lower height' due to the shortage of timber in Syria which meant that the ceiling had to be stone vaulted and lower.

T.S.R. Boase, the most recent of these authorities, quotes a lengthy extract from a letter of 1909 written by Lawrence to his mother in which he enthusiastically praises Saone's keep, gates, moat and support pinnacle. Boase seconds Lawrence's opinion of the last two features by adding, 'It is indeed a strange and overpowering spectacle'[17].

It is clear that subsequent authorities have accepted Lawrence's main conclusion — that Saone is a Western-style castle containing some Eastern features — as well as many of his more detailed remarks.

Even when compared to the work of recent archaeologists, *Crusader Castles* has sometimes proved to be surprisingly accurate. Lawrence writes that 'At Belvoir, Rey declares that there are traces of a square keep inside the ditch and wall' but that 'neither Mr. Pirie-Gordon nor myself ... could find the slightest trace of its existence. Rey was probably deceived by the wall of some Arab house' (*CC*, p.78). In 1985, Benjamin Kedar and Denys Pringle noted that 'the castle of Belvoir was for many years thought to have had a keep until excavations in the 1960s decisively proved otherwise.' They say that 'The originator of this heresy seems to have been E. Rey. ... It is repeated in Conder and Kitchener' and although 'it was considered skeptically by T.E. Lawrence', it appears to have continued to exert an influence over writers on the castle as late as 1956'[18] such as R.C. Smail. For a BA work Lawrence's thesis is indeed remarkable and promised what might have been a bright archaeological future for its author.

Lawrence's second season at Carchemish began in February 1912 under C. Leonard Woolley. This photograph dating from the spring of 1912 shows, front row, left to right, Gregori, Lawrence, Woolley, the Turkish Imperial Commissaire Fuad Bey, and the village sergeant-major. Gregori, a Cypriote head-man at the dig, had worked with D.G. Hogarth on other occasions.

In August 1911 the poet James Elroy Flecker became the British vice-consul in Beirut and it was probably in the following December that Lawrence met him and his wife Helle, who later wrote that 'One day T.E. Lawrence turned up early in the morning. As we enquired how he had got to Areya, there being no train at that hour, he quietly explained that he had arrived by the night train but not wishing to disturb us had slept on the floor in the station to the scandal of the station-master. My husband was delighted to be able to talk literature and Oxford again, and to hear of the "amazing boy's" astonishing adventures in Asia Minor. The photo [is] ... of the "amazing boy," as Roy sometimes spoke of him, by my husband.'

Carchemish, 1911–14

After finishing his thesis Lawrence was given a 'demyship' or small fellowship by Magdalen College. This decision was prompted by Hogarth, Lawrence's mentor and the director of the Ashmolean Museum in Oxford. Hogarth wanted him to participate in the dig he was running in Jerablus, Syria, the site of Carchemish, Viceregal city of the ancient Hittite Empire. Biblical references to the Hittites are many: Abraham bought the Cave of Machpelah from Ephron the Hittite (Gen.23) and both David and Solomon enlisted Hittites among their soldiers. Solomon apparently had Hittite wives and, in an ancient version of the modern 'arms deal', even sold the Hittites military equipment — chariots and horses from Egypt. The Hittites dominated much of the Middle East from around the thirteenth to the ninth century BC when their rule was challenged by the invasion of the Sea Peoples, including the Philistines. They eventually succumbed to Assyrian power early in the eighth century.

Left: During the Carchemish period, Lawrence struck up a very close friendship with Salim Achmed or Dahoum. Dahoum took this photograph showing Lawrence wearing Dahoum's clothes.

Right: Writing home around 18 September 1912 Lawrence reported 'I have carved a great sun disk, with crescent moon, & wings, on our store door-lintel — the dining room door that is. As I had no chisels I carved it with a screw-driver and a knife. It is a Hittite design and use, and looks very fitting...'. In this photograph, Lawrence bends over to wash photographic plates near his 'Hittite' door-lintel.

At Carchemish, Lawrence worked under Hogarth and later C. Leonard Woolley. Hogarth was one of the leading archaeologists of his day and Woolley, then in his early thirties, was in time to win fame as excavator of Ur of the Chaldees. If these men had not respected Lawrence's skill, they would not have allowed him to participate in their research.

Lawrence's role in the Carchemish dig was less independent than his *Crusader Castles* field-work. At Carchemish he was clearly an assistant undergoing apprenticeship for what might have become his life's work. He looked back on the Carchemish period as the best of his life; he learned a lot about the Middle East and the Hittites (not previously his area of expertise) and about managing a large group of men. Besides serving as foreman, his work involved 'squeezing & drawing the inscriptions and sculptures' (*HL*, p.141) and photographing antiquities; he also performed a myriad of odd jobs that required mechanical ingenuity.

During 1911 and 1912 the dig produced poor results and seemed always on the verge of losing its funding. It was apparently saved when Hittite remains were unearthed (as might be expected) close to the bottom of the mound. Carchemish never equalled the attraction of more ancient sites but should not be dismissed as 'negligible', as Yardley suggested. Nor should Lawrence's part be overlooked.

Woolley describes the Carchemish dig in detail in his *Dead Towns and Living Men:* 'Very magnificent must Carchemish have been when its sculptures were gay with colour, when the sunlight glistened on enamelled walls, and its sombre brick was overlaid with panels of cedar and plates of bronze ...'. It is clear that he, at least, found the place impressive and the dig important. John Garstang, one of the most authoritative Hittite experts of his day, devoted nineteen pages of his 1929 book to Carchemish, dominated by a discussion of the finds Hogarth, Woolley and Lawrence made. His praise is unequivocal:

'This first impression of a radical distinction in the art-products and culture of Carchemish has been amplified and confirmed in a notable fashion by subsequent investigations. In 1912 the British Museum resumed its excavations.... . The work was begun by the late Mr. David G. Hogarth and continued under the experienced supervision of Mr. C. Leonard Woolley, who with his collaborators has also published a complete and instructive record of the results'[19].

Lawrence and Woolley standing near some carved slabs and the dig's light railway. This picture was apparently taken by Dr Heinrich Frank, who during 1912-13 was a photographer with a German research expedition to central Mesopotamia.

Garstang's positive impression is confirmed by O.R. Gurney, who reviews the work on Carchemish up to 1952 and writes:

'The British Museum ... had in the years 1911–14 been enriched by the accession of many stone monuments and hieroglyphic inscriptions excavated by a second expedition to Carchemish under the direction of D.G. Hogarth, C.L. Woolley, and T.E. Lawrence. Thus it came about that while there developed an entirely German science of Hittitology devoted to the study of cuneiform tablets, the small band of British enthusiasts tended to concentrate on the decipherment of the hieroglyphic script and the study of Hittite art'[20].

In other words, the finds of the expedition set the direction for much future British study of the Hittites.

Since the publication of Gurney's book, the value of the dig has been reaffirmed several times. H.G. Güterbock writes about the third volume of *Carchemish* (1952), 'This rich and beautiful volume fills a long-felt gap and lets Carchemish, and especially the city of Katuwas emerge in all its greatness'[21]. While angrily denying that the dig was used for a spying mission on the nearby German railway, R. D. Barnett of the British Museum (a co-author of this third volume) wrote in 1969: 'That Carchemish ... was a first class Hittite imperial site has recently been demonstrated by the discovery of letters in Hittite cuneiform script in the French excavations of Ras Shamra, showing that in the fourteenth–thirteenth centuries B.C. it was the seat of the Hittite Viceroy of North Syria. Hogarth's prescience has thus been fully vindicated'[22].

Clearly the Carchemish dig was not unimportant but what of the precise value of Lawrence's role? In 1980, P.R.S. Moorey published his monograph *Cemeteries of the First Millenium B.C. at Deve Hüyük, near Carchemish, salvaged by T.E. Lawrence and C.L. Woolley in 1913*. It is interesting to note that Moorey puts Lawrence's name before Woolley's, reversing the order in their archaeological publications. Moorey's book is a catalogue of objects that Lawrence and Woolley had 'salvaged' from a cemetery near Carchemish which was being looted by the local peasants. Moorey confirms the value of these objects. He also quotes letters from Woolley and Lawrence to Hogarth, and adds that one of 'the most interesting points to emerge from this correspondence' is 'Lawrence's recognition of graves from the Parthian period amongst the earlier ones ...'[23]. Because 'Lawrence recognised intrusive graves of the Parthian period cut into Deve Hüyük', Moorey is able to see 'a close affinity to the graves excavated at Dura-Europos, downstream on the Euphrates.' Here, then, is another clue to the acuity and archaeological skill of the young T.E. Lawrence, who learned from and contributed to the Carchemish work no small amount. Soon he was to survey the northern Sinai desert on an equal footing with Woolley, and to produce with him a book of permanent archaeological value.

The Wilderness of Zin, 1914-15

Just before Christmas 1913 Woolley and Lawrence were directed by a telegram from the British Museum to join Captain Stewart Newcombe of the Royal Engineers in Beersheba, Palestine, for a six-week survey. The purpose was, ostensibly, to study Biblical, Nabataean and Byzantine remains in the northern Sinai and southern Negev for the Palestine Exploration Fund; but as Lawrence wrote to his mother, the real object was to spy on the Turkish defences in southern Palestine, not far from the Suez Canal. Among other feats, he and Dahoum were to make a foray into the Akaba area which was outside the officially Turkish-approved survey region. They evaded Turkish police and conducted an exploration of the Ile de Graye (also called Jezirat Faroun and Coral Island) seven miles south of Akaba, as well as looking closely at the city of Akaba itself.

As Neil Silberman points out, Lord Kitchener had, as a young lieutenant, conducted the first survey of the Holy Land with Lieutenant Claude Conder of the Royal Engineers in 1874, mixing archaeological and military purposes[24], and later as Secretary of State for War would value the usefulness of the new survey. From exploring the Nabataean and Byzantine fortifications in the area, Lawrence himself learned that 'the Turks' preparations were basically fruitless'[25] because 'fortresses are of little avail against a mobile enemy in a desert country where roads run everywhither.' This remark (which forms the germ of Lawrence's later guerrilla theory) is also respectfully quoted in a recent article on ancient Middle-Eastern banditry[26].

When war broke out, Lawrence and Woolley were in England where they were told to finish the book quickly in order to make the trip seem archaeological in intent. The surprising thing is that this rushed book, based on a very quick spying survey, remains of permanent importance in Biblical studies: it correctly identified the Kossaima district and especially Ain el-Qudeirat rather than Ain Kadeis as the site of Kadesh-Barnea, where the Hebrews settled and from whence Moses sent men to spy out the land of Canaan. Indeed, Rudolph Cohen points out that Lawrence and Woolley 'were the first to study the remains on the tell'[27] of Ain el-Qudeirat, and in recounting his reasons for identifying this site as the true one Cohen repeats almost verbatim those reasons given by Lawrence and Woolley in *The Wilderness of Zin* and in Woolley's preliminary article of 1914[28].

Nor is this Lawrence and Woolley's only contribution to Biblical research in *The Wilderness of Zin*. In another article, Cohen summarizes approvingly their work on the fortresses of the first millenium BC:

'The remains of several fortresses (Qasr er-Ruheibah, Bir Birein and Tell Ain el-Qudeirat) were first observed in 1914 by C.L. Woolley and T.E. Lawrence. ... On the basis of potsherds found in the debris they dated the fortresses to sometime in the late second to early first millenium B.C. In addition, they identified the pottery as "Syrian" in type, concluding from this that the fortresses had not been Egyptian outposts. ... Concerning their specific historical background, they suggested that these fortresses may have belonged to the Patriarchal age, or that they were connected with the Red Sea "adventures" of one of the "Jewish" kings. ... According to the Bible Solomon established a maritime base at Ezion-Geber, near Eilat, in order to carry out trade with Ophir (1 Kgs 9:26), and Jehoshaphat and Uzziah both attempted later to repeat his success (1 Kgs 22:49, 2 Chr 20:36). Thus, in the view of Woolley and Lawrence, the fortresses had probably served as 'military police stations' designed to guard the caravan routes. ... Although in many respects their phraseology and descriptions are now obsolete, their discoveries and conclusions have provided a solid basis for further study.'[29].

In yet another article on this region, Cohen respectfully quotes Woolley and Lawrence's opinion about the date of the 'army camp' at the Nabataean-Byzantine city of Avdat[30].

In his investigation of the Negev and northern Sinai desert antiquities, Nelson Glueck praises Lawrence and Woolley's survey as a pioneering effort and the direct predecessor of his own, but writes that 'Through no fault of their own, neither Woolley nor Lawrence nor anyone else of their time could conduct a proper archaeological exploration of the Negev or Sinai or Transjordan, because they lacked the simple but indispensable tool of pottery identification. That tool was not really developed and sufficiently refined for scientific use until almost a generation after their archaeological venture in Sinai and in the Negev'[31]. This point is also made by Philip C. Hammond in his book on the Nabataeans.

Nevertheless, Woolley and Lawrence were praised by Rudolph Cohen for their pottery identification:'At both Bir Birein and Tell el-Ain el-Qudeirat. ... Woolley and Lawrence observed the presence of "rough hand-made wares" and were thus evidently the first to have identified the "Negev" pottery. It was "rediscovered" by Glueck ... and subjected to a more formal study'[32].

The Wilderness of Zin contributed not only to solutions to Biblical problems but also to our knowledge of the Nabataean and Byzantine cities that dot the desert around Beersheba. The Nabataeans were a group of desert dwellers who appear in Greek and Roman sources in the fourth century BC. Their kingdom in southern Palestine was annexed by the Romans in 106 AD, and they subsequently disappeared from history. Marvellous water engineers, desert farmers and traders, they established a chain of cities from Petra (now in Jordan) across the desert to the Mediterranean. Their cities continued to be important even after the passing of Rome; the Byzantine rulers who inherited the Eastern Roman Empire fortified them, implanted churches, and continued to rely on these cities as trading sites. They repaired and augmented the Nabataeans' great dams and water systems, adopting their method of terrace farming and extensive agriculture. So when Lawrence and Woolley surveyed the area, it was the Byzantine 'layer' they saw. Lack of time and the pottery key meant they were unable to probe beneath the surface and examine the Nabataean ruins in detail, although they did find some Nabataean remains.

Shivta (or Subeita) is the largest of these once-prosperous cities, which contain some impressive cathedrals and are generally situated near extensive dam systems. Avraham Negev writes that 'In 1914, C.L. Woolley and T.E. Lawrence drew a more accurate plan of the town, as well as plans of the churches, and of several houses'[33]. In his introduction to the 1936 edition of *The Wilderness of Zin*, Sir Frederic Kenyon quotes T.J. Colin Baly of the 1934-38 Colt expedition to Shivta as correcting only minor details of Lawrence and Woolley's work[34], and Arthur Segal of Haifa University writes that they were not satisfied with a superficial description of surface remains but attempted a comprehensive understanding of the city. According to him, 'their major achievement was, without doubt, the preparation of a city plan that remains one of the most precise and comprehensive to date'[35].

Sir Frederic Kenyon praises *Zin's* 'most valuable features':

'... the account of the central area of Ain Kadeis, the discussion of the climatic conditions in the past, the elucidation of the routes from Palestine to Egypt in biblical times, and the exposition of the way the Byzantine government, in spite of the most unfavourable circumstances of soil and climate, was able to spread over the whole district a veneer of settled civilization, of which the remains are everywhere discoverable today'[36].

Lawrence and Woolley's exposition of climatic matters remains especially impressive. Some authorities before the First World War claimed that the climate of the Negev and Sinai had altered over the years, and that fluctuations in rainfall accounted for changes in the population of the Negev. Lawrence and Woolley countered this theory by noting that there is an absence of wood in Byzantine dwellings, which indicates that in the Byzantine period, as now, there was a lack of trees. They also saw that after rain the water in the Byzantine and Nabataean cisterns rises exactly to the water level of Byzantine times, as indicated by the rings around the cistern walls. They remarked that the Byzantine storehouses the bedouin continued to use were still capable of keeping grain good for several years. Finally, they pointed to the elaborate Byzantine terrace system and to the fact that Byzantine iron ploughs cut deeper than the wooden ones used by the bedouin, thus keeping seeds farther from the sun and closer to the moisture hidden in the ground. They explained the end of Byzantine rule as the result of the Arab incursions, not a change in the climate or water supply.

Forty years later Professor Glueck came to the same general conclusion about the early Negev dwellers:

'[They] succumbed to conquest by arms and not to uncontrollable forces of nature. The resulting diversion of trade to other regions and routes drained away their economic lifeblood, and not the drying up of their lands because of sudden lack of water. The conclusion seems inescapable, wherever it has been possible to check, that the major factors affecting the course of human history certainly in the Near East, and probably elsewhere, during the last ten thousand years, are those over which in general there is a large measure of human control'[37].

Since Lawrence and Woolley discussed their notes and conclusions about the different areas they studied, neither can be demonstrated to be wholly responsible for any chapter or section. The twenty-six year old Lawrence must fully share with Woolley the praise of later scholars for the contributions in *The Wilderness of Zin*, which have stood the test of time.

After the start of the war when Lawrence became a map officer in Cairo, his *Zin* work helped him draw up some of the maps of Sinai that were to be used later by General Allenby's victorious army. During his *Zin* explorations, he had also become familiar with the terrain and defences around Akaba, and this was to be of value during his successful attack on that city with bedouin forces in 1917. A recent issue of the *Jerusalem Post* adds the fascinating postscript that Lawrence's wartime cartography (based on his pre-war survey) concerning the boundary between Egypt and Ottoman Palestine today forms one basis of the competing claims by Egypt and Israel to the Taba area of Sinai.

Chapter two

The Intelligence Agent

Precisely when Lawrence first undertook intelligence work has not yet been determined. The actor Peter O'Toole, who portrayed Lawrence in the 1962 film, is actually a distant relative of his. O'Toole offered the view, based on family gossip, that Lawrence's father was also in intelligence but this idea has never been confirmed.

Preparation, 1909-14

D.G. Hogarth, who was highly placed in the secret service and whose role as archaeologist allowed him to travel to distant sites without arousing suspicion, became aware of Lawrence from the time the young man began working as a voluntary assistant at the Ashmolean Museum. Desmond Stewart has suggested that Hogarth enlisted Lawrence before his 'Crusader Castles' walking tour of 1909 and H.V.F. Winstone (whose book *The Illicit Adventure* surveys Western intelligence activities in the Middle East around the time of the First World War) agrees with him. Amongst other factors, Winstone points out that Harry Pirie-Gordon, an archaeologist and intelligence agent related to Hogarth, gave Lawrence maps to be updated during his 1909 trip. Indeed, Pirie-Gordon is mentioned in *Crusader Castles* but always in an innocently archaeological context.

Knightley and Simpson pointed out that Lawrence was equipped with a very expensive telephoto lens when he went on the Carchemish dig and also noted the proximity of the dig to the railway that the Germans were building for the Turks. The allegations that Carchemish was a cover for espionage activities by Hogarth and Lawrence were denied by R.D. Barnett of the British Museum in 1969 and by John Mack on the basis of an interview with Hogarth's son. But Lawrence was certainly spying by the time of the Zin expedition in January 1914 when he was under the command of the Military Intelligence (and Royal Engineers) officer, Captain Stewart Newcombe. However speculative the issue of precisely when Lawrence's intelligence activities began and what they were in this early period, certain facts remain incontrovertible.

In the first place, the Carchemish dig was at least partly financed by Walter Morrison, 'a wealthy Oxford benefactor and Unionist M.P., who was also one of the founders of the Palestine Exploration Fund', which was frequently used as a cover for spying activities.

When most of Lawrence's contributions to the secret Arab Bulletin were republished in 1939 as Secret Despatches from Arabia, this photograph served as the frontispiece. Probably taken by B.E. Leeson, who had joined X Squadron at Rabegh in January 1917, it shows Lawrence at the aerodrome there and is dated March 1917.

Gideon Gera points out that Morrison's 'contribution was kept confidential at the time, for some reason' and further that 'The executive of the fund included — among others — Walter Morrison, Hogarth, and Colonel Hedley, head of the Geographical section — General Staff — Newcombe's superior'[38].

Moreover, Robin Bidwell, in his introduction to the 1986 reprint of the secret *Arab Bulletin*, writes, 'It is clear that before the war, through their consuls and through Hogarth and the younger archaeologists associated with him, the British had established an extremely efficient intelligence network in Syria and there are indications that they were in contact with the secret nationalist societies'[39]. And, as Gera points out, during the 1911–14 period Lawrence supplied information and even arms to these Consuls.

Sir Leonard Woolley readily admits that the Zin trip was a cover for Newcombe's mapping of the Turkish fortifications. He then recounts the lesser known story of his expedition with Lawrence in May 1914 along the planned route of the German railway, during which they secured all the blueprints for the railway from a disgruntled Italian engineer! Woolley comments, 'It is the only piece of spying I ever did before the War'[40], but he says nothing of Lawrence's previous experience.

It is certainly interesting that almost as soon as the war began Woolley, Newcombe, Lawrence and Hogarth found themselves acting as intelligence officers in Egypt. Interesting, too, is the fact that in Cairo, Lawrence began work in a map section set up by Captain L.B. Weldon, who was, like him, later transferred to more active espionage activities. In his book *"Hard Lying"*, Weldon reveals the methods used by British Naval Intelligence to plant and pick up agents along the Palestine coast, including the 'Nili' spies and Charles Boutagy who would fifty years later claim not only to have worked with Lawrence, but that Lawrence had recruited some agents before the war.

Further evidence indicating the nature of Lawrence's early spying work can be found in the Ransom Humanities Research Center at the University of Texas, where there are many photographs of the Hejaz Railway and its rolling stock ascribed to him and taken before the war. If we are not to see these photos as the result of military curiosity, then we must assume Lawrence to have been very interested indeed in the aesthetic quality of railways! The use to which he put his telephoto lens becomes clear; Mal Read's film is accurate at least when it shows Lawrence photographing railways before the war. His pre-war knowledge of the Turkish railway system would, of course, be very useful during his wartime raids upon it, which is probably one reason his superiors chose him for work with the Arab forces.

Finally we have Gertrude Bell's opinion, expressed in 1911 in a letter to her stepmother, that Lawrence, whom she had just met at Carchemish, was 'going to make a traveller'. Is this simply a judgement of character, or did such an experienced agent know that Lawrence was in fact already primed for (or indeed engaged in) 'travelling' or spying?

In short, although the theory that Lawrence was an official or semi-official agent before the war cannot be fully explored, there are far more grounds for suspicion than Mack, Barnett or J.M. Wilson allow. At the very least, it was for Lawrence a time of intense intelligence apprenticeship.

Cairo and Kut, 1915-16

Lawrence began his formal intelligence career in GHQ Cairo. In a letter to Hogarth on 15 January 1915, he writes that he is 'in an office all day & every day, adding together scraps of information, & writing geographies from memory of little details' (*L*, p.191). A little later he wrote to A.B. Watt about his work. 'No spying: Intelligence is mostly topography, (guiding, advising as to products, routes, people, etc.) and interpretation: interrogation of prisoners' (*L*, p.199).

Lawrence's cartographical work was not so simple as it might appear from these letters. According to Jon Kimche, during Lawrence's visit (unauthorized by the Turks) to the Akaba region in the course of the Zin survey, he made a sketch from memory of the Taba area. This sketch — called 'Sketch 23' — was unclear because of the conditions under which Lawrence worked and did not show the position of the border between British Egypt and Ottoman Palestine. In 1915, when the British and Turks were at war, a final map based partly on this ambiguous sketch was drawn up by Lawrence. In Kimche's words:

'[this map] ... managed to improve the British geographical position opposite Taba by carrying out a significant alteration of the boundary at Taba. The completed 1915 map — drawn by Lawrence and edited by Newcombe — showed, for the first time, a boundary post just where the British wanted it, and a new boundary placed in relation to Akaba, again just where the British wanted it. As it happened, this map became established as the mother of all Sinai maps, British, Egyptian, French, German, Russian and much later also Israeli. It came with such impressive credentials that it was never questioned until very recently'[41].

This falsified map has signified in the recent contention between Egypt and Israel over Taba. Kimche describes Lawrence along with Woolley and Newcombe as one of 'the best intelligence-geographers the British could muster'.

When the revolt of the Sherif of Mecca looked like becoming a reality, a special Cairo 'Arab Bureau' was created in Whitehall on 6 January 1916 to co-ordinate the uprising's activities as well as all Middle-Eastern intelligence work outside the Mesopotamian area, which fell under the purview of the Indian authorities. The members of this Arab Bureau eventually included among others, D.G. Hogarth, Philip Graves (former correspondent of the *Times* in Constantinople and half-brother of Robert Graves), Colonel Stewart Newcombe, Kitchener's nephew Lieutenant-Colonel A.C. Parker, George Lloyd, MP (later High Commissioner of Egypt), Aubrey Herbert, MP (an expert on the Ottomans) — and T.E. Lawrence.

H.V.F. Winstone adopts a critical view of these 'Intrusives' as they were known, and of Lawrence in particular. Winstone claims, with some exaggeration, that they 'set themselves illicit tasks that were unique in the annals of war' because they chose to disregard Indian and Mesopotamian opinion and run their own Sherifian campaign almost free from outside supervision.

What he does not consider is that the Indian and Mesopotamian authorities made serious blunders during the war and were unable to control the activities of the skilful German agent Dr Konrad Preusser and the even more exceptional Wilhelm Wassmuss. By these failures they had forfeited the respect of many, including Lawrence. Moreover, Winstone fails to appreciate that intelligence agencies (even within the same government) are notorious for their sense of rivalry and for their tendency to act as 'rogues' outside government rules — and that therein lies their attraction.

The 'Intrusives' were not altogether free from authoritative scrutiny; they consistently won the support of Whitehall for their covert activities. In her study of the Sherifian revolt, Sheila Ann Scoville concludes that it was able to displace Indian opinion because 'The Easterners in the War Office, the Prime Minister himself, the intelligence network in Egypt, policy-makers behind the scenes like Kitchener and Sykes, and the influence of the Zionist organizations world-wide, all had their effect on focusing the British Empire's raison d'etre in the Middle East on the Hejaz and Syrian campaign. The Turks themselves had brought this refocus into being by forcing on ethnic groups within the Ottoman empire a pan-Turanism which left them lacking in national dignity ...'[42].

In the course of his praise for the 'Intrusives', the departing High Commissioner of Egypt, Sir Henry McMahon, pointed to the manner in which their role inevitably expanded:

'The Arab Bureau has been called upon to perform duties of a far more varied and onerous nature than were ever contemplated when its establishment was decided upon and its functions laid down. In addition to all the political and research work involved, the Bureau was compelled by force of circumstances to undertake the forwarding to the Hejaz of all military supplies and munitions from the commencement of operations up to the 4th of November 1916. ... The Arab Bureau has been indispensable to me in the conduct of the Arab Question'[43].

Among these brilliant men and one woman (Gertrude Bell, who joined them for a brief period at the beginning of the war) Lawrence was, in the words of the hypercritical Winstone, 'brilliant and assertive' and 'the catalytic junior'. He quotes a German Intelligence report of the period which described Lawrence as 'A dreamer, a man of fantasy, a secretive scholar' but also, and incorrectly, as 'Not a man for deeds. No soldier, no natural leader of men'[44]. Lawrence was soon to prove how well he could unite the roles of soldier and scholar. However, an early report from French Intelligence describes Lawrence as 'brilliant'.

Lawrence's brilliance stemmed from natural gifts, hard work, and a taste for the exotic and unusual inspired by such books as Charles Doughty's great *Travels in Arabia Deserta* (the centenary of whose publication also falls in 1988). The book 'helped guide us to victory in the East' wrote Lawrence in his introduction to the 1921 edition. During his Cairo period Lawrence acquired the only copy available in the city and Hogarth tells us how he and others in the Arab Bureau made use of this unusual book:

'The *Arabia Deserta* volumes were in daily use in ... Cairo. ... When Sherif Husein's messages about adherence of fresh tribes or occupation of new districts or villages came in, one turned for light first to *Arabia Deserta*, and often found there the only light! ... As was said with astonishment by an officer who, having just crossed Arabia, was persuaded in Cairo to look up what *Arabia Deserta* had to say about the regions on his route, everything about Arabia seemed to be in the book, if one only read enough of it!'[45]

Indeed, so informative is Doughty's book that British Intelligence continued to employ it in the Second World War as well[46].

Because of his book knowledge and natural aptitude, Lawrence was chosen to accompany Aubrey Herbert on a top-secret mission during the Cairo period, in March 1916. Lawrence and Herbert had the delicate task of trying to ransom with first one million, and then two million pounds sterling, the trapped force of General Townshend at Kut. The report he wrote for the *Arab Bulletin* makes it clear that although he and Herbert failed at this task, Lawrence used the undercover mission to ascertain the Turkish attitude towards the Arabs fighting in the Turkish army. He was also able to gauge the level of support in Mesopotamia for an Arab uprising against the Turks (*L*, pp.208-10).

The Arab Revolt, 1916-18

During the Arab Revolt, which began in June but which he formally joined in November 1916, Lawrence naturally engaged in many of the activities of the intelligence operative:he received secret reports from agents and from intercepted Turkish correspondence;he developed his own agents and gathered a good deal of information on his own account. He writes that the Revolt's 'intelligence service was the widest, fullest and most certain imaginable' (*SP*, p.394). Despite charges that he publicized his exploits too much in *Seven Pillars of Wisdom*, he may, in fact, have told us very little about the extent of his intelligence activities. Winstone, for instance, writes that at the time of Lawrence's initial ride to meet Feisal in October 1916:

'... Parker sent Lawrence on an extensive survey of the Wejh coastal region, still garrisoned by the Turks. It was a dangerous exercise and Lawrence, who combined a courageous spirit with an alert if over-inventive mind, was in his element. The map work that he had done on and off for a year or more since his arrival in Cairo had made him a nimble cartographer and he completed a detailed survey of the Wejh-Yanbo-Rabegh coastal region ...'

Lawrence says nothing of this mission-within-a-mission in *Seven Pillars of Wisdom*. Parker commented that Lawrence was chosen because 'he will do it as well or better than anyone else.'

Perhaps his most outstanding deed, however, was his secret trip behind enemy lines during the expedition to Akaba. For two weeks in early June 1917 Lawrence travelled with only two companions, hundreds of miles behind Ottoman lines — from Wadi Sirhan on the edge of Arabia right up to and beyond Damascus. Here he had a clandestine interview with the General Officer Commanding in the city, Ali Riza Pasha al-Rikabi — a secret Arab nationalist ostensibly working for the Turks.

Although in 1986 Suleiman Mousa would admit that his political opinion of Lawrence had 'mellowed'[47], he continued to insist that the northern journey never took place. He based this view on the memory of Nasib al-Bakri and on the contemporary letters of Sherif Nasir (the leader of the Akaba expedition) in which the trip is not mentioned[48].

On the other hand, an impressive body of evidence shows that this journey did take place. In addition to Lawrence's report to Clayton (reprinted in *L*, pp.225-31), there exists in General Wingate's personal papers a letter in which he states that 'Lawrence's exploit in the Syrian Hinterland was really splendid and I hope you will have an opportunity of putting in a word that will help him to get the V.C., which in my opinion he has so thoroughly earned. Clayton and G.H.Q. are now digesting the information he has collected ... .' The reason Lawrence did not receive a Victoria Cross is that no officer

Captain Lawrence in late 1916 or early 1917.

witnessed his feat. But Knightley and Simpson and Mack have quoted Lawrence's war diary as evidence that it did occur. Morsey and Scoville show on the basis of British archival documents that the knowledge gained on Lawrence's northern trip definitely influenced future British strategy and policy-making. For his exploit, Lawrence was made a Companion of the Bath and congratulated by the War Cabinet in London.

If, as now seems evident, Lawrence made this journey, why did he (and the British authorities) not reveal its details? During the war, it is obvious that al-Rikabi's name would have had to be kept absolutely secret lest the Turks learn that he was an Arab sympathizer and spy. Moreover, as Gideon Gera suggests, Lawrence was probably ascertaining the level of Feisal's support in Syria without his knowledge, which is tantamount to spying on an ally — a delicate matter in any circumstances. Also, the trip encroached on the area of French interest and might have caused political friction. Gera notes further that had Lawrence expanded on his deeds even after the war, he might inadvertently have revealed details that would have 'blown the cover', or led to the unmasking of British-affiliated agents in the area who had helped him and might still have been operating when *Seven Pillars* was issued in 1922 and 1926[49].

Yet in *Seven Pillars*, Lawrence had at least to mention this amazing trip in the interests of accuracy and for it to have some permanent public record. He could recall it safely only by failing to give details about it. Changing his story to Lowell Thomas, Robert Graves and Liddell Hart in turn, also created some mystery and ambiguity which Lawrence undoubtedly enjoyed.

Lawrence first met George Lloyd either late in 1914 or early in 1915. On 12 February 1915 Lawrence wrote home from the Intelligence Office, Cairo, describing his colleagues, including Lloyd: '... there is Lloyd, an M.P. (I should think probably Conservative, but you never know) who is a director of a bank, and used to be attaché at Constantinople. He is Welsh, but sorry for it: small, dark, very amusing ... speaks Turkish well, and French, German & Italian: some Spanish, Arabic & Hindustani ... also Russian. He is quite pleasant, but exceedingly noisy.' This photo was taken at Batra during the raid on which Lloyd accompanied Lawrence in late October 1917.

As impressive as this trip was, Lawrence's written work constitutes his lasting contribution to intelligence methods. His 'Twenty-seven Articles', published in the *Arab Bulletin* on 20 August 1917, have been judged 'permanently valid' by the military writer Hillman Dickinson: 'They are well worth study even today and far excel in general usefulness and detail Mao's later but more widely known "Eight Points"'[50]. Specifically applicable to the bedouin, many of these rules of behaviour would nonetheless be useful to a clandestine agent working among any foreign national group. Lawrence stresses the importance of detailed knowledge. 'Learn all you can about your Ashraf and Bedu. Get to know their families, clans and tribes, friends and enemies, wells, hills and roads. Do all this by listening and by indirect inquiry. ... Get to speak their dialect of Arabic, not yours.' He writes that once the agent dresses in Arab clothes he 'will be like an actor in a foreign theatre, playing a part day and night for months, without rest, and for an anxious stake.' He concludes, 'The beginning and ending of the secret of handling Arabs is unremitting study of them ... hear all that passes, search out what is going on beneath the surface, read their characters, discover their tastes and their weaknesses, and keep everything you find out to yourself. Bury yourself in Arab circles, have no interests and no ideas except the work in hand, so that your brain shall be saturated with one thing only, and you realize your part deeply enough to avoid the little slips that would undo the work of weeks'[51].

That Lawrence put into practice the principles set down in this document becomes evident in *Seven Pillars*. He was sent two telegrams from Cairo informing him that Auda abu Tayi and other Howeitat sheikhs were in treasonable correspondence with the Turks,

Lawrence, Lloyd and a raiding party left Akaba on the evening of 24 October 1917. They soon entered Wadi Itm, where Lawrence was photographed, probably by Lloyd. Lawrence later wrote of the 'fearful heat of the granite walls of Itm'.

The Arab Bureau, Cairo. Lawrence was promoted Lieutenant-Colonel early in March 1918 and is shown here holding that rank He stands at left with Commander D.G. Hogarth, who was made the first chief of the Bureau in 1916. To the right is Colonel Alan Dawnay of the Akaba base, about whom Lawrence wrote: 'Dawnay was Allenby's greatest gift to us .... He married war and rebellion in himself; as, of old in Yenbo it had been my dream every regular officer would. Yet, in these years' practice only Dawnay succeeded.' On 12 May 1918 Lawrence wrote home from the Arab Bureau: 'I sent you a wire about a week ago, as I passed through Cairo on my way up to Palestine. Since then I have been travelling at red hot speed, but tonight have finished. Tonight I am going to spend in Cairo, and I got here last night. It is the first time in six weeks that I have spent two nights running in one place.'

even after the capture of Akaba. He took Auda (and another sheikh, Mohammed) to the ruined fort at Akaba, to speak privately. 'When we were alone I touched on their present correspondence with the Turks. ... They were anxious to know how I had learnt of their secret dealings, and how much more I knew. We were on a slippery ledge. I played on their fear by my unnecessary amusement, quoting in careless laughter, as if they were my own words, actual phrases of the letters they had exchanged. This created the impression desired' (*SP*, p.334). This makes an interesting parallel to Article 12 published just fifteen days after this exchange had taken place 'Cling tight to your sense of humour. ... A dry irony is the most useful type, and repartee of a personal and not too broad character will double your influence with the Chiefs. Reproof if wrapped up in some smiling form will carry further and last longer than the most violent speech.' In 'Twenty-seven Articles' Lawrence defined for all time the theory governing how an outsider can effectively 'melt' into a native background.

Lawrence showed more intellect, subtlety of approach, and sympathy with indigenous forces than did any of his colleagues. Perhaps this is why he was one of the few wartime British operatives in the Middle East who brought his political, military and intelligence effort to a completely successful conclusion — when Feisal's army marched into Damascus in October 1918.

The collection of pieces he wrote for the *Arab Bulletin* (of which 'Twenty-seven Articles' is one) reveals his acuity in the gathering and evaluation of information. Perhaps the other most impressive piece in this collection is an analysis of the ethnic diversity of Syria, written in 1915 and entitled 'Syria — the Raw Material'. In this Lawrence expressed the opinion that only an outside force could unite Syria at all. Gera comments that 'The measure of the quality of the analysis contained in this article is that some of its insights on the region are as valid and pertinent today as they were almost seventy years ago'[52].

In a portion of a secret despatch dated 15 February 1917 and entitled 'Feisal's Table Talk', Lawrence relates a discussion between Feisal and Baron Max von Oppenheim, the head of German Middle-Eastern Intelligence, about a projected German-Turkish expedition into Persia. With the death of the German chief strategist and victor of Kut,

Field-Marshall von der Goltz, this proposed expedition never became a reality. In the event it would have been almost unnecessary, as from the start of the war the Germans had a very important agent working in Persia, sometimes single-handedly, and getting superb results. His name was Wilhelm Wassmuss.

Wassmuss and Lawrence

The parallels between these two men were remarkable, as is evident from Christopher Sykes's *Wassmuss: 'The German Lawrence'*. Just as Lawrence's job was to foment rebellion against the Turks and Germans by the Hejaz and Syrian tribes in order to divert men from the Palestine front, so Wassmuss's 'object was to rouse the Persian hatred of Russia and England, thus to set up an agitation at best obliging the British to undertake a separate expedition, at least to divert large numbers of valuable troops'[53].

Like Lawrence, Wassmuss disliked routine. He achieved his goals and succeeded in remaining uncaptured throughout the war because he disregarded orthodox opinion and 'worked alone and out of reach of instructions'. Like Lawrence, he had a knowledge of the tribesmen's language and culture. Even the men he helped to lead appear very much like Lawrence's Arab companions in the Revolt. Zair Khidair Khan, for instance, seems very much like Auda abu Tayi in Sykes's portrait:'A robber, a tyrant, monstrously cruel, he was like a mixture of Homeric hero and a boy playing at Red Indians. Yet though he was as trustworthy as a viper he also conceived a really noble loyalty to Wassmuss. He faltered gravely in it, unlike Sheikh Husain, but that was after three years of profitless warfare.' The Persian Sheikh Husain seems a counterpart to the Emir Feisal. Just as Lawrence lived familiarly with the rank and file of the Arab Revolt (unlike the other English officers) so Wassmuss 'knew and was loved by the ordinary people'. Moreover, again like Lawrence, Wassmuss 'began to wear their dress' without hesitation.

Spies and liaison officers must wear their consciences lightly. Neither Lawrence nor Wassmuss could achieve this indifference. Sykes writes about Wassmuss that 'As his calling demanded, he lied daily, but to his love of Persia he was true always. It was for him the first of all things, and so, in a manner, he was untrue to no man.' Wassmuss may have known that he was serving Germany at the expense of bringing hardship and possibly disaster on his tribal allies but by his second year 'he really began to believe in the hallucination he had created', that he was serving Persia as well as Germany. Lawrence salved his conscience about his need to reconcile the demands of 'two masters', England and the Arabs, by telling himself that if the Arab Revolt succeeded well enough, England would put aside the treaty she had made with France and allow the Arabs some form of independence after the war. Both Wassmuss and Lawrence were deceived. The Persian tribes gained nothing from their revolt against England, and Feisal was evicted from Syria by the French General Gouraud in 1920.

The two men worked well with the seemingly intractable war material of the tribes. Lawrence used them for small raids, and it took Wassmuss five months to persuade the Persian tribesmen to take part in the 'pathetic' battle of Bushire, in which almost nothing happened. However small and unheroic, these results were of greater significance than other outsiders managed to elicit from the tribes.

Out of many such small victories, both Lawrence and Wassmuss achieved spectacular overall results. Lawrence brought the Arabs into Damascus, while the Kaiser himself praised Wassmuss and his compatriot Niedermayer for having 'saved Baghdad' from the British 'for a year', and having 'made possible the fall of Kut'. Just as the Turks put a price on Lawrence's head, so the British offered £3000 and later £14000 for the capture of Wassmuss. It would have been worth the money had the British ever succeeded in capturing this master of propaganda and deception permanently (he was captured once by a Captain Noel but quickly escaped). Not every agent could have convinced his Persian allies, as Wassmuss did, that German forces had not only invaded England but had publicly executed King George!

Sykes writes that Niedermayer 'was put in command of a Turkish force for operations against the Arabs and while in this command he fought, though he did not know it at the time, against Lawrence. He was successful in one engagement against his more famous antagonist, to whose career his is so parallel.' Unfortunately, Sykes does not specify this battle — but we do know that Niedermayer was at the head of the combined Turkish and German force that took the city of Tafileh from the Arabs (who had gained it under Lawrence's direction). Lawrence, however, was not present during this second battle.

If we are to compare the relative effectiveness of Wassmuss and Lawrence we must take into account the fact that Wassmuss worked in the field for four years, as opposed to Lawrence's eighteen months, and that as early on as the autumn of 1917 Wassmuss had no support team and no money, while Lawrence could rely on a steady stream of gold and supplies from British headquarters and worked with a highly efficient French and British army and navy crew.

Even the two men's final position with respect to the tribesmen has a certain similarity, although Lawrence proved to be the better survivor, just as he appears to be when placed against the British operatives Leachman (assassinated by a tribesman), Captain Shakespear (shot while watching an Arabian battle), and Gertrude Bell (who committed suicide). After the war, Wassmuss became head of the Eastern Department of the German Foreign Ministry. In this position, he received news that the Persian hinterland was the same as it had been before the war and that the tribesmen's four years of fighting at his instigation had brought them only grief. He began to see himself as a liar, and when the sheikhs' demand for the £5000 that he had promised them was received in Berlin, he felt obligated to repay it. The impoverished German government refused at first, and then capitulated under pressure from friends of Wassmuss. He foolishly insisted upon taking the money to start a farm in Persia, in order to 'uplift' the tribesmen, rather than repaying them immediately. For years he and his wife toiled on their farm before it failed, due to the sheikhs who were jealous of his leadership and systematically sabotaged his crops. They also involved him in a lawsuit that ended only when he was already back in Berlin, a broken and destitute man. Sykes visited the Wassmuss farm near Bushire in 1934 to find wasted equipment covered with dust.

Lawrence too was not the same after the 1919 Paris Peace Conference, when France was finally awarded control over Syria. His mother reports that he was in a highly depressed state. He campaigned against British imperialism in Mesopotamia and remained loyal to the Hussein family, helping to put Abdulla on the throne of Transjordan and Feisal on the throne of Iraq once he had been evicted from Syria. Lawrence then quit the Colonial Office, despite Churchill's possible offer of the High Commission of Egypt, and joined the RAF as a private, declaring himself finished with the Middle East. Sent to a base in what is now Pakistan, he never ventured beyond its confines despite sensational newspaper reports of spy activity. Unlike Wassmuss, Lawrence was too realistic to return to the Middle East after the war, except in an official capacity, and he soon grew tired of that. He was no doubt spared Wassmuss's final disillusionment as a result.

How effective was Lawrence as an intelligence agent? Gideon Gera writes that 'During World War I, British intelligence chiefs grew aware of the different qualities required from operatives in the field and from those engaged in long-range evaluative work. Lawrence seems to have been a rare combination of these two distinct sets of qualities. This was probably due to personal ability, suitable training, and political circumstances in which his special talents could be articulated .... Lawrence was one of the last "generalist" agents in the nineteenth century tradition'[54]. In Ronald Seth's words 'the British had a brilliant agent of their own in Colonel T.E. Lawrence, who was assisted by an outstanding group only a little less endowed with the genius that made Lawrence such an exceptional operative'[55]. Moreover, Lawrence's secret work extended beyond a momentary victory: it produced a set of permanently useful writings for subsequent agents.

R.H. Kiernan also points out that the cartographer and traveller Lawrence, like his model Doughty, made important contributions to our knowledge of Arabian geography:

> 'Lawrence's fighting has naturally attracted more interest than his geographical work, which covered great areas of new country. Less known than his ride to Akaba are his journeys from Wejh to Wadi Ais and his description of the confluence of Hamdh, Jizil, and Ais. It was Lawrence also who contributed a most important piece of information gathered in the first place from a remark of the Emir Feisal's during a conversation on the physical features of the Hejaz. Feisal said that the Wadi Akik, which rises south-west of Taif, passed well east of Mecca and went northward as far as Medina. It was already known that pilgrims on the way to Rabegh had to cross a *wadi* of this name south-west of Medina, but this valley had not been connected with the channel near Taif, three hundred miles away. These data were specially important because they showed that the main divide of the peninsula lay inland of Taif.'

Lawrence also confirmed the fact, later proved by air mapping, that one section of the Hejaz railway line had been placed twenty miles too far east on British maps[56]. Thus, in the course of his known and unknown activities as a spy and covert agent, Lawrence became a noteworthy Arabian explorer, too!

Chapter three

The Guerrilla Leader

In Arabia, Lawrence conducted a most unusual guerrilla campaign, which deployed bedouin fighters to best advantage. He codified the basic principles of irregular warfare, becoming one of our century's most important military theoreticians.

What Lawrence Accomplished

In his memoir *Five Years in Turkey*, General Liman von Sanders, German Commander-in-Chief of the Turkish armies in Palestine, in effect sums up Lawrence's achievement as a guerrilla leader very succinctly when he writes that because of the Arab Revolt, the British 'were fighting under conditions as though in their own country, while the Turks in defense of their own country had to fight amongst a population directly hostile'[57]. He twice mentions the strategic importance of the capture of Akaba and the crippling effect of the Arab attacks on the Hejaz Railway, especially late in the war when spare parts were no longer available.

Liman von Sanders also notes that 'The failure of all means of communication' among the Turkish forces was 'unintelligible to German conception'[58], and his words could apply equally to the thinking of orthodox British generals, who could not imagine waging war with a group of bedouin under conditions unknown to modern Western military science. Lawrence's strength as a leader was precisely that nothing was unintelligible to his mind: he proved completely adaptable to the special conditions of his war and the qualities of the bedouin. In his period, only a Lawrence could write that:

> 'Arab processes were clear, Arab minds moved as logically as our own, with nothing radically incomprehensible or different, except the premiss: there was no excuse or reason, except our laziness or ignorance, whereby we could call them inscrutable or Oriental, or leave them misunderstood. They would follow us, if we endured with them, and played the game according to their rules' (*SP*, p.227).

Owing precisely to this flexibility of approach, Lawrence was able to take a poorly organized band of warring bedouin tribes and turn them (and the civilian population of the Hejaz and Syria) into an unorthodox weapon that helped bring about the collapse of

---

Written in only six weeks, Graves's book contains many errors, including the caption 'Lawrence at Versailles' for this photograph, which actually shows Lawrence on the balcony of the Victoria Hotel, Damascus, on 2 October 1918. The photographer was John Finlay, Chairman of the American Red Cross in Palestine and the Near East. On 26 January 1935 Lawrence wrote to Bruce Rogers 'Should you meet Finlay ever, will you give him my regards and thanks? If you say Victoria Hotel, Damascus, he will smile and remember our meeting in character, him in khaki, me in skirts; but deadly tired, I was: unable to talk, or at least to think before I talked.'

the Turks. Under Lawrence's direction, the Arabs developed a strategy, took the important port of Akaba, kept the Turks bottled up in Medina for the whole war, preoccupied them with the problem of somehow keeping their railway running, and made them the targets of civilian wrath. Thus the Turks' confidence was undermined and they were transformed from all-powerful occupiers into worried and isolated garrisons in a hostile land. Lawrence assisted Allenby's forces in Palestine by providing a strategic port, by causing a constant drain on the enemy's resources and morale, and by diverting a good number of Turkish troops from the Palestine front. Once the Arabs had captured Akaba and moved up into what is now Jordan, Lawrence served as the liaison officer between the British and Arab forces, and helped to organize a regular Arab army. When the Arabs marched into Damascus on 1 October 1918 (just two years after he predicted that they would) Lawrence's theory that an unconventional force could be valuable received its final proof.

With hindsight these events seem simple but to achieve victory Lawrence had to overcome orthodox British opinion, which demanded regular troops in the Hejaz and doubted the value of guerrilla forces; he also had to convince the Emir Feisal (chief of the most important Sherifian army) of his ideas and win his confidence; prove to the bedouin themselves that he was as tough as they were; short-circuit Arab attempts to double-deal with the Turks; and undergo a good deal of physical and mental agony in the service of not one but two masters (the British and the Arabs) with different goals in mind at once (British victory and Arab semi-independence). By March 1917, when he was evolving his theory of deploying the bedouin forces, the British had lost men in huge massed battles in Europe, in Gallipoli, in Kut, and in Gaza. Seen against this background of routine thought and routine failure, his use of unconventional warfare seems even more daring.

Did Lawrence Tell the Truth?

Did Lawrence tell the truth about his exploits in *Seven Pillars of Wisdom*? Although the Deraa incident in particular remains in dispute, Lawrence's leading part in all of the major *actions* in which he was engaged (the secret northern ride, Akaba, the train demolitions, the attack on Deraa, and the assumption of government in Damascus) has been confirmed by many documents or by the memoirs of witnesses. Only concerning the Battle

Lawrence photographed, probably by B.E. Leeson, at the Rabegh aerodrome in March 1917.

The Royal Flying Corps' presence had early been felt in the Hejaz with the arrival at Rabegh of X Squadron. Later, at Wejh, Lawrence joined B.E. Leeson on a journey by car up Wadi Hamdh looking for a crashed plane. The trip probably took place late in April and this photograph shows Lawrence (right) with the Crossley car used on this occasion. Captain T.E. Henderson later wrote that Lawrence 'always looked upon these jobs as a sort of picnic and seemed to thoroughly enjoy himself. He was a most economical companion, needing very little water for his personal requirements; no matter how badly we prepared our food, he relished it. In the Wadi Hamdh, when the progress of the car was reduced to about one mile per hour on account of thick thorn bushes and large boulders, and in a very unpleasantly hot temperature — we measured it once, 131° in shade — his temper remained as imperturbable as ever.'

of Tafileh does there remain any substantial doubt (expressed in the books of Subhi al-Umari and Captain Charles Blackmore) about Lawrence's role. He himself admitted that his report on this battle was a 'parody' of what actually occurred and commented that 'We should have more bright breasts in the Army if each man was able without witnesses, to write out his own despatch' (*SP*, p.492). On the other hand, it is worth noting that when Lawrence was present the Arabs took Tafileh, but when he was not, a mixed German and Turkish column succeeded in recapturing it.

In *Seven Pillars of Wisdom*, Lawrence may have condensed events to make them more dramatic and interesting; he may have presented a subjective autobiographical, rather than an objective historical, view of events — and he may also have done his best to show the Sherifians in a positive light. Yet there is no longer any doubt on the part of most scholars that (with the possible exception of Tafileh) he carried out the major actions that he claimed for himself in the Arab Revolt.

The raid on Akaba was a daring operation requiring a several-hundred mile trek through almost impassable desert and guarded mountain passes in order to attack the port unexpectedly from the rear. The issue of precisely who — Lawrence, Sherif Nasir, Auda abu Tayi, or Feisal — was most responsible for this conception remains clouded. Nonetheless, it is impossible to deny Lawrence a very important part in this outstanding victory. Scoville states, for instance, that 'various British and Arab accounts give corroborating data'[59] which confirm Lawrence's story of the taking of Guweira and the advance from Guweira to Akaba. This advance was helped by Lawrence's previous notation in his diary of a predicted eclipse that enabled the Arabs to surprise the Turks (*SP*, p.316). Newcombe, whose own part in the war was nothing short of heroic (he served on demolition teams with Lawrence, was captured leading a diversionary action during the British breakthrough at Beersheba, and twice escaped from Turkish captivity in Istanbul) has confirmed to Jean Béraud-Villars that Lawrence was entirely responsible for the conception of the Akaba attack — just as stated in *Seven Pillars*. Although the attack was discussed earlier with Feisal and other parties in the Hejaz and Cairo, in Lönnroth's and Morsey's view the precise plan of action was probably decided on the road, as the tactical situation became clear. Even so, they stress that Lawrence as advisor would have been consulted at every important turn and most probably was the driving force behind the expedition.

Elie Kedourie has questioned Lawrence's claim that the Arabs arrived in Damascus before the British, countering that the British allowed them to do so. Kedourie, however, has great difficulty determining exactly who reached Damascus and when, because the situation and the documents are so confused[60]. Lawrence himself once criticized the modern historical reliance on documents with the comment that 'documents are liars' (*L*, p.559). The fact remains that the Arabs were the first to assume political leadership in Damascus (von Sanders testifies that Sherifian flags were flying in the city before the Turks retreated from it) and that Lawrence played a leading part in setting up the city's government, just as he claims in *Seven Pillars*. Indeed, Konrad Morsey concludes that although *Seven Pillars* is not an objective, third-person documentary history, it is 'not justifiable to deny its importance as an historical source'.

Lawrence's Role

One indication, albeit oblique, of Lawrence's ability and primary role in almost all events is simply the fact that once he was out of the area and no longer available as an advisor, Feisal lost his position in Syria and his father, Sherif Hussein, lost Arabia to Ibn Saud. But there are more direct testimonies to Lawrence's importance.

Alec Kirkbride was assigned to the Revolt as a representative of the Eastern Mediterranean Special Intelligence Branch. He was both knowledgeable and a trained military expert who was first given a briefing by Wyndham Deedes:

'... it was thought advisable to warn me about a curious situation which had arisen amongst the British personnel who were attached to the Arab Army. The senior British officer was a Lieutenant Colonel G. [sic — should be Pierce C.] Joyce but another member of the staff, Major (later Colonel) T.E. Lawrence, was stealing the limelight and acting as though he was independent of local control. ...owing to the distinguished part which he had played in the capture of Aqabah, he had obtained direct access to the Commander in Chief and had thereby established a position in which he was able to exert great influence. He was enhanced in Arab eyes by the fact that one of his duties was to disburse the golden subsidy to the Amir Feisal'[61].

Kirkbride adds that gold alone cannot account for Lawrence's success where so many other advisors failed.

Lawrence emerges as a semi-rogue agent (and therefore interesting) but not as a liar. Moreover, his qualities of courage and leadership come through clearly in Kirkbride's balanced account:

'The position of Lawrence was difficult to define. The only men directly under his command were a bodyguard of gaudily clad "bravos", whom he recruited personally from the same types that joined the mercenaries, but his influence with both Arab and British Commanders in Chief, plus his undoubted courage and strong personality, make it inevitable that he should take effective control in operations undertaken by the tribal formations in which he participated'[62].

Allenby himself commented on Lawrence's role in a BBC broadcast in 1935, stating that 'Lawrence was under my command, but, after acquainting him with my strategical plan, I gave him a free hand. His co-operation was marked by the utmost loyalty, and I never had anything but praise for his work, which, indeed, was invaluable throughout the campaign ... there shone forth a brilliant tactician, with a genius for leadership.'

While Lawrence was away in Egypt, Kirkbride witnessed a bedouin attack on Wadi Jardun Station on the Hejaz Railway. His account matches Lawrence's statements of similar raids and reveals the danger through which Lawrence had to pass almost every day:

'Several hundred of them charged ahead, some on foot, some on horses, and some on camels; those in the front line fired their rifles from their hips as they ran. This was the quite dangerous charge which they were prepared to make once in every affair. ... There were some casualties on both sides, including some Turks who were shot by the tribesmen after they had surrendered[63].

Lawrence gives plentiful details of many such raids, making it clear that he was as much at risk from the bedouin as from the Turks. Concerning an attack on Mudowwara Station he comments on his companions: 'For my private part he [Zaal] was the only one to be trusted further than eyesight. Of the others, it seemed to me that neither their words nor their counsels, perhaps not their rifles, were sure' (*SP*, p.368). Charging with the bedouin was itself no easy matter, yet he managed to survive and went on to participate in such actions time and again.

Kirkbride also confirms Lawrence's 'extraordinary habit of wanting to do everything himself' both before and after his arrival in Damascus (during which Kirkbride was present) and his equally extraordinary openness of mind on military questions. The bedouin 'taught Lawrence desert strategy and tactics. He applied the lessons and by so doing earned praise, as a natural military genius, from some members of the higher command in Cairo. Perhaps it was a touch of genius on his part to recognise that advice from his followers might be of more practical value than the dogma of staff college graduates'. In Kirkbride's eyes at least, 'Lawrence was no ordinary man'[64].

Kirkbride's testimony to Lawrence's primacy and the value of the Arab Revolt to Allenby has been echoed by more recent military experts such as Robert Asprey, who writes that 'thanks to linguistic ability, imagination, perception, intellectual and moral honesty, and, not least, immense energy' Lawrence 'went to the tribes, found a leader, determined a viable goal, weighed capabilities, and hit on a type of war compatible to leadership, capabilities, and the political goal'[65].

Similarly, Brian Gardner finds that 'Despite von Sanders' own incontrovertible admission that the railway attacks were his bane, critics have continued to suggest that Lawrence was employed on spectacular but unimportant sorties:in fact, he and the other British demolitionists were seriously undermining the whole Turkish force. ... the iconoclasts were unable to destroy the pure nugget of solid achievement in Lawrence's career'[66]. Douglas Orgill concludes that Lawrence was a 'classic' guerrilla commander: 'Aqaba alone was an achievement such as few men have to their credit. The whole handling of Feisal and the Arabs, and their brilliant use as an instrument of war, seem hardly to have been within the scope of any other individual'[67].

Lawrence's Guerrilla Theory

As impressive as these expert assessments are, Lawrence's claims to our consideration must rest not only on his actual achievements in his time but also on the usefulness and validity of his guerrilla theory today. In this respect, what Lawrence has left us are: the article on guerrilla warfare that B.H. Liddell Hart compiled from Lawrence's writings (used in the *Encyclopaedia Brittanica* from 1929 until 1957); parts of the *Secret Despatches*, including 'Twenty-seven Articles'; his pieces on the 'evolution of a revolt'[68]; and, most important, chapter 33 of *Seven Pillars of Wisdom*. Lawrence admitted that this chapter profited from some retrospective thinking but Konrad Morsey has demonstrated that Lawrence certainly operated according to most of these principles during the Arab Revolt itself. In any case, no one before or after Lawrence has ever set down the principles of guerrilla warfare so effectively.

Lieutenant Colonel Frederick Wilkins writes that 'Whatever the truth about Lawrence may finally be, he was the first man to reduce guerrilla warfare to a set of rules. ... He was the first leader to see that the true objective of guerrilla warfare is not necessarily fighting ...'[69]. The German military historian Werner Hahlweg states that 'The guerrilla led by Lawrence against the Turkish lines of communication was, in outward appearance, in organization, in method of fighting as in its kind of political-strategic objectives, trend-setting — at least in the region of the Western world ...'[70].

In the famous chapter 33 Lawrence begins by explaining that, as he lay sick with dysentery in a tent in the Emir Abdulla's camp in Wadi Ais in March 1917, he passed his idle time by looking 'for the equation between my book-reading and my movements' (*SP*, p.193). Like the philosopher René Descartes, who discovered the principle of the x and y axes of algebra while resting on his cot in an army camp and trying to fix the position of a fly on the ceiling, Lawrence reveals a rare ability to think in terms of pure abstractions that ultimately have practical significance.

Lawrence was of course well informed:

'In military theory I was tolerably read, my Oxford curiosity having taken me past Napoleon to Clausewitz and his school, to Caemmerer and Moltke, and the recent Frenchmen. They had all seemed to be one-sided; and after looking at Jomini and Willisen, I had found broader principles in Saxe and Guibert and the eighteenth century. However, Clausewitz was intellectually so much the master of them, and his book so logical and fascinating, that unconsciously I accepted his finality, until a comparison of Kuhne and Foch disgusted me with soldiers ...' (*SP*, p.193).

Aldington considers this passage pompous and claims that Lawrence learned of these writers' principles only through the Oxford 'Kriegspiel' club. But the important points are that Lawrence apparently understood these men's ideas very well and that the line of thinking he developed from them proved to be successful in practice. Brigadier Shelford Bidwell writes that Lawrence is able to say 'as much in one paragraph as Clausewitz says in a chapter'[71].

As Lawrence applied his academic percipience to matters of warfare some startlingly original ideas emerged. He discovered that the 'maxims on the conduct of modern, scientific war' would not fit the situation in which the Arabs found themselves in the Hejaz. For them, what could be the value of large massed attacks on fixed points like Medina, well-defended by the Turks? The Arabs had no organized forces and could not endure casualties. What the Arabs had to do instead was to control territory and population — which they already did since the Turks were concentrated in Medina and had no effective power over any other place. In those terms the Arabs had the upper hand almost from the beginning. It was not necessary to kill masses of the enemy in what Lawrence contemptuously names a 'murder war';such a war had killed two of his own brothers on the Western front.

For him, warfare contains an 'Algebraical element of things, a Biological element of lives, and the Psychological element of ideas' (*SP*, p.197). The algebraical element of the Hejaz war could be formulated precisely in terms of numbers of men and the amount of territory to be controlled. In these purely material terms, the Arabs and Turks were contending for perhaps 140 000 square miles. The Turks would need at least 600 000 men to put a post of approximately twenty men into every four square miles of this now-hostile territory — far more than the 25 000 they had at Medina plus the few thousand scattered along the railway and at other posts. The Arabs had 50 000 men dispersed throughout the Hejaz. They could be like 'an influence, an idea, a thing intangible, invulnerable, without front or back, drifting about like a gas' against which a regular soldier would be powerless, since he would own 'only what he sat on' and could control only what he could poke his rifle at! In purely material terms, the Turks did not have enough men to control a rebel uprising throughout the Peninsula, while the Arabs could strike when and where they pleased.

Lawrence then turns to the biological, or human, element in war, whose 'components were sensitive and illogical' (*SP*, p.199). In dealing with the bedouin, who feared artillery, aeroplanes, and large numbers of casualties, morale was a particularly difficult problem. Lawrence therefore devised a method to make massed attack and the resulting Arab casualties unnecessary. In Lawrence's 'war of detachment', the Arabs would concentrate for only a brief moment, striking at a particular material point (like the railway track) rather than a human target, and then disappear again. At his most inventive, he writes, 'We might ... develop a habit of never engaging the enemy' (*SP*, p.200), which is the precise opposite of the conception of the generals on the Western Front.

The third element, the psychological or 'diathetical', Lawrence considered his most important tool. He advocated 'arranging' not only the minds of his men in terms of motivation but also 'the minds of the enemy, so far as we could reach them; then those other minds of the nation supporting us behind the firing line, since more than half the battle passed in the back; then the minds of the enemy nation awaiting the verdict and of the neutrals looking on; circle beyond circle' (*SP*, p.201). Thus he stresses the power of propaganda and of undercutting the enemy psychologically.

Lawrence's guerrilla theory may seem familiar, because later in the twentieth century we have become accustomed to the use of partisan actions by many groups around the world. Types of guerrilla warfare were certainly also practised as long ago as ancient times but Lawrence was the first to set down on paper, for all time, a truly comprehensive theory of such warfare.

Lawrence's Influence

Undeniably, Lawrence's theory of war has had an incalculable effect on the events of our times. B.H. Reid notes Lawrence's great effect on Sir Basil Liddell Hart, whose theory of the 'indirect approach', consisting of quick, oblique strokes against the enemy[72], has been used by many armies since the 1930s. Through his contact with A.P. Wavell, Lawrence had direct influence on the conduct of guerrilla actions in the Second World War. Wavell (who served in the First World War under Allenby and was given control of all Near-Eastern operations at the beginning of the Second World War) employed Lawrence's strategy of quick strikes:

'In the summer of 1940 the Long Range Desert Group ... began penetrating far behind the Italian lines, and attacked lines of communication, in much the same way Lawrence had done. Like Lawrence, they were not always successful, but again like Lawrence, they spread confusion and alarm among the enemy. This was a direct result of what Lawrence had wanted to do with armoured cars. After the First World War Wavell had continued his friendship with Lawrence, and he listened to Lawrence's theory of irregular warfare. They had arranged to meet at Lawrence's cottage for further discussion in May, 1935, but Lawrence's death intervened. One of the most notable L.R.D.G. exploits was the destruction of the isolated desert airfield at Murzuk, five hundred miles south of Tripoli, which had been reached in temperatures of 160° Farenheit and with water rationed to a pint a day. Lawrence would have appreciated it'[73].

It was not only in desert operations that Lawrence's ideas were to be applied. Baljit Singh and Ko-Wang Mei state that 'Lawrence's concept of guerrilla warfare was accepted enthusiastically in later decades. The partisan movements in France, Russia, the Balkans and south-east Asia during World War II were mostly of this type'[74].

In the last week of December 1917 Lawrence joined the Hejaz Armoured Car Company in a raid on the railway. Captain L.H. Gilman, who commanded the car company, took this photograph and wrote on the back of the print: 'On way to 1st. Mudowwara — Lawrence next to Col. Joyce with back against tender. I took the picture. One of the few occasions when T.E. was not in full Arab dress.'

The Chinese have understood Lawrence's value very well. Canadian Lieutenant-Colonel J.A. English writes that 'As early as 1936 a Western observer noted that General Lu Cheng-ts'ao, commander of the Central Hopei Communist guerrillas, had a copy of *Seven Pillars of Wisdom* at his elbow. The general reputedly stated at the time that he and other guerrilla commanders considered it to be "one of the standard reference books on strategy"'[75]. Colonel James A. Mrazek goes farther, accusing Mao Tse-Tung of plagiarizing Lawrence's principles[76].

Geoffrey Fairbairn has described T.E. Lawrence as 'that strange man of genius' and goes on to say that 'there are three reasons for discussing Lawrence's concept of guerrilla warfare: first, there is good reason to suppose that in fact it has not gone unnoticed in the Communist countries; secondly, he first raised guerrilla warfare on to the plane of strategy; and thirdly, in the light of his thought, revolutionary guerrilla warfare more readily surrenders its meaning ...'. Fairbairn claims that 'To an astonishing degree Lawrence's doctrine and practice anticipate many of the features to be found in the military guerrilla campaigns in China and, on a much smaller scale, in Indo-China.' Lawrence understood so many vital elements: 'retention of the initiative through mobile concentration, ... the need for perfect intelligence, the forcing of passive defence on the enemy, the importance of a base (Akaba)', as well as the inter-relation between distance and strength, and between space and time. He 'avoided attacking enemy garrisons. ... The parallels go down to the smallest things.' Most of all, however, 'Lawrence understood something altogether more relevant ... something that troubles even the finest counter-insurgent experts of the West today: he understood "motivation"...'[77].

It is no wonder, then, that the 1986 edition of the *Encyclopaedia Brittanica* lists Lawrence along with Lenin, Trotsky, Mao, Che Guevara, Ho Chi Minh and General Giap as one of those leaders 'with extraordinary intelligence and courage' and one of the 'unusual, unorthodox personalities, generally with civilian backgrounds' who have created modern guerrilla warfare[78]. Lawrence himself thought that Lenin was 'the greatest man' because Lenin had realized his ideology in a concrete fashion.

At the same time, M. Kagramanov, a modern Russian propagandist, has worked hard to 'prove' that Lawrence was a pathological liar and exhibitionist[79]. If his article is any indication, the Russians desire to discredit Lawrence as a strategist. Perhaps they simply do not want to acknowledge that they, too, used the guerrilla doctrine of an 'imperialist' in the Second World War. Ironically, Kagramanov's attack might be another indication of Lawrence's effectiveness.

In an article of 1976, British military writer Anthony Burton points out that although Vietnamese General Giap (like other Communist generals) was an admirer of *Seven Pillars*, some Westerners currently have a tendency to denigrate Lawrence. Yet for Burton, Lawrence 'was ahead of his time in understanding the larger questions of the use of force for political ends'; and Lawrence also understood that 'war was a total activity involving the use of violence combined with deception, espionage, corruption, propaganda and promises designed to destroy the enemy's will to continue.'

Burton concludes with a message for Britain today:

'We in the West — and more particularly in Britain — have been accustomed to possessing military strength and technological proficiency; as our economy declines, however, and the cost of military technology rises we shall become progressively weaker relative to the U.S.A. and the U.S.S.R. ... This deficiency can only be repaired by a greater attention to Lawrence's "psychological dimension". Hitherto we have studied guerrilla warfare primarily in order to defeat it; in our new comparative weakness we shall have to study it yet more intensively so that we can utilize it in order to offer a potential aggressor total opposition'[80].

Whether we accept such a pessimistic analysis of Britain's future or not, Burton's statement is proof that Lawrence's strategy continues to affect British military thinking in our time.

Perhaps the most important praise of Lawrence as a commander comes from Kirkbride, who points out that although the Bolt film depicted Lawrence 'as wallowing in blood, his views were that war should be avoided, if possible; and, if inevitable, be waged and won with as little damage to either side as could be managed.' This philosophy might be recommended to all government and military leaders today.

This photograph, which dates from around 15 September 1918, shows (left to right), Major Winterton, Lawrence and Major Hubert Young. Winterton had arrived in the Arabian theatre with the Imperial Camel Corps earlier in 1918 and Young's presence had been requested by Lawrence, who needed help with his work.

Chapter four

The Diplomat

The major players in the Middle-Eastern game of the First World War period had very divergent goals and all sides were treacherous. Lawrence's own policies and accomplishments were based on a fragile political situation during the Arab Revolt of 1916-18, the Paris Peace Conference of 1919 and in 1921-22 when he was a member of Winston Churchill's Colonial Office. But a deep concern for logic, responsibility and conscience underlies all of Lawrence's policies, as Hannah Arendt saw when she wrote of him that 'Never again was the experiment of secret politics made more purely by a more decent man'[81].

The Great Game in the Middle East, 1914–22

In this period of Middle-Eastern politics, during and immediately after the First World War, no side could be trusted, and each party's motives and hoped-for gains were extremely labyrinthine.

Great Britain wanted, first and foremost, to win the war by defeating Germany's ally Turkey. One means to this end (embodied primarily in the correspondence of Egyptian High Commissioner Sir Henry McMahon with Sherif Hussein) was the promise of Arab independence in Syria, Palestine and the Hejaz as a reward for rebelling against the Turks. In addition it was deemed vital to protect the Suez Canal (to ensure control of India) by creating a buffer in Palestine and possibly Syria. The British also sought control of the oil fields of Mesopotamia for their ships. Moreover Britain was determined to make quite certain that no single, large Arab power would arise to challenge British control of these oil fields and the Canal, and that any independent Arab countries eventually created would remain in the British orbit. To win Jewish support during the war, Britain issued the Balfour Declaration of 1917, offering the Jews a 'national home' in Palestine. At the same time, good relations were to be maintained with France (the Russians dropped out of the fighting after the Revolution in 1917) by agreeing to French control of Syria, as embodied in the Sykes-Picot Treaty of 1916. In short, Britain wanted to win a most desperate and cruel war and ensure that it emerged with a commanding position for the future, even if this entailed making contradictory promises to the Arabs, Jews and French.

Government House, Jerusalem, 28 March 1921. Lawrence (left) with Abdulla, RAF Commander-in-Chief Middle East Sir Geoffrey Salmond, and (in civilian clothes) Brigadier General Sir Wyndham Deedes, the Chief Secretary to the Administration in Palestine.

William T. Ellis, Feisal and Lawrence in London, late 1918 or early 1919. Ellis was special correspondent in the Balkans, Turkey, and Egypt for the New York Herald. He later wrote that 'this mildmannered and inconspicuous young Briton ... is far less fastidious about his uniform and his hair than is the usage in the British army. He has no parlor tricks .... Lawrence confided to me his two ambitions — one to retire to Oxford on a fellowship; and the other to own, by gift from Feisal, the site of Carchemish, the ancient Hittite capital, that he may explore it in the name of scholarship and Great Britain.'

Of course 'Britain' consisted of many conflicting voices and final policy was sometimes the skewed result of the combination of all these voices, or the outcome of an arbitrary decision rendered by a single powerful individual. The Government of India, for instance, was never enthusiastic about either the Arab Revolt or Sherif Hussein (or his backer the Arab Bureau in Cairo) and preferred to work with Ibn Saud, the Wahabi (or Islamic purist) ruler of central and eastern Arabia. Until Lawrence suggested early in the Revolt that no British troops need be dispatched to help the Arabs, the idea of the Arab Revolt was unpopular even in British GHQ Cairo. The Arab Bureau, for its part, vigorously opposed French control of Syria, while the Foreign Office proved itself ready to recognize such control in the Sykes-Picot Treaty. Actually, the final settlement of Syria on the French and Mosul on the British was the product of a brief chat in a taxi-cab between Lloyd George and Clemenceau during the Paris Peace Conference, without any consultation with the experts or the Arabs. As Barbara Anne Presgrove writes, no less than 'Eighteen persons, two Civil Departments, the Government of India and the War Committee could produce or criticize suggestions concerning the Middle East. Apparently the only factor which they had in common was the belief that their suggestions were correct and that everyone else's were wrong'[82].

The fact that many of these individuals and agencies changed their minds on important political issues as the war evolved served only to confuse the British position in this period. Mark Sykes (English co-author of the Sykes-Picot Treaty) felt toward the end of the war that the treaty had been a mistake and wanted it renegotiated. Lawrence himself, who strenuously opposed the treaty throughout the war period, was ready to accept it in 1919 when it seemed as if it were the best deal the Arabs were going to get. That Lawrence was able to accomplish as much as he did in this shifting maze of bureaucratic conflicts is remarkable in itself.

The French meanwhile had few soldiers to spare for the Middle East, since the Western war was taking place primarily on France's own soil. Yet, despite her lack of serious participation in the Middle-Eastern campaigns, she regarded territorial spoils there as her due for sacrifices on the Western front. At the start of the war, France was already Syria's largest trading partner; control of Syria would increase French foreign trade and complement France's empire in North Africa. Furthermore, there was a feeling on the part of French officials that just as Britain was consolidating her control over Iraq, Palestine and Egypt, so France deserved Syria as a balance to British power. She therefore signed the Sykes-Picot Treaty quite readily and after the war doggedly insisted that Britain fulfil all its terms.

Sherif Hussein revolted against the Ottoman government because, having lived under virtual house arrest in Constantinople for much of his life and having finally been allowed to become Sherif of Mecca and guardian of the Holy Cities, he feared that the Turks would replace or assassinate him. He preferred working with the Arab Bureau in Cairo because he disliked the pilgrimage policies of the Government of India. He was an Arab nationalist who desired Arab independence but was sufficiently self-interested to want to be the sole ruler of all Arab areas liberated from the Turks — despite an obvious lack of political ability. His sons Feisal, Abdulla, Zeid and Ali were less religious, more Western, more able, and more willing to compromise with the Western powers and as a consequence did not always get along well with their father. As late as the summer of 1918, however, Feisal was in secret correspondence with the Turks concerning a separate peace, and even revealed to them that a major British offensive was about to take place. After the war, in 1920, when King Hussein was receiving a British subsidy and Feisal was still ruling in Syria and counting on British (and Lawrence's) help to free Syria from French designs, father and son both secretly gave substantial funding to the revolts against the British that took place in Iraq. Feisal's role in this was probably not known to the British at the time. King Hussein did not hesitate to use British money to foment a revolt against Britain in Iraq because he felt betrayed by British policy toward Palestine and Syria which contradicted the deliberately ambiguous British promises given him during the war[83]. During two months in 1921 Hussein refused, despite Lawrence's best diplomatic efforts, to sign a treaty recognizing British interests in the Middle East and Jewish settlement rights in Palestine in exchange for British protection against Hussein's troublesome neighbour Ibn Saud.

During and after the war, the Syrian Arabs were divided by loyalty according to sect and politics. Maronites (Lebanese Christians) favoured France; *Fatah* and *Ahd* (secret society) nationalists were for Sherifian rule; the Damascene urban notables opposed this and supported either continued Ottomanism or purely Syrian nationalism. Even Damascus and Aleppo, the two leading cities of Syria, were divided by rival political ambitions.

Meanwhile Zionists were looking towards a Jewish state but assimilationists, like Edwin Montagu in the British Cabinet, were opposed to that goal. Palestinian Jewry was forced to serve in the Turkish army, and some Zionist leaders advocated neutrality in the First World War. Many Jews in fact worked for a British victory since they saw Britain as the power most able to bring about a Jewish return to Palestine. Aaron and Sarah Aaronsohn led the important 'Nili' spy ring in Palestine, while the chemist and Zionist leader Chaim Weizmann, living in London, discovered a means of synthesizing an all-important gunpowder ingredient needed by Britain when the supply of raw materials was cut off. Vladimir Jabotinsky headed the Jewish Legion which fought in the British army. These helpful contributions to the war effort (and Britain's desire to enlist Jews everywhere to her cause) eventually led to the British government's Balfour Declaration of 1917. While working for a Jewish majority in Palestine, the Zionists attempted to placate hostile Arab opinion.

The Turkish war aim was to maintain the Ottoman Empire in the face of British and Russian threats, and to overthrow the humiliating system of 'capitulations', under which foreigners were above Ottoman law. Turkey even hoped to push Britain out of Egypt. She offered the Arabs the promise of post-war independence in exchange for wartime support, while cracking down hard on Arab nationalists. Turkey's calls for a holy war were not successful, however, due to Sherif Hussein's alliance with the British.

The Germans lent support to their ally Turkey in order to weaken Britain in Europe as well as in the Middle East, and to win the wider war. Some of Germany's finest commanders, men and weapons were supplied to the Turks in order to divert the British from the Western front.

Any individual stepping into such a nest of scorpions, into this mêlée of clashing motives and goals, could scarcely expect to emerge unscathed. Lawrence's own thoughts were that 'anyone who pushed through to success a rebellion of the weak against their masters must come out of it so stained in estimation that afterward nothing in the world would make him feel clean' (*SP*, p.682).

Lawrence's Dilemma

During the Revolt, Lawrence was the man on the spot, the one who had to reconcile the McMahon-Hussein correspondence, which the Arabs interpreted as giving them complete post-war control over most of Syria and Palestine as well as Arabia, with the Sykes-Picot Treaty, which assured France of the Mandate over Syria, and with the Balfour Declaration, which guaranteed the Jews a national home in Palestine. These documents are still argued over today; but Lawrence was forced to face their contradictions at the moment with no external guidance:

> 'Clear sight of my position came to me one night, when old Nuri Shaalan in his aisled tent brought out a file of documents and asked which British pledge was to be believed. ... My advice, uttered with some agony of mind, was to trust the latest in date of the contradictions.' (*SP*, p.283)

Lawrence's solution to his moral dilemma was to try to realize the goals of both his 'masters' (as he puts it) at once: military victory for the British, military and political victory for the Arabs. To this he was to add attempts at Arab-Jewish compromise. He seemed to have succeeded in all these goals when the Arabs helped the British take Damascus, and Feisal set up an Arab government there and proved ready to work with the Zionists. Yet within two years of the victory, France had evicted Feisal and assumed total control, thus negating Lawrence's wartime political work as well as the hope embodied in the Arab Revolt. Furthermore, in 1924 Ibn Saud defeated Sherif Hussein, driving him into exile in Cyprus and consolidating control of what became Saudi Arabia. Was Lawrence's work therefore misguided from the start and the total failure that its detractors have held it to be — or is there some logic and accomplishment to be discerned in it after all?

Lawrence and the French

Why did Lawrence oppose French rule in Syria? He was not alone in his espousal of an anti-French policy: the entire Arab Bureau and the War Office in London concurred. These agencies understood that French colonization of Syria would necessitate Britain's keeping a much larger post-war army in Palestine and Transjordan than would otherwise be the case. In Syria the French would always be astride Britain's Middle-Eastern lines of communication and could even threaten the Suez Canal.

In strictly political terms, too, there were some grounds for worry. The majority of the Syrian population, the Sunni Muslims, hated being under French control from the start, and there was constant friction. The French accomplished little or nothing in Syria apart from some improvement in the general standard of living during their lackadaisical twenty-five year rule, which ended in 1945 when they bombed the Syrian parliament building and the newest quarter of Damascus. The British army stationed in the area at that time was forced to take control of the situation and to order the French forces back to their barracks[84].

Of course, the same charge of maladministration can be levelled against the British in Egypt, Palestine and Iraq, where many uprisings occurred during the same period. Perhaps if a pro-Hashemite policy had been allowed to prove itself in Syria and other countries from the start, through the installation of Hussein's sons, much of this tension might have been avoided. Certainly the Middle-East situation calmed down after the 1921 Cairo Conference, when Britain adopted a Hashemite policy.

Military events that took place in Syria during the Second World War were to prove Lawrence's dogged opposition to French rule there completely correct. In a letter of 18 March 1915 to Hogarth, Lawrence pointed out that a hostile French government in Syria could position 100 000 troops on the Suez Canal within twelve days of a declaration of war and that 'One cannot go on betting that France will always be our friend' (*L*, p.193). As a student of French culture and politics, he was aware that France, although relatively cohesive during the war, was not politically stable. In fact, as Philip Khoury points out, in France between 1920 and 1940 'the office of Premier changed hands no less than 33 times and was filled by 19 different men. At the Quai d'Orsay, responsible for French Mandates, 14 different men became Foreign Minister'[85].

Soon after the beginning of the Second World War the Vichy regime installed the pro-German General Dentz as High Commissioner in Syria. In 1941 Dentz's government offered Syrian airbases to German aircraft, to be used to attack the British position in the Middle East! Fortunately a British and Free French invasion of Syria culminated in Allied control of the country for the duration of the war.

The Arab Bureau and Lawrence had been entirely correct in fearing the possible uses to which a French Syria might be put, although they could not, of course, have foreseen the Franco-Nazi alliance that actually occurred.

Lawrence and the Hussein Family

Probably the most repeated criticism of Lawrence and the Arab Bureau is that they supported the Hashemites rather than Ibn Saud, the able ruler who drove King Hussein into exile in 1924. Although to some degree valid, this criticism is largely partisan comment emanating from British Government of India and Mesopotamian bureaucracy, which viewed the Arab Bureau as a rival agency to be defeated at all costs; Lawrence was never forgiven by the 'Mesopotamians' for his vitriolic report criticizing their handling of military operations, including General Townshend's disastrous campaign. Among Mesopotamian partisans are H. St. John Philby, H.V.F. Winstone and David Howarth who writes that:

'The British in Cairo had no option but to choose the Sherif as the nominal leader of their Arab Revolt against the Turks, and once having made their choice, to offer him ever-increasing rewards in gold and arms and power. The misfortune of Arabia was that they believed that their choice of a man was right in Arab eyes ... with Lawrence's genius and Britain's wealth, the revolt went from strength to strength. Yet it was always hollow: it was always an expression of Lawrence's will and of British power, and never of any permanent Arab aspiration'[86].

Despite Howarth's criticism, the Arab Bureau's decision to support the Hashemites rather than Ibn Saud was logical in many ways and confirms Lawrence's political judgement.

In the first place, Hussein came forward and solicited British support for the Revolt of his own accord. It was his son Abdulla who contacted Kitchener in February 1914, long before Ibn Saud offered to act against the Turks. Besides, it was Hussein, as guardian of the Holy Cities, who enjoyed a religious prestige in the Islamic world that Ibn Saud, the leader of an extreme sect from inner Arabia, could not match. Having Hussein on Britain's side defused any possible *Jihad* (holy war) that the Turks and Germans might hope to inspire. Both Lawrence and Hogarth stressed this religious factor above all others as an explanation for their choice of Hussein.

In addition, several influential Syrian Arabs had come forward and asked for Hussein's support and accepted his leadership; and Feisal had long been in contact with Arab nationalist circles in Syria. Thus, although not all Syrian Arabs supported a potential Hashemite government, many did. Ibn Saud enjoyed no such support outside of his immediate area and he was totally preoccupied with tribal battles against the Ibn Rashid dynasty of Hail.

It should also be remembered that the Hashemites were knowledgeable of Ottoman manners, diplomacy and the wider world. They were therefore more amenable to, and used to working with, foreign powers and cultures. In Feisal's case, religious observance was at a minimum; he once said in a speech that he was an Arab before he was a Muslim. Such liberality would naturally be congenial to the British, while Ibn Saud's religious exactitude made him a less attractive foreign ally, whatever his prowess as a fierce warrior. It was only after he conquered Arabia that Ibn Saud looked like the obvious candidate for British support even though as early as 1917 Feisal had expressed to Lawrence his belief that Ibn Saud would eventually triumph over his father in Arabia. Whatever the speculation, commitments were made to Hussein under the pressure of war, and there was no easy way to retract these. As Hogarth wrote in 1925, 'In adopting this [Hashemite] policy we were not looking beyond the war'[87].

Even if we do look beyond the war, however, the results of Britain's wartime Hashemite policy were more positive than negative. Sherif Hussein was never respected by the British, and rightly so; his rule in the Hejaz after the war was marked by economic oppression, charlatanry and arbitrary decision-making — reinforced by a personal torture chamber under his house. During two long months in 1921 Lawrence attempted without success to persuade him to agree to British policy in Palestine and Iraq in exchange for British protection from Ibn Saud. Hussein's obstinacy in refusing to endorse what he saw as a British betrayal of the Arabs in Palestine and Syria might be admirable in terms of principle but it led in 1924 to his losing the kingdom that he was too weak to protect; it must therefore be seen as politically foolish. Hussein's sons, however, were to adopt a very different attitude.

After his eviction from Syria by the French in 1920, Feisal was made ruler of Iraq by the British, and Abdulla was given the kingship of Transjordan, which was separated from Palestine. Feisal remained on the throne of Iraq until his death in 1933, and Abdulla on the throne of Transjordan until he was shot in 1951. Iraq stayed in the British orbit until 1958 when Nuri al-Said, the last important member of the Arab Revolt to hold political power, was overthrown. Although Nuri al-Said was a dictator, and Feisal and Abdulla kings rather than democratic rulers, from the British point of view the continued rule of the Hashemites or their associates guaranteed a measure of Western influence in the Arab countries well beyond the Second World War. And by the standards of the Middle East, Feisal and Abdulla were long-lived rulers who brought a measure of stability and calm to their countries. If not the best heads of state compared to Ibn Saud, they were the only reasonable ones available to the British for use *outside of Arabia* during the war and in the immediate post-war period. Today, King Hussein of Jordan (Abdulla's grandson) remains a voice of reason and moderation and the country represents a fairly stable, pro-Western force.

Zionism and Arab Nationalism

Lawrence's third policy, unfortunately less lasting than his part in creating Jordan as a pro-Western country, was to attempt Arab-Jewish co-operation. This policy resulted in the first agreement signed between Jewish and Arab nationalists in this century. Perhaps because he is called Lawrence 'of Arabia', many people are unaware that he was in favour of Zionism. In August 1909 he wrote to his mother that Palestine in the time of Jesus was a 'decent country' and 'could easily be made so again. The sooner the Jews farm it all the better: their colonies are bright spots in a desert' (*L*, p.74). Replying to Dr McInnes, the Anglican Bishop of Jerusalem in 1922, Lawrence called Dr Chaim Weizmann, leader of the Zionist movement, 'a great man whose boots neither you nor I, my dear Bishop, are fit to black' (*L*, p.343). In his own memoirs, Weizmann says that Lawrence visited his house in London many times and was most favourably inclined toward Zionism. In *Seven Pillars*, Lawrence noted that 'Galilee did not show the deep-seated antipathy to its Jewish colonists which was an unlovely feature of the neighbouring Judea' (*SP*, p.340).

Lawrence's interest in Zionism began long before the First World War, but during the war his interest became more practical: if the Jews and Arabs could be induced to work together, they might form a bulwark against French expansion in the area. The Balfour Declaration offered a 'national home' to the Jews, in the hope that they would support the British war effort in all countries in which they lived and prove loyal allies once the war was over. Although Lawrence noted — with some distaste for the slipperiness of British policy — that in the Balfour Declaration the Jews were only 'promised something equivocal in Palestine' (*SP*, p.572), in his view it would be convenient to have both Syria *and* Palestine in the hands of pro-British national freedom forces who could also co-operate, and this would be a boon for the Arabs and Jews themselves.

Under British tutelage Weizmann and Feisal first met near Akaba in June 1918. There they exchanged casual expressions of support, according to Colonel P.C. Joyce who was present. Military operations caused Lawrence to miss this event but he had met Weizmann a few days earlier. Feisal and Weizmann were photographed together at Feisal's request.

The second Feisal-Weizmann meeting proved much more fruitful. It took place in early 1919 at the Carlton Hotel in London and Lawrence was present as interpreter and moderator. On the 3rd (or 4th) of January 1919 an agreement between Feisal and Weizmann, which resulted from this meeting, was signed. Although later Arab historians such as Suleiman Mousa and A.L. Tibawi have attempted to throw doubt on the importance of this meeting (and others like it) the full text of the agreement appears as an appendix in *The Arab Awakening* by the Arab nationalist writer George Antonius.

The preface to the agreement states that Feisal and Weizmann as the leaders of the Arab Kingdom of the Hejaz and the Zionist Movement, respectively, realize that 'the surest means of working out the consummation of their national aspirations, is through the closest possible collaboration in the development of the Arab state and Palestine' and are 'desirous further of confirming the good understanding which exists between them'. Article IV states 'All necessary measures shall be taken to encourage and stimulate immigration of Jews into Palestine on a large scale.' The agreement concludes with a pledge on the part of both sides to 'act in complete accord and harmony in all matters embraced herein before the Peace Congress'. For the first time, Arabs and Jews had agreed to support one another's national aspirations.

Weizmann was to write in *T.E. Lawrence by His Friends* that Lawrence 'was instrumental in drawing up the Treaty. ... That, whatever the subsequent result, was a very great service on his part to the cause of Zionism.' It was also a service to Arabism, but was unfortunately dissipated by Feisal's failure to hold on to power in Syria, from which he might have exerted some influence on Palestinian politics. Whether Lawrence tilted more toward the Jewish or Arab side, or was attempting to block the French and forward the Arab Bureau's programme of a Hashemite state in Syria without much serious regard for Arab-Jewish co-operation, as Knightley and Simpson charge, is speculative. The undeniable fact is that he alone could and did draw the two sides together not merely to exchange pleasantries but to sign an agreement.

Both Tibawi (the Arab historian) and Amram Scheyer (an Israeli writer on Lawrence) suspect that Lawrence's Arabic-English translations between Feisal and Weizmann on the occasion of the negotiations for the agreement were less than perfect, and deliberately so. There are, after all, precedents for Lawrence's useful forgeries, such as his falsified placement of the Egypt-Palestine boundary on the Taba map, and his doctoring of the telegrams between Feisal and his father to make them seem more conciliatory than they actually were (*SP*, p.598). But Lawrence could not have forged the entire Feisal-Weizmann agreement, which was widely published.

However unlikely it may seem today that the Jews and Arabs would ever have signed a joint agreement, especially one supporting Jewish immigration to Palestine, even more amazing is the fact that Feisal wanted Israel Sieff (Weizmann's personal secretary) to join him immediately as Jewish representative in Damascus[88]! But then, a contingent of Jews from Baghdad had actually fought in the ranks of the Arab Revolt, and positions had not yet hardened in the Arab and Jewish movements. These facts do not however diminish Lawrence's unusual capacity for reconciliation.

Sadly, the movement toward understanding, which Lawrence had been instrumental in starting, did not continue in later years. But when he took over Transjordan, Abdulla proved more willing to negotiate with Zionism than did many other Arab leaders. Without Lawrence's advice in the latter half of 1921, when he was the Chief British Representative in Amman, Abdulla might never have kept his throne and Jordan never have become a state. Abdulla had little capacity for administration, and H. St. John Philby, succeeding Lawrence in his role as advisor in 1921, reported that although the financial and administrative situation had been 'as bad as it could be' the 'storm cleared with amazing suddenness' once Lawrence was on the scene, and that he had enormously improved Abdulla's economic, civil and military administration[89]. Because Lawrence was able to put order into Abdulla's government, he was also able to convince the Colonial Office, which was ready to recommend Abdulla's removal, that Transjordan should continue as a state separate from Palestine[90].

Lawrence's influence on Middle-Eastern politics must not be underestimated. In particular, his work with the Hussein family had positive long-term results — and had Feisal and Weizmann been able to continue in the path of Arab-Jewish understanding, who knows what fruitful developments might have taken place?

Lawrence the Anti-Imperialist

Unlike the Prime Ministers Lloyd George and Clemenceau, Lawrence appreciated that the old-style imperialism would not endure long after the First World War. At the Paris Peace Conference he appeared in Arab headdress, argued Feisal's case eloquently in French as well as in English and even forced the powers to allow representation for the Hejaz, which France strongly opposed. Obviously motivated by genuine support for the Arab cause, Lawrence became involved in vigorous pro-Feisal 'dinner party' diplomacy and a newspaper campaign. It was all in vain. France was awarded the mandate for Syria, and a year later, on 24 July 1920, the French deposed Feisal. Earlier in the month riots had broken out against British rule in Iraq. In *The Observer* for 8 August 1920, Lawrence made clear his opposition to both French and British policy:

'Yet we really have no competence in this matter to criticise the French. They have only followed in very humble fashion, in their sphere in Syria, the example we have set in Mesopotamia. It would show a lack of humour if we reproved them for a battle near Damascus, and the blotting out of the Syrian essay in self-government, while we were fighting battles near Baghdad. ... It is odd that we do not use poison gas on these

Following the Paris Peace Conference Lawrence set off for Cairo with a Handley-Page bomber squadron, but the aircraft in which he was travelling crashed while landing at Rome. Both pilots were killed, but Lawrence escaped with a broken collar-bone and rib. Carl Dixon, a member of the squadron, later wrote of Lawrence that he was 'the most unlikely-looking hero I ever saw; wearing sandals, a lieutenant's jacket and hat, and a pair of civilian slacks.' This photograph shows Lawrence (left) at Foggia aerodrome soon after the crash, probably with Captain T.E. Henderson, who led one of the squadron's flights.

occasions. ... By gas attacks the whole population of the offending districts could be wiped out neatly; and as a method of government it would be no more immoral than the present system.'

This is Swiftian opposition to direct imperialism in the clearest and most public form possible. Yet Lawrence did not believe that in his time the Arabs could unify themselves or succeed in complete self-government, and he remained concerned about the defence of the British position in the Middle East.

Lawrence's synthesis of these disparate philosophies, adopted by Churchill in the Cairo Conference of 1921 (called expressly to sort out Britain's future in the Arab world), was to suggest that Feisal be placed on the throne of Iraq and Abdulla in the rulership of Transjordan. The result of their kingships in those countries was several years of tranquillity not enjoyed by the French in Syria, and the feeling of Lawrence that he had fulfilled the claims of loyalty to the Arab Bureau's Sherifian vision, if not in Syria.

Despite attempts to portray Lawrence as a rabid imperialist, there is very little basis anywhere in his writings, public or private, for such a view, although he understood and supported Britain's need to retain at least indirect control of certain areas. He vaguely subscribed to the position of Lionel Curtis, who envisioned a future for the British Empire as a commonwealth of nations. In a letter to Lord Curzon of 27 September 1919 he stated 'My own ambition is that the Arabs should be our first brown dominion, and not our last brown colony.' To D.G. Pearman he wrote in 1928 that:

'... you can gauge the good fortune of England in having had Winston Churchill as its Colonial Secretary in 1921, by comparing the cost of Irak, since then, with the cost of Syria: and the happiness of Irak with the misery of Syria. French pride is engaged, and they refuse to learn by their mistakes. We turned over a new leaf ... my objects were to save England, & France too, from the follies of the imperialists, who would have us, in

When the Cairo Conference closed on 22 March 1921, Churchill and Lawrence proceeded to Jerusalem. There on 28 March at Government House, Churchill met with Abdulla and formally offered the throne of Transjordan to him. Photographer G. Eric Matson noted on the back of this print that it was 'taken as the three were on a private walk, outside the building for some confidential talk, when I waylayed them and obtained this important, unposed picture.'

1920, repeat the exploits of Clive or Rhodes. The world has passed by that point. I think, though, there's·a great future for the British Empire as a voluntary association: and I'd like it to have Treaty States now, from Nepal downwards: let's have Egypt and Irak, at least, to add to them.' (*L*, pp.577-78)

In a letter of 1927 to his mother and brother M.R. Lawrence, he mused 'We used to think foreigners were black beetles, and coloured races were heathen: whereas now we respect and admire and study their beliefs and manners. It's the revenge of the world upon the civilization of Europe.'

Even D.G. Hogarth, whom Knightley and Simpson unjustly accuse of being anti-democratic, actually wrote in a memorandum to the Foreign Office in 1918 that if it were not for Britain's moral obligations to the Hashemites, he would like to see republican institutions installed in both Syria and Iraq. In 1925 Hogarth even said that during the years 1914–15 'and indeed after them, schemes for imperial expansion or post-war predominance, whether formed in India or France, seemed futile or worse; and in light of post-war events in both Mesopotamia and Syria, perhaps it will be agreed that this view was not far wrong'[91].

Barbara Anne Presgrove sums up Lawrence's progressive views when she writes about the entire Arab Bureau that:

'The world was in a state of flux at the end of the war. Great power imperialism was dying out and small power nationalism was growing. Consciously or not, the Arabists attempted to use these two forces to advance their own ideas, and in the Middle East made one of the few attempts to combine imperialism and commonwealth in a practical and concrete form. Certainly they used ideas based on colonial imperialism to advance British interests in the Middle East. Yet at the same time they combined imperial thought with the new ideas of commonwealth so that the possible additions to the Empire would not be in the position of eighteenth or nineteenth century colonies, but eventually could take their places as full-fledged members in a future British Commonwealth. ... Lawrence was one of the more far-seeing in his desire to have Arab dominions established which eventually could stand alongside the white dominions in the Commonwealth'[92].

Lawrence's position between old-world imperialism and complete self-determination, as well as his typically British role of middleman between warring parties, guaranteed that he would be reviled by extremists on all sides in the conflict. Right-wing Zionists could attack him for recommending the separation of Jordan from Palestine. Extreme Arab nationalists would see his support of any kind of Zionism as a betrayal. British policymakers looked askance at his work for the Arabs at the Paris Peace Conference. The French could not view his opposition to their goals in a favourable light.

The Israeli political scientist Aaron Klieman sums up Lawrence's role by commenting that he 'genuinely sought independence for the Arabs as a means of righting earlier wrongs. But he functioned as a servant of Great Britain and British interests, particularly when in the employ of Churchill and the Colonial Office's Middle East Department. Moreover, in performing his responsibilities, like any other member of the policymaking establishment, he was asked to respond not to an idealized situation but to an imperfect reality'[93].

The most recent judgement of the Jordanian historian Suleiman Mousa is really remarkably similar:

'... was Lawrence a friend of the Arabs or not? In my considered opinion, Lawrence was an Englishman, naturally owing his loyalty and allegiance to his own country. Within the framework of that loyalty he was the friend of the Arabs and helped them in war and peace to the best of his ability. He visualised a series of Arab states bound to England by the strongest of ties. He was not the friend of the Arabs to the extent of supporting them in their aim of establishing a great united and fully independent state, either because he thought that the realisation of that aim was premature, or because he simply did not believe in it. ... I think that he betrayed his friendship to the Arabs in the question of Palestine, unless we take the view that he honestly believed that the example Jewish colonisation would give to the Arabs would stimulate them to achieve speedy progress and regeneration'[94].

Perhaps the best testimony to Lawrence's ability to retain the admiration of all *moderate* parties is that Feisal in a telegram of 1921 to his father called Lawrence 'the most sincere and greatest supporter of the Arab cause'[95], while Weizmann repeatedly praised his devotion to Zionism and Churchill believed him one of the greatest Englishmen of the century. Even the French have always been fascinated by Lawrence, and recent French thought about him is favourable.

Stephen H. King remarks that Lawrence had always relied 'upon the primacy of intelligence and his greatest strength was knowing how to employ that knowledge to gain political ends'[96]. In his political failures no less than in his successes, Lawrence's strengths of knowledge, vision and determination are always apparent.

Lawrence spent much of the time from October to early December 1921 in Transjordan and this photograph, which shows him at Faraifra, probably dates from this period.

Chapter five

The Mechanic

Lawrence served in the Royal Air Force under the name John Hume Ross as a simple airman from August 1922 to January 1923, when newspaper disclosure of his identity led to his discharge. In March 1923 he succeeded in being allowed to enlist in the Tank Corps as a private and remained there until August 1925 when he was transferred back to the RAF. In August 1927 he formally changed his name to T.E. Shaw. He served in the RAF at Cranwell, Karachi, Mount Batten (earlier named Cattewater), and Bridlington until he retired, with great regret, on 26 February 1935.

Most of Lawrence's intellectual friends, including Robert Graves and George Bernard Shaw, looked upon his years in the ranks as a waste of talent, and his biographical detractors have been quick to second their opinion. Desmond Stewart emphasizes Lawrence's flagellation but has practically nothing to say about his very real accomplishments during this period, when he achieved more than most other people do in a lifetime. In addition to finishing and producing the 1926 edition of *Seven Pillars of Wisdom*, writing a then unusually frank autobiographical account of service life in *The Mint*, and translating Homer's *Odyssey* from the Greek and one modern novel from the French, Lawrence became a first-class mechanic with several important innovations to his credit. He participated in the design of a seaplane tender that would save the lives of many crashed pilots in the Second World War. More spectacularly, with the engineer Edward Spurr he designed a ram-wing craft, a precursor of both the hydrofoil and the hovercraft.

In addition to these innovative activities, Lawrence also maintained a series of Brough motorcycles, passed his Rolls test in the Tank Corps with especially high marks, helped to organize the Schneider Cup seaplane races of 1929 — in which a Spitfire prototype defeated its European and American competitors — and in July 1932 drove armoured target launches during dangerous aircraft bombing practice. He learned to fly a Gypsy Moth and became an accomplished sailor — who once ran 500 miles before a gale while delivering an RAF boat.

Lawrence working on RAF launches, in a photograph which probably dates from 1932, around the time he published a foreword to Bertram Thomas's Arabia Felix.

Through his contact with Sir Hugh Trenchard, first chief of the RAF, Lawrence helped do away with unnecessary service hardships, including the useless pith helmet in tropical climates, bayonets and sticks, and buttoning of the top button on airmen's greatcoats. He also advised Trenchard from time to time about Middle-Eastern affairs, suggested the crossing of the Empty Quarter of Arabia by airship, and helped devise anti-insurgency air patrols for Iraq. In a letter of 1934 to Lionel Curtis, he predicted that the navy of the future would be vulnerable to air attack and suggested a change to 'small, high-speed, manoeuverable mosquito craft, none larger than the destroyers of today'. His final career thus proved no less distinctive, if much less spectacular, than his Arabian adventures. It is this last, highly productive phase of Lawrence's life which has been underappreciated by many biographers and has only recently begun to receive full attention.

On 4 February 1935, just twenty-two days before he was finally discharged, Lawrence wrote a letter to Graves justifying his twelve years in the Royal Air Force '... the conquest of the last element, the air, seems to me the only major task of our generation' (*L*, p. 851). Despite the fact that he had broken his collarbone in an air crash on his way to Egypt in 1919, he never missed an opportunity to pilot a plane and loved performing even the most menial labour involved, such as washing aeroplanes down and cleaning their hangars. Ironically, his main innovations were in the design of Royal Air Force boats and in the last six years of his RAF career he was in the water far more often than he was in the air.

At first sight, the 'mechanical' phase of Lawrence's life may seem unexpected but in fact Lawrence had demonstrated a marked mechanical ability from his earliest years at home. His brother M.R. Lawrence remembers that it was 'Ned' who always changed light bulbs or did any little mechanical jobs around the house. He learned yachtsmanship and photography from his father.

An undated photograph probably taken by Sergeant Pugh, who was of Lawrence's flight, showing Lawrence on his Brough Superior outside B Flight's hangar at Cranwell.

Aircraftman Shaw at RAF Karachi where he was attached to the Engine Repair Shops.

On 24 August 1929 Lawrence left Cattewater for Calshot, at the mouth of Southampton Water, site of the Schneider Cup Trophy Race. The press photographers who attended the race were warned by the Publicity Chief of the Air Ministry to avoid Lawrence. But the Daily Herald's photographer James Jarché, who was present and took this picture, wrote in 1934 that 'One day Aircraftman Shaw was standing talking to Lord Thomson .... They were in front of the Italian racing planes which were out for trial. They were keenly interested. Aircraftman Shaw gesticulated, talking with animation. He would have made the ideal picture .... So Aircraftman Shaw was shot at from all angles. The photographs appeared all over the world.'

While on a bicycle trip to the family's old home in Dinard in 1906, he wrote to his mother:'I have been wrestling with the tyres of Will's old bicycle here, I removed three outer covers (without the one minute removers) took out and exchanged 3 inner tubes; changed two valves, tightened a chain, and adjusted the bearings of a wheel, all in two hours' (*L*, p.44).

Five years later at Carchemish, 'My faculty of making and repairing things has recently demonstrated how to make paint (black and red) for marking antiques, how to render light-tight a dark slide, how to make a camera obscura, how to re-worm a screw (difficult this without a die), how to re-fit a plane-table, and replace winding mechanism on a parafin lamp. Also, I have devised a derrick, and a complicated system of human-power jacks (out of poplar poles, & rope, and Arabs) which has succeeded in setting an Ishtar on her legs again. The Romans or Assyrians had broken her off at the knees, and the men could not shift the slabs back again, with any delicacy: so Mr. Hogarth & myself set to, and with our brains, & the aid of 90 men, put all right again. Before this there had been 120 men playing about with the ropes quite ineffectually' (*HL*, p.146).

During the Arab Revolt, Lawrence developed the use of explosives into a mechanical science:

'Joyce rushed down in his tender with more gun-cotton, and hastily we set about the bridge, a pleasant little work, eighty feet long and fifteen feet high, honoured with a shining slab of white marble, bearing the name and titles of Sultan Abd el Hamid. In the drainage holes of the spandrils six small charges were inserted zigzag, and with their explosion all the arches were scientifically shattered; the demolition being a fine example of that finest sort which left the skeleton of its bridge intact indeed, but tottering, so that the repairing enemy had a first labour to destroy the wreck, before they could attempt to rebuild.' (*SP*, p.611)

Like any soldier with field experience, Lawrence respected greatly men who could calmly repair (as well as destroy) things under the enormous pressure of battle. He relished working on war machines himself, as shown in the bridge-blowing episode when his armoured car broke down during escape:

'The front bracket of the near back spring had crystallized through by the chassis, in a sheer break which nothing but a workshop could mend. We gazed in despair, for we were only three hundred yards from the railway, and stood to lose the car, when the enemy came along in ten minutes. A Rolls in the desert was above rubies: and though we had been driving in these for eighteen months, not upon the polished roads of their makers' intention, but across country of the vilest, at speed, day and night, carrying a ton of goods and four or five men up, yet this was our first structural accident in the team of nine.

Rolls, the driver, our strongest and most resourceful man, the ready mechanic, whose skill and advice largely kept our cars in running order, was nearly in tears over the mishap. ... At last he said there was just one chance. We might jack up the fallen end of the spring, and wedge it, by baulks upon the running board, in nearly its old position. With the help of ropes the thin angle-irons of the running boards might carry the additional weight ... we ... jacked up the spring and the chassis, lashed in the wooden baulks, let her down on them (they bore splendidly), cranked up, and drove off. ... In camp we stitched the blocks with captured telegraph wire, and bound them together and to the chassis; till it looked as strong as possible, and we put back the load. So enduring was the running board that we did the ordinary work with the car for the next three weeks. ... Great was Rolls, and great was Royce!' (*SP*, pp.611-12)

At RAF Cattewater Lawrence's commanding officer, Wing Commander Sydney Smith, shared a Moth Seaplane with his friend Major A.A. Nathan. Lawrence took an interest in the plane and Smith later wrote, 'Shaw looked after the Moth in his spare time. During the weekends he flew a lot with Nathan as his passenger, and I remember they made several flights to the Channel Islands, and also to the Scilly Isles. In fact they explored most of the inland waterways of the South-West coast of England.' The photograph shows Lawrence and the Moth at St. Helier, Jersey, 1929, and was probably taken by Nathan.

The common denominator of Lawrence's interest in machines was always his love of speed. While in the desert, he was attracted to what would now be known as off-the-road vehicle racing, as he tells us in *Seven Pillars*: '... the occupation of pushing cars and motor-bicycles through the desperate sand about Wejh was great. The fierce difficulty of driving across country gave the men arms like boxers. ... With time they became skilled, developing a style and art of sand-driving, which got them carefully over the better ground and rushed them at speed over soft places' (*SP*, p.177).

From his first term in the RAF, he rode a Brough Superior motorcycle, the best that money could buy at that time. Before he was sent to India in 1926, he wrote a letter to George Brough, informing him that he had completed 100 000 miles on five successive Superiors and found that the latest 'machines are as fast and reliable as express trains, and the greatest fun in the world to drive. ... The S.S.100 holds the road extraordinarily. It's my great game on a really pot-holed road to open up to 70 m.p.h. or so and feel the machine gallop: and though only a touring machine it will do 90 m.p.h. at full throttle' (*L*, p.500). *The Mint* contains the exciting story of Lawrence's motorcycle race with a Bristol Fighter aeroplane:

'An approaching car pulled nearly into its ditch at the sight of our race ... I gained ... gained steadily: and was perhaps five miles an hour the faster. Down went my left hand to give the engine two extra dollops of oil, for fear that something was running hot: but an overhead Jap twin, super-tuned like this, would carry on to the moon and back, unfaltering.' (*M*, p.201)

While Lawrence and the Sydney Smiths were at the Schneider Cup Race they stayed in the yacht Karen owned by the Smiths' friend Colin Cooper. During this period, Cooper and Lawrence took many rides on the small speed-boat, a Biscayne Baby, that accompanied the yacht. Cooper liked Lawrence's enthusiasm for the boat and gave it to him and the Smiths. Soon after the Schneider Race the Karen called at Cattewater and delivered the Biscuit as they had named her. Lawrence and Clare Sydney Smith (seen here) frequently used this boat, and Lawrence spent a lot of time overhauling it during 1930-31.

Lawrence at the wheel of the first of the 200 series boats which he helped develop, and which were to save the lives of many crashed pilots in the Second World War.

Despite the technical awareness in this passage, written around 1927, he could still call himself, perhaps too modestly, 'a non-technical man, very vague as to the function of a camshaft or inclined drive' (*L*, p.514). By 1935, however, he could speak to Brough as an equal in engine mechanics and design, responding to his query about fan problems:

'About your fan. Our propeller experiments were all marine, and they showed how little was known yet, even in that much exercised branch. Air propellers (of the suction type) have been, I am sure, very little studied. Large diameter of course means noise, as do broad tips. Four blades are quieter than three and as efficient. You can push an air-prop pitch up to great steepness, so long as the revs are not extravagant. But frankly I cannot help you. Our props had so different an intention. The water is so solid an element. Have you considered Ethylene glycol for cooling? Or is the engine getting too hot for its oil?'

Then, interestingly, Lawrence flashes back to a makeshift device he used in the desert campaign, which reveals that he had some expertise with engines even then:

'In the desert I ran a tiny condenser for our old Fords, and so boiled all day without using a pint of water, and with great thermal advantage. Later they doubled the Leader-tank [sic; should be Header-tank], increased the pump output, and carried on without boiling. Petrol consumption then increased.' (*L*, p.867)

It was during the autumn of 1929, when Lawrence had returned from India and was serving at Mount Batten, that he really taught himself to become a first-rate mechanic. Singlehandedly, he overhauled a Biscayne Baby speedboat, the *Biscuit*, which an English millionaire, Colin Cooper, had given to him and his base commander. In November 1930 he participated in a number of seaplane rescue operations and became interested in the development of fast boats for this purpose, continually petitioning the RAF about its weaknesses in this area. Then in February 1931, in the presence of Clare Sydney Smith, he witnessed the crash of an Iris III seaplane into Plymouth Sound. Six men drowned, but six were saved — largely through Lawrence's own exertions, which included directing the rescue operation spontaneously and diving into the water himself. Lawrence was deeply moved by the loss of life on this occasion and wrote 'Six of us crushed together in the crushed canister of the hull were bubbling out their lives. Great belches of air spewed up now and then, as another compartment of wing or hull gave way' (*L*, p.713).

As Lawrence's interest in fast rescue boats grew, he was assigned to the Hubert Scott-Paine shipyard at Hythe near Southampton to tune, test and develop new engines, and to help Scott-Paine design a new faster boat. On 13 April 1931 Lawrence wrote to Liddell Hart that 'My two-year war with the Air Ministry over the type of motor boats suited to attend seaplanes is bearing results now, and experimental boats are being offered by the contractors. I've become a marine expert, and test the things for them ...' (*L*, p.718). On 19 April, he was more specific in a letter to Dick Knowles: 'The engine test is now on. It's the 100 H.P. engine used in the Invicta car, and the Vickers tank. We buzz it up and down Southampton Water, the Spit and the Solent, each of us ... taking the wheel in turn, while the other checks gauges' (*L*, pp.720-21).

By the end of June 1931 Lawrence had written a good deal of his eighty-page technical manual on the '200 Class Royal Air Force Seaplane Tender', the rescue boat that resulted from his pressure on the Air Ministry and his tests. The manual, completed and issued in 1932, covers all aspects of the boat's maintenance and handling in various weather conditions, and is written with respect for the craft's quality and well-being:

'212. The 200 class was designed to be as directionally stable as possible in all runs of sea and windage; and with that in view the after part of the hull has been kept high to balance the high forepart in side winds. Plenty of dihedral was also allowed to give side area or keel area, so that with very little draft they do not weathercock or blow sideways as readily as would otherwise have been the case.

214. The primary purpose of the class is to save life or Service equipment from a crash at sea. Between emergencies they will serve for general duty; but they must always be kept in trim for high-speed work. The coxswain's constant duty is to save the engines, by intelligent reading of the dashboard instruments and by moderation in use of the throttle'[97].

Boats like the 200 class seaplane tender were to save many downed pilots in the Second World War, and with its speed and manoeuverability it was the prototype for the PT (patrol torpedo) boat.

Lawrence expressed his satisfaction with this 37½ foot cruiser in a letter of 22 March 1932 to Geoffrey Dawson:

'... a big crash a year ago in Plymouth Sound ... showed me convincingly that we had nothing in the service fit to help marine aircraft in difficulties. ... So the R.A.F. (partly ... at my prompting) went into the science of it, and have had produced for them ... an entirely new type of seaplane tender. They are 37 foot boats, twin engined, doing 30 m.p.h. in all weathers, handy, safe, and very cheap. ... All this has been done through the admiralty, in the teeth of its protests and traditions. Now ... the sailors are beginning to take notice, and wonder if there isn't something in it'[98].

On 20 December 1934 he was to sum up his achievements in the RAF to John Buchan by claiming that 'In four or five years we have trebled the speed and yet reduced the prime cost and running cost of all the R.A.F. boats: and now the War Office and the Admiralty are borrowing our boats and copying or adapting our designs for their purposes' (*L*, p.837). He later pointed out that 'the German, Chinese, Spanish and Portugese Governments have adopted' these new boats too.

In addition to teaching crews how to use the 200 class tenders, he piloted armoured target launches during aeroplane ship-assault practice — attempting to evade dummy bombs dropped from low-flying aircraft. This sport gave rise to wild rumours, one being that he had invented and designed the boats used, but this he always denied. The 200 class seaplane tender was apparently the only RAF boat in whose design he had played a major role, and he was the first to admit that it was the product of many minds.

An unpublished seventy-nine page report by Lawrence, entitled 'Power Boat Hull Reconditioning', covering speedboat overhauls done at Bridlington between November 1934 and February 1935, is now in the possession of the University of Texas. This report testifies to Lawrence's mechanical expertise just before he left the RAF:

'Item I. Taken from the water. Armoured roof sent to Messers. Hadfield. Cab, engines, trays tanks onezote removed. Bilges treated with Hack varnish to water line and with white paint above. Topsides burnt off where necessary and rubbed down where sound. Painted black. Bottom not burnt off but repainted with red anti-fouling composition. Hull, skin-fittings, shafting propellers rubber steering gear exhausts rubber fenders etc. overhauled and removed as necessary. Superstructure painted and chromium plate checked for defects.'(p.1)

By this time Lawrence foresaw the need to bolster the Air Force since Germany was in the ascendant: 'When Germany wings herself — ah; that will be another matter, and our signal to reinforce: for the German kites will be new and formidable ...' (*L*, pp.792-93). He suggested to Lionel Curtis that more aerodromes and aircraft plants should be built, and 'research made into flying boat development ... and wireless-controlled aircraft' as well as anti-aircraft gunnery.

By far the most impressive technical development with which Lawrence was involved in this period was a hovercraft/hydrofoil prototype — yet this project is not mentioned in the Mack, Stewart, Montgomery Hyde or Yardley biographies, and Lawrence apparently told no one about it, perhaps because he wanted it patented first.

In an article that appeared posthumously in the London *Evening Standard* on 20 May 1935, Lawrence stressed (as H.F. King points out[99]) that in contrast to the old naval-style boats that existed when he began working on RAF marine craft in 1929, the new boats that he had helped to design and test 'rise out of the water and run over its face' as their speed increases. 'They cannot roll nor pitch, having no pendulum nor period, but a subtly modelled planing bottom and sharp edges.'

These very features were to reappear in a revolutionary form when in May 1938, three years after Lawrence's death, a new type of craft named *Empire Day* was displayed. This had been designed by T.E. Lawrence and Edward Spurr, a young Bradford engineer whom Lawrence met in 1932 when they were both working with Scott-Paine at the British Power Boat Company yard in Hythe.

'[H.F. King's] investigations suggested or established that the craft had been built in secret by the engineering firm of R. Malcolm Ltd., of Slough ...; that the work had been given to this company because of its experience in *aircraft* construction; that Spurr and Lawrence had worked together on "new theories of speedboat design"; and that since Lawrence's death in 1935, Spurr had continued the researches which had led to the building of *Empire Day*. It emerged also that Lawrence and Spurr had made nearly 70 miniature models for this craft; that these had been subject to "innumerable tests"; and that Lawrence was "heart and soul in the work"'.

According to King, *Empire Day* was 'beyond any doubt, a form of air-cushion vehicle — a true forerunner, in its general principles, of craft recently constructed and projected, employing dynamic lift and ram effect to reduce their displacement or raise themselves clear of the water.' The Lawrence-Spurr invention had something of the properties of both the hydrofoil and the hovercraft. King comments that 'lift at high speed was obtained principally by aerodynamic, rather than hydrodynamic, means.' He goes on to say that in 1935 a Finn, T.J. Kaario, had experimented with ram-wing watercraft too but that when it appeared, *Empire Day* was far more sophisticated than any of Kaario's models.

Kevin Desmond and Leo Villa have also investigated this unique boat, and find that it embodied 'the most complete attempt at aerodynamically streamlining a boat yet made', but that 'the most revolutionary idea of all was in the choice of power units, because this "hover"-craft was designed to take two totally different engines', the 150 hp Spurr engine and the 960 Napier Lion aero-engine[100].

Lawrence died three years before Spurr was granted a patent for *Empire Day* in May 1938. When the new craft was shown to the press, its prow bore the dedication 'To L. of A.: a compte' — 'To Lawrence of Arabia: on account'. *Empire Day* was intended to travel at 80 mph but failed in its speed trials on Lake Windermere in August 1938 because of 'water-cooling defects, transmission defects and repeated stalling'[101] of the Spurr engine. On 9 September 1938 Spurr succeeded in making one run at 73 mph before his propeller flattened out. Early in 1939 the boat, now fitted with the Napier Lion engine and renamed *Empire Day II*, was scheduled to assault the world's water-speed record. Unfortunately, some unusual transmission parts could not be built in time and Spurr had to withdraw from the race.

The posthumous collaboration of Lawrence with Spurr went on beyond the *Empire Day* project. Lawrence had envisioned a fleet of fast torpedo boats for coastal defence. Spurr designed some that (like *Empire Day*) would have aerofoil hulls so they could shoot torpedos out in the space between the hull and the water, which would greatly improve their storage and delivery. During the Second World War Spurr worked in the aircraft industry and was granted several patents but the whereabouts of his pioneering boat are at present unknown.

Lawrence's design imagination, mechanical skill and love of machinery make him almost as extraordinary a mechanic as he was an archaeologist, intelligence agent, guerrilla leader, diplomat and writer. His love of and contribution to aeroplane, speedboat and motorcycle racing are clear; he may also have made a small contribution to horse-racing as well, by lending his name to the Arab Horse Society as an honorary member from 1919 to 1930[102]. What was Lawrence's attitude toward horses, and did he actually own a horse himself?

He certainly preferred machines to animals, as he tells us on more than one occasion. 'A skittish motor-bike with a touch of blood in it is better than all the riding animals on earth, because of its logical extension of our faculties, and the hint, the provocation, to excess conferred by its honeyed untiring smoothness' (*M*, pp.244-45). 'Poor Arabs wondered why I had no mare, and I forebore to puzzle them by incomprehensible talk of hardening myself, or confess I would rather walk than ride for sparing of animals: yet the first was true and the second true. Something hurtful to my pride, disagreeable, rose at the sight of these lower forms of life' (*SP*, pp.175-76). Yet Lawrence states that he occasionally rode to a host's tent on a blood mare (SP, p. 271). He also notes that during the Arab Revolt, staff officer 'Stirling's passion for horses was a passport to intimacy with Feisal and the chiefs' (*SP*, p.558).

Middle-East researcher Andrew Carvely reports that in Cairo he met a British doctor named Stevens who had known Lawrence during the war period. According to Stevens, Lawrence was 'overwhelmed' by horses for some reason. Stevens, however, said that

Lawrence had been offered or given Arabian horses by the sheikhs of many bedouin tribes. Carvely also spoke to Dr Rowland Ellis, an archaeologist and student of the Middle East who knew Lawrence. Dr Ellis said that Lawrence was never as fond of horses as he was of camels (in *Seven Pillars* he calls the camel 'that intricate, prodigious piece of nature', p.346) but that Lawrence did claim to have owned a horse. Carvely explains that a mare rather than a stallion is usually given and the recipient leaves the horse with the tribe; then, in a few years, he has not one horse but many.

This would explain the rumour about Lawrence very well: possibly he was offered a horse, left it in its tribal habitat and never collected this magnificent gift. Thus he may have 'owned' a horse without actually having possessed it. Those who study Lawrence know that he never quite yields up all his secrets! The precise details of all his mechanical work, too, are largely unknown but that it was an absorbing facet of his life and yet another field in which he had the capacity to achieve excellence is undeniable.

Chapter six

The Writer

Throughout his entire adult life Lawrence recorded his experiences and ideas on paper: in one form or another he was a writer. Besides his thesis on Crusader castles, his diaries and intelligence reports, his translations and his own books, there were also various reviews and introductions (most notably to Doughty's *Arabia Deserta*) and countless letters — literally hundreds, if not thousands, of them. Although his archaeological, intelligence and technical reports are most valuable for the factual information and skillful assessments they convey, his letters, translations and two autobiographies, *Seven Pillars of Wisdom* (1926) and *The Mint* (1928), best reveal his attitudes toward life and himself as well as his intense attention to style.

Letters and Translations

Witty, profound, scholarly, tortured and self-revealing by turns, Lawrence's letters form one of the great collections of the century and, as they continue to be discovered and published, an ongoing autobiography. His epistolary models were Byron, Keats, Horace Walpole and Lord Chesterfield. 'There are few good letter-writers,' he once commented, 'as few as there are good sonnetteers: for the same reason: that the form is too worn to be easy, and there are too many who try' (*L*, p.583). In a letter of 1934 to Eric Kennington, Lawrence blames a delay in responding on the laziness that afflicts many letter-writers, but then reveals the care with which his letters were composed: 'I write them in great batches, on the days when at length (after months, often) the impulse towards them eventually comes. Each tries to direct itself as directly as it can towards my picture of the person I am writing to: and if it does not seem to me (as I write it) that it makes contact — why then I write no more that night' (*L*, p.857).

Three months before his death, he actually had 'a lovely little card printed "To tell you that in future I shall write very few letters"' and said that 'I'm going to tuck one into each letter that I write for the next six months' (*L*, p.857) but whether such an inveterate correspondent could have maintained his resolve not to write letters is doubtful. Had he lived, he most probably would have continued in the love-hate relationship with letter-writing that seems to be an essential characteristic of this literary form.

Lawrence's career as a writer began in March 1904 when, at the age of 16, his essay 'An Antiquarian and a Geologist in Hants' was published in the Oxford High School magazine. A second essay, 'Playground Cricket', followed in July. Lawrence's first work of substance — his Oxford B A thesis, which won him First Class Honours — was researched and written in 1909-10. Lawrence is seen here as he appeared in 1910, along with his four brothers: from left to right, Lawrence, Frank, Arnie, Bob and Will.

Lawrence's major wartime writings were the reports he published in the Arab Bulletin. He originated the idea of this secret publication, the first issue of which appeared on 6 June 1916. Most of his contributions were later reprinted in Secret Despatches from Arabia, and one entitled 'A Raid' begins 'I left Akaba on October 24, with Captain G. Lloyd, Lieut. Wood, R.E., and the Indian Machine Gun Company ... We marched into Rumm (October 25) ...' En route to Rumm they camped in the Wadi Itm where Lawrence was photographed by Lloyd.

Lawrence's attitude toward translation was also ambiguous. He looked forward to translating Adrian Le Corbeau's *Gigantesque* because 'it would be nice to play with words again' (*L*, p.408), and derived the 'deepest satisfaction' from the musical sequences of vowels and consonants he achieved during this translation, which he began in 1923. Later he expressed satisfaction about the prospect of translating Homer's *Odyssey*. But Lawrence undertook the translation of both works principally to earn money, and had to labour in the difficult conditions of the Tank Corps and RAF barracks. It is therefore perhaps no wonder that he lost interest in both authors, commenting that it was better to do nothing than to write like Le Corbeau, and that he was 'tired of all Homer's namby-pamby men and women', a controversial opinion that shows originality if not objective literary judgement.

Even so, the classics scholar Maurice Bowra has praised Lawrence's *Odyssey* translation, which appeared in 1932:

'... two qualities seem to emerge and give it a special distinction. The first is that he enjoys the story for its own sake and spares nothing to keep it clear and lively, to make the details illuminate and strengthen the whole effect and never to allow the plot to be lost in undue emphasis on the wrong point. The second is that he sees the whole Homeric world with a clear vision as Homer himself saw it'[103]

A subsequent appreciation by James Notopoulos has sustained this opinion[104], and Lawrence in a letter of 1931 to his publisher Bruce Rogers explains the underlying experiences that would make his translation unique, however tedious Lawrence found it: 'For years we were digging up a city of roughly the Odysseus period. I have handled the weapons, armour, utensils of those times, explored their houses, planned their cities. I have hunted wild boars and watched wild lions, sailed the Aegean (and sailed ships), bent bows, lived with pastoral peoples, woven textiles, built boats and killed many men' (*L*, p.710).

A similar first-hand knowledge of France informed his translation of Le Corbeau's *Gigantesque*, which Lawrence with accuracy and good taste Anglicized as *The Forest Giant* (1924). Maurice Larès, recalling Lawrence's childhood education in the French city of Dinard and his continuing love of French literature and architecture, writes that Lawrence had 'an excellent knowledge of written French and a great capacity for appreciation of the nuances of the original. One does not find even a single ridiculous error in his translation. In addition, its quality is uniform'[105].

Lawrence was also asked to translate Pierre Custot's novel *Sturly* but although he liked its style much more than that of Le Corbeau's work, he became exasperated with the task and in 1924 burned the chapters he had translated. He sent the publisher, Jonathan Cape, a cheque 'towards the fee for a substitute-translator' and eventually wrote just the blurb for the new translation. It was by Richard Aldington[106].

Seven Pillars of Wisdom

Ultimately Lawrence's literary reputation rests on the work that most powerfully reveals his character. *Seven Pillars of Wisdom* is perhaps the finest British autobiography of the twentieth century and one of the world's great books, no less enduring than the masterpieces Lawrence consciously set out to equal, Doughty's *Arabia Deserta*, Melville's *Moby Dick*, Nietzsche's *Thus Spake Zarathustra*, Cervantes' *Don Quixote*, Rabelais' works, Whitman's *Leaves of Grass* and Tolstoy's *War and Peace*.

In 1927 Herbert Read disputed the stature of *Seven Pillars of Wisdom*, seeing in it a 'core of darkness' and 'divided aims' while he contended that 'Great books are written in moods of spiritual light and intellectual certainty.' In answer to Read's strange assertion about light and certainty, Lawrence rightly wrote 'I would maintain against him that these moods never produced an imaginative work the size of a mouse.' Yet Read caught a certain truth about Lawrence:his book does contain darkness and divided aims although this is not the whole truth.

In October 1922 Lawrence intimated to Edward Garnett: 'I've made some rather poor notes, which show me how hard it would be to bring off a picture of the R.A.F. Depot.' Some of these notes were later used to compose The Mint. Early in November he was posted to RAF Farnborough where he is shown (left) in this photograph.

D.H. Lawrence, in his *Studies in Classic American Literature*, separates writers into two groups: those like Poe, obsessed with death and ruin, who tear down, and those like Whitman, interested in procreation and unity, who attempt to build up. T.E. Lawrence's book is a unique combination of both tendencies: he painfully works to construct the Arab Revolt yet he shows himself falling apart in the process because of the wounds, torture and mental strain he had to undergo. Even as he wrote and rewrote the book (from 1919 to 1926) he knew that the Revolt had ended in failure when France evicted Feisal from Syria in 1920, and felt therefore that his personal sacrifices had been in vain: particularly at Deraa, he had 'prostituted' himself in the service of an alien race, as he says in his first chapter, echoing Conrad in *Lord Jim*[107]. Lawrence's book is great partly because of the constant tension between these two contrary sets of knowledge — the military victory in which 'the lone hand had won against the world's odds' and the personal and political trials which caused Lawrence to feel 'so stained in estimation that afterward nothing in the world would make him feel clean' (*SP*, p.682).

In contrast to the relative fluency with which he produced his other works, it was very painful for Lawrence to compose *Seven Pillars of Wisdom*. Working alone in a garrett in an architect's house in Barton Street, Westminster, for long stretches of time without food or sleep, he came perilously close to a nervous breakdown as he relived on paper the most painful events of the Revolt. He wrote the book not once but again and again and again, especially his account of the Deraa incident, in which he could never seem to reveal exactly what had happened but could not conceal it either. He lost most of the first manuscript at Reading railway station; possibly he half-wanted to continue concealing his emotions. He rewrote the book from memory, rewrote it a third time and in 1922 printed up eight copies of this third version on the press of the *Oxford Times*. He spent another four years revising this version and seeing it into print in 1926 as a limited edition 'book beautiful' in the tradition of William Morris. This was followed by the editing labour that resulted in the abridgement *Revolt in the Desert* of 1927 (which omits the profound introspective and speculative passages of the unabridged work). Upon Lawrence's death in 1935 the first public edition of *Seven Pillars of Wisdom* was published by Jonathan Cape.

From the start, the leading writers of his own period were in no doubt about its quality. H.G. Wells called *Seven Pillars* 'the finest piece of prose that has been written in the English language for 150 years.' Arnold Bennett preferred Lawrence's writing to that of his namesake D.H. Lawrence, and found T.E. 'a better writer than Winston Churchill. He is one of the best English prose writers living. ... Seemingly he has passed unscathed through a world bristling with clichés.'

Winston Churchill, E.M. Forster, John Buchan, Wyndham Lewis, Siegfried Sassoon, Robert Graves, George Bernard Shaw, Thomas Hardy, C. Day Lewis and Rex Warner were among the other admirers of Lawrence's book in its prime and it has remained continuously in print from 1935 until now.

In recent years it has steadily accrued the respect of literary scholars. For Stanley Weintraub 'the reason why the attempts to imitate Lawrence in literature appear so unsuccessful — or, at best, modest achievements — is that his own self-portrait is so rich in its resonances. In its narrative power, ambiguity of characterization, vivid prose, and epical sweep, Lawrence's writing, particularly in *Seven Pillars of Wisdom*, overwhelms the challenges it evokes'[108]. Jeffrey Meyers sees *Seven Pillars* as 'essentially and primarily a literary work of genius, beauty and insight ... a masterpiece of psychological analysis and self-revelation, and' one of 'the finest books of the modern age'[109]. For Keith Hull, *Seven Pillars'* 'greatness hinges on its mysteries'[110].

Some readers find Lawrence's personality as revealed in its pages every bit as irritating as his military superiors in Cairo found him in person, while others think his character admirable. Ultimately, what makes Lawrence a great autobiographer is the fact that fifty years of readers have felt as if they had known him personally. When he wrote *Seven Pillars*, and to a lesser extent *The Mint*, he became his own best image-maker, far exceeding Lowell Thomas and his other biographers in wit, subtlety and power.

The most intriguing aspect of the book is its recurring element of paradox. Unlike the works of his biographers, who must each 'interpret' or 'understand' Lawrence, sometimes smoothing over the contradictions to do so, Lawrence's own work has the ambiguous quality expressed in these lines by Walt Whitman:

> 'Do I contradict myself?
> Very well then I contradict myself.
> (I am large, I contain multitudes)'.

Lawrence was far too intelligent to take a simple-minded view of the world, and if the Revolt was a 'triumph' (as his sub-title claims) he also felt by 1920 that it was a failure. The very title 'Seven Pillars of Wisdom' can refer to a completed solid structure as well as to a ruined temple or palace lying in the desert sands like Shelley's Ozymandias. Lawrence gives us not one certain view of any character, event or thought but at least two, and then leaves the reader to try to strike a balance.

For instance, Edward Said accuses him of creating racialist stereotypes of Arab culture, while Western writers have found him all too ready to praise Arab ways at the expense of British customs. But what does *Seven Pillars* actually say? In Chapter 3 (which serves as a summary description of desert religion as Lawrence saw it) the bedouin's 'sterile experience robbed him of compassion and perverted his human kindness to the image of the waste in which he hid. ... He saved his own soul, perhaps, and without danger, but in a hard selfishness' (*SP*, p.40). Yet Lawrence recounts that while he was swimming in a pool in the Wadi Rumm, he met an old man who cried out that 'The love is from God; and of God; and towards God' (*SP*, p.364). With no attempt to suppress or avoid contradiction Lawrence comments openly that he 'had believed Semites unable to use love as a link between themselves and God' but that 'the old man of Rumm loomed portentous in his brief, single sentence, and seemed to overturn my theories of the Arab nature' (*SP*, pp.364-65). Does Lawrence, then, believe Arab religion to be hard and selfish, or capable of reaching out to others? He leaves it to us to decide.

The same contradictory quality informs his view of the people with whom he worked for so long. Sometimes he is accused of portraying Feisal in a brave romantic way and then undercutting him:

> 'I felt at first glance that this was the man I had come to Arabia to seek — the leader who would bring the Arab Revolt to full glory. Feisal looked very tall and pillar-like, very slender, in his long white silk robes and his brown head-cloth bound with a brilliant scarlet and gold cord'. (*SP*, p.92)

Much later on in the book, Lawrence describes him as 'a brave, weak, ignorant spirit, trying to do work for which only a genius, a prophet or a great criminal, was fitted. I served him out of pity, a motive which degraded us both' (*SP*, p.582).

This is clearly a change, although Lawrence from the very first described Feisal with some complexity as 'hot-tempered and sensitive, even unreasonable' and noted that 'Appetite and physical weakness were mated in him' and that there was a 'pathetic hint of frailty' (*SP*, p.98) in his character.

Several biographers have accused Lawrence of inconsistency or insincerity but perhaps he simply held both heroic and unheroic views of Feisal, or perhaps his perception of Feisal changed as the Revolt progressed. Since almost no one is either a paragon of virtue or a pit of vice, his differing views of Feisal actually sum up the strengths and weaknesses of a man, not a stereotype. If Lawrence's characterization of Feisal were only heroic, then

Lawrence would be the mere propagandist for the Revolt that Aldington and Kedourie have assumed. If his portrayal of Feisal were simply negative, Lawrence might be only the Western racialist that Said posits. Neither view gives Lawrence credit for the genuine complexity of his literary vision.

Equally one might wonder if Lawrence saw war as a noble or an ignoble enterprise. The Battle of Tafileh seems a glorious victory over the Turks but 'The Arabs on their track rose against them and shot them ignobly as they ran' (*SP*, p.491). Although a 'battle might be thrilling at the moment for generals', for Lawrence immediately after Tafileh 'there was no glory left, but the terror of the broken flesh, which had been our own men, carried past us to their homes' (*SP*, p.491). In the aftermath of a train attack, Sergeant Stokes proudly 'strolled through the wrecked bridge, saw there the bodies of twenty Turks torn to pieces by his second shell, and retired hurriedly' (*SP*, p.380), shocked at what he had seen and not wishing to enquire too deeply into his own handiwork. During the charge at Aba el Lissan, Lawrence is among the first camel riders to attack the Turkish defences, fulfilling the role of heroic victor, but then falls and just as suddenly becomes the underdog, wondering 'what a squashed thing I should look when all that cataract of men and camels had poured over me' (*SP*, p.311). A war of national liberation is for Lawrence at first a wonderful thing, for he and the Arabs were 'devoted to freedom, the second of man's creeds |the first, according to Shakespeare, is life, and the third, happiness|, a purpose so ravenous that it devoured all our strength, a hope so transcendent that our earlier ambitions faded in its glare' (*SP*, p.27). On the other hand, in his intellectual mood he thinks that 'To man-rational, wars of nationality were as much a cheat as religious wars, and nothing was worth fighting for: nor could fighting, the act of fighting, hold any meed of intrinsic virtue' (*SP*, p.565).

Does Lawrence favour the British or the Arab side in the conflict with the Turks? On the final march to Damascus:

> 'I could feel the taut power of Arab excitement behind me. The climax of the preaching of years had come, and a united country was straining towards its historic capital. In confidence that this weapon, tempered by myself, was enough for the utmost of my purpose, I seemed to forget the English companions who stood outside my idea in the shadow of ordinary war. I failed to make them partners of my certainty' (*SP*, p.603).

Yet five days later, when the Arabs fill up Azrak on their way toward victory at Damascus:

> 'The crowd had destroyed my pleasure in Azrak. ... and I went off down the valley to our remote Ain el Essad and lay there all day in my old lair among the tamarisk, where the wind in the dusty green branches played with such sounds as it made in English trees. It told me was I tired to death of these Arabs; petty incarnate Semites who attained heights and depths beyond our reach, though not beyond our sight' (*SP*, p.607).

In five days he swings from neglecting his English comrades who do not understand the Arabs' motives and from pride in his leadership of the Arabs, to accusations against them reminiscent of Charles Doughty's 'The Semites are like to a man sitting in a cloaca to the eyes, and whose brows touch heaven.' At the end of Lawrence's campaign, he actually feels at home with neither side:'... the efforts for these years to live in the dress of the Arabs, and to imitate their mental foundation, quitted me of my English self, and let me look at the West and its conventions with new eyes: they destroyed it all for me. At the same time I could not sincerely take on the Arab skin: it was an affectation only' (*SP*, p.30).

Similar divisions affect Lawrence's view of his own personality. In his self-portrait Lawrence appears contradictory and unpredictable, a man difficult to deal with, yet one able to assume many roles precisely because of the multitude of personalities he harboured within. In the chapter 'Myself' he writes overtly 'I was a standing court martial on myself, inevitably' (*SP*, p.583), and he states that after the Deraa beating he felt himself dividing into parts. This is only an extreme extension of what was apparently his normal feeling of self-division. Lawrence experienced at least four major contrary tendencies: to lead and to be led; to be active and to be introspective; to deny his body and to give in to it; to reveal and to conceal his feelings and foibles.

He seems unable to decide whether he prefers the position of leader or follower. After the capture of Akaba, Lawrence tells his superior, Director of Military Intelligence Gilbert Clayton, that the port 'had been taken on my plan by my effort. The cost of it had fallen on my brains and nerves. There was much more I felt inclined to do, and capable of doing — if he thought I had earned the right to be my own master' (*SP*, p.331). Lawrence craves and demands more responsibility, and reluctantly settles for Colonel Joyce's formal seniority on condition that Joyce will allow him a free hand. In the book's opening poem 'To S.A.', he writes very commandingly that:

> 'I drew these tides of men into my hands
> and wrote my will across the sky in stars'.

But after Emir Zeid spends the gold that Lawrence wanted for an offensive, he decides to leave, baring his soul to Hogarth:'I complained that since landing in Arabia I had had options and requests, never an order: that I was tired to death of free-will, and of many things beside free-will' (*SP*, p.514). In his reflections on his thirtieth birthday, he writes that 'Always in working I had tried to serve, for the scrutiny of leading was too prominent' and 'I followed, and did not institute' (*SP*, p.582).

He fills the roles of man of thought and man of action, but not without conflict. When Clayton likes Lawrence's report on the potential of the Arab Revolt and tells him that he must go back as Feisal's advisor, Lawrence urges his 'complete unfitness for the job'. However, Clayton insists, 'So I had to go: leaving to others the Arab Bulletin I had founded, the maps I wished to draw, and the file of the war-changes of the Turkish Army, all fascinating activities in which my training helped me' (*SP*, p.117). He seems happy with a desk job and no practical responsibility. Lawrence tells us that even later when he had been in the field for eight months, 'I felt mean, to fill the place of a man of action; for my standards of value were a wilful reaction against theirs, and I despised their happiness' (*SP*, p.284).

Yet again and again he shows that he was a very capable man of action. 'I had a heavy bout of fever on me, which made me angry, so that I paid no attention to Rahail's appeals for rest. That young man had maddened all of us for months by his abundant vigour, and by laughing at our weaknesses; so this time I was determined to ride him out, showing no mercy. Before dawn he was blubbering with self-pity; but softly, lest I hear him' (*SP*, p.460). Lawrence later adds, 'For a year and a half I had been in motion, riding a thousand miles each month upon camels with added nervous hours in crazy aeroplanes, or rushing across country in powerful cars' (*SP*, p.514). Despite his complaint in this passage about so much motion, Lawrence loved crazy aeroplanes and powerful cars and almost never neglected a chance to ride in one. He also complains that he is not a soldier but then immediately adds that he had read practically everything available about strategy.

One of his most powerful internal conflicts springs from the attempt to suppress and deny his bodily urges: 'I so reverenced my wits and despised my body that I would not be beholden to the second for the life of the first' (*SP*, p.547). He writes of himself that 'There was no flesh' (*SP*, p.581). It seems that by an act of the will Lawrence is consciously forcing himself to forget hunger, tiredness and sex, almost like a medieval monk.

Yet, he writes approvingly of Arabs 'quivering together in the yielding sand with intimate hot limbs in supreme embrace' (*SP*, p.28) and remembers 'a delicious warmth, probably sexual' (*SP*, p.454) swelling up in himself after his beating at Deraa. In the

During his service in the Tank Corps, Lawrence translated Adrien Le Corbeau's Le Gigantesque. He also wrote an introduction, dated 24 May 1924, for a new edition of Richard Garnett's The Twilight of the Gods and Other Tales. He is shown here outside Hut 12 at Bovington Camp.

1922 'Oxford' text, he writes that after this beating, an attraction to pain 'had journeyed with me since, a fascination and terror and morbid desire, lascivious and vicious, perhaps, but like the striving of a moth towards its flame.' (The struggle between his desire to experience pain and his wilful attempt to resist it continued long after the Deraa incident, as the details surrounding his post-war flagellation sessions seem to indicate.)

Finally, he seems simultaneously to want to tell all concerning his inner nature and yet to be unable to do so. He will reveal his feeling of sexuality after the torture at Deraa but in the public edition of the book does not state his full attraction to pain. He will describe what happened to him in the Bey's headquarters but not clearly enough for us to understand it precisely. He will say that the 'citadel of my integrity had been irrevocably lost' at Deraa but not clarify what that means. He will write a very sensual poem to 'S.A.' but not tell us who that was or if he harboured homosexual feelings. He will say he took a trip behind Turkish lines but not what he did there.

In these four basic conflicts resides the essence of Lawrence's character in *Seven Pillars*, and the main reason that the book has remained 'alive' for half a century after his death. In some of his biographers' versions, Lawrence has become a puritan or a perverse sado-masochist, a great man of action or merely a pretentious talker, an important leader or really only a follower who exaggerated his role, a man undergoing tortured self-revelation or a misleading liar. Viewed objectively as a character in *Seven Pillars*, Lawrence *is* his contradictions — both self-revealing and self-concealing, attracted to masochistic and homosexual feelings but repelled by them, a man of action who also thinks too much, and a superb leader who craved the follower's freedom from responsibility.

All the same, if we over-emphasize Lawrence's conflicts in *Seven Pillars*, we forget what is perhaps his most under-rated quality as a writer, his sense of humour. That element does much to restore the balance to his portrayal of himself. The incident in which he mistakenly shoots his own camel in the head during the charge at Aba el Lissan is especially revealing in its comic import, both visually (in the Eric Kennington sketch Lawrence chose to illustrate it) and verbally. After a long assault on the Turks' position on a particularly hot day, Lawrence goads Auda abu Tayi into a camel charge, and then proceeds to take part in it himself:

> 'My camel, the Sherari racer, Naama, stretched herself out, and hurled downhill with such might that we soon out-distanced the others. The Turks fired a few shots, but mostly only shrieked and turned to run: the bullets they did send at us were not very harmful, for it took much to bring a charging camel down in a dead heap.
>
> I had got among the first of them, and was shooting, with a pistol of course, for only an expert could use a rifle from such plunging beasts; when suddenly my camel tripped and went down emptily on her face, as though pole-axed. I was torn completely from the saddle, sailed grandly through the air for a great distance, and landed with a crash which seemed to drive all the power and feeling out of me. I lay there, passively waiting for the Turks to kill me, continuing to hum over the verses from a half-forgotten poem, whose rhythm something, perhaps the prolonged stride of the camel, had brought back to my memory as we leaped down the hill-side. ... While another part of my mind thought what a squashed thing I should look when all that cataract of men and camels had poured over.
>
> After a long time I finished my poem, and no Turks came, and no camel trod on me. ... My camel's body had laid behind me like a rock and divided the charge into two streams: and in the back of its skull was the heavy bullet of the fifth shot I had fired.' (*SP*, pp.310-12)

This incident must have been anything but funny to Lawrence when it happened; and his relation of how his mind reacted under the pressure of imminent death proves the authenticity of his experience to anyone who has been through a similar life-threatening situation. Yet he chooses to relate this incident with a wry attack on his own pretensions. The fierce military commander is abruptly transformed into a helpless Oxford aesthete who seems absurdly out of place reciting Ernest Dowson's poem 'Impenitentia Ultima' while waiting to be crushed by a horde of camels and riders. The great epic hero charging forward is suddenly turned into a foolish bungler who has caused his own slapstick troubles by shooting his camel in the head. Had Lawrence simply been intent upon glorifying himself, he would have omitted this incident. Instead, he has used humour here, as elsewhere in his book, as the best way of counteracting any situation in which he threatens to become too proud of himself.

Early in *Seven Pillars* Lawrence makes fun of his spoken Arabic, commenting that his 'fluency had a lack of grammar, which made my talk a perpetual adventure for my hearers. Newcomers imagined I must be the native of some unknown illiterate district; a shot-rubbish ground of disjected Arabic parts of speech' (*SP*, p.240). Nowhere is self-denigration employed to greater effect than at the end when an Australian medical major blames Lawrence for the filth of the Turkish military hospital which Lawrence has just tried to clean up. Instead of returning insult for insult, Lawrence merely 'cackled out like a chicken, with the wild laughter of strain; it did feel extraordinarily funny to be so cursed just as I had been pluming myself on having bettered the apparently hopeless' (*SP*, p.682). Lawrence even takes a slap on the face and believes he deserves it, for having had to do many disagreeable things in the course of the Revolt. Thus, time and again in *Seven Pillars* his humour restores a sense of proportion when he begins to portray himself as a hero.

If he can be humorously harsh with himself, he is just as severe to others, especially military men with pretensions. Authorities unworthy of their rank in his view come in for his most aggressive 'taking down'. He writes 'My instinct with the inevitable was to provoke it' (*SP*, p.658), by which he means that he could not resist challenging unjust authority and never allowed authority to stand in the way of his plans. When GHQ determines to keep him away from the Arab Revolt, he 'became ... quite intolerable to the Staff on the Canal. I took every opportunity to rub into them their comparative ignorance and inefficiency in the department of intelligence (not difficult!) and irritated them yet further by literary airs, correcting Shavian split infinitives in their reports' (*SP*, p.65). Yet, when he supports their political objectives by recommending that no British soldiers except a few advisors be sent to support the Arab Revolt he suddenly becomes popular and mocks Headquarters for this about-face. 'My popularity with the Staff in Egypt, due to the sudden help I had lent to Sir Archibald's prejudices, was novel and rather amusing. They began to be polite to me, and to say that I was observant, with a pungent style, and character. ... I was hugely amused, inwardly, and promised to be good ...' (*SP*, pp.114-15).

When Lewis the Australian thinks he is better than the Arabs because of his skin colour, Lawrence remarks that 'It added humour to the situation that he was browner by far than my new followers ...' (*SP*, p.354), and he delights in using his Arab dress to confound the routine and subconscious racialism of the military police:

'A mixed body of Egyptian and British military police came round the train, interrogating us and scrutinizing our passes. It was proper to make war on permit-men, so I replied crisply in fluent English, "Sherif of Mecca — Staff", to their Arabic inquiries. They were astonished. The sergeant begged my pardon: he had not expected to hear... . They looked at my bare feet, white silk robes and gold head-rope and dagger. Impossible!' (*SP*, p.327)

On the whole, Arab authority fares no better than British. Lawrence parodies Auda's epic style (*SP*, pp.285-87) to his tribe's amusement, and at Aba el Lissan tells Auda that his tribe shoots a lot but hits a little. Sherif Hussein, Feisal's father, portrayed as an obstinate old man lacking in humour, never realizes that Lawrence doctors his telegrams to Feisal to make them more acceptable. By contrast, Feisal has a fine sense of the comic which Lawrence portrays as quiet wit. When Lawrence retouches Sherif Hussein's telegrams, Feisal, knowing this, gently remarks that his father's apology (forged by Lawrence) has 'saved all our honour' but then corrects this to 'I mean the honour of nearly all of us' (*SP*, p.598), referring to Lawrence.

Often, Lawrence uses humour seriously and ironically to ease the passage of painful events. When the bedouin cut a shepherd across the soles of his feet to prevent his running to the Turks with information about their whereabouts, Lawrence comments 'Odd as was the performance, it seemed effective, and more merciful than death' but that the shepherd's 'gratitude was not coherent' (*SP*, p.300). In the Turkish military hospital in Damascus, Lawrence finds that decomposing bodies look grotesquely funny:'Many were already swollen twice or thrice life-width, their fat heads laughing with black mouth across jaws harsh with stubble' (*SP*, p.677). His humour here has become surrealistic and, as in many Gothic works, mixes the macabre with the comic. When the Bey at Deraa, whose homosexual intentions have been repulsed by Lawrence, pulls out a bayonet, Lawrence comments calmly 'I thought he was going to kill me, and was sorry' (*SP*, p.452). For Lawrence grim humour has become a survival tool.

The failure of his detractors to understand the value of irony as a means of distancing the mind from unpleasantness has led them sometimes to charge Lawrence with sadism or a failure to appreciate the suffering of others. Few, if any, see Lawrence as an early twentieth-century practitioner of the art of black humour, which seeks to make us laugh at genuine horrors as a means of keeping them at bay.

The absurdity of Lawrence's whole situation as he saw it is summarized with good humour in the scene at Isawiya in which he feasts with the Abu Tayi tribe:

'Oxford or Medina had tried to cure Nasir and me of superstitious prejudice; and had complicated us to the point of regaining simplicity. These people were achieving in our cause the height of nomadic ambition, a continued orgy of seethed mutton. My heaven might have been a lonely, soft arm-chair, a book-rest, and the complete poets, set in Caslon, printed on tough paper: but I had been for twenty-eight years well-fed, and if Arab imagination ran on food-bowls, so much the more attainable their joy' (*SP*, p.278).

Neither the Western nor the bedouin 'ideal of bliss' is exalted here at the expense of the other; rather they exist in a wise balance.

Calm balance is not often found in *Seven Pillars*: there would be even less of it without Lawrence's comic touches. He was not and could not present himself as a simple unified personality and in the chapter 'Myself' he does not mention his sense of humour at all, preferring to dwell on his darker qualities. Yet at the end of the book we remember not only the tortured self-questioning Lawrence but the young high-spirited captain always ready to mock himself, authority and the necessary terrors through which he passed.

True to the divisions in his self-portrait, Lawrence never believed with a whole heart that his book was any good. He called it the 'mangy skin' of his will, 'dried, stuffed and set up squarely for men to stare at' (*SP*, p.581) — in a metaphor possibly inspired by Michelangelo, who depicted himself in the Sistine Chapel as a flayed skin. Yet, like Michelangelo's strange self-portrait, Lawrence's is still very much with us.

The Mint

The Mint, composed between 1922 and 1928 but not made publicly available until 1955, tells the story of Lawrence's life as a private in the RAF from the time of his enlistment through his experiences in Cadet College. The book has had its advocates, including E.M. Forster and David and Edward Garnett, and its critics — among whom L.P. Hartley and V.S. Pritchett are prominent. Its subject cannot match the political, military and cross-cultural interest of the Arab Revolt and Lawrence's many trials during that period, nor is its prose as exciting as that of *Seven Pillars*. Yet the interest of Lawrence's character remains in *The Mint* and the book shows his development as an artist.

Its clipped style and brief, abrupt chapters remind one of the photographs that Lawrence studied at the RAF photography school at Farnborough. It seems like a very artistic documentary film, and may be the first autobiography to attempt to compete with this medium, as in this passage of direct but sensitive visual and auditory description:

'Our sun-softened asphalt declines into a dusty gravel. Shuffle shuffle goes the loose crowd of us, past another gate. The wall gives place to park-paling and wire: there are khaki men in the park, distant. A third gate.' (*M*, p.21)

Lawrence's movement from the highly-emotional late romantic style of *Seven Pillars* to *The Mint's* sharply-focussed twentieth-century realism reflects his continuing literary development and his attempt to remold himself in the 'mint' of the service and make himself into a rather more ordinary person. To a large degree he succeeds. He was later to comment in another context to John Buchan that 'You have in me a contented being, and no literature arises out of contentment' (*L*, p.736), a remark which can be applied to the picture of satisfaction that he gives in 'Service', the final Part 3 of *The Mint*. This section strikes many readers as too bland but it contains superb moments, such as the description of the funeral of Queen Alexandra, which he had attended, and his motorcycle race with an aeroplane. The final scene in the book, in which Lawrence and his airmen companions utilize an unexpected respite from work for a welcome rest period, shows that he retained the ability to produce good if not great writing even from moods of unalloyed happiness:

'We were too utterly content to speak, drugged with an absorption fathoms deeper than physical contentment. Just we lay there spread-eagled in a mesh of bodies, pillowed on one another and sighing in happy excess of relaxation. The sun-light poured from the sky and melted into our tissues. From the turf below our moist backs there came up a sister-heat which joined us to it. ... Everywhere a relationship: no loneliness any more.' (*M*, pp.205-6)

In passages like this, Lawrence convinces us that in his later years in the RAF he was frequently able to still his mind and to find the companionship that was available in no other way to a self-questioning intellectual like himself.

Yet he was certainly not without mental and physical torments in the RAF, especially during the early years. *The Mint's* first two parts, 'The Raw Material and 'In the Mill', vividly portray much of this suffering in realistic detail:

'Again unlucky. I've been picked for kitchen fatigue which we know by experience to be the worst, after shit-cart, of our drudgeries. ... Kitcheners crawl out of bed into overalls and go straight over at the dark reveille, unwashed, to work till the guard have had their suppers after seven at night. These are long hours, and the tepid dishwater: the smooth evil of grease: the having to hump great quarters of chilled beef, smelling like corpses, from meat lorry to cutting bench: the inevitable sodding of hands, and hair and clothes with a reek which will cling to them for days ...' (*M*, p.84)

Of his flagellation, we are now aware. In *Seven Pillars*, Lawrence had admitted his feeling of sexual pleasure after the beating in Deraa, and (especially in the 1922 'Oxford' version) had hinted at its lingering shadow. But in *The Mint*, which concerns the period during which his flogging compulsion was active, he never refers to the matter at all (although his obsession with self-degradation is apparent). Neither does he explain why he joined the RAF as a simple aircraftman. Lawrence probably could not satisfy himself as to the reasons for his enlistment in the ranks any more than he could have explained his need for humiliation, and has bequeathed these questions to his interpreters. *The Mint* thus contains an element of Lawrence's ultimate unknowability that makes it a suitable

A photograph taken at Miranshah in December 1928, which shows, left to right, Corporal A.G. Stone, Aircraftman H.G. Hayter, Lawrence and Corporal J.W. Easton. Easton later wrote of Lawrence, 'Although I saw him every day in my wireless cabin, and talked to him, I never pressed him to have his photo taken even in the group before they left Miranshah.' Stone later wrote of Lawrence that 'He spent most of his spare time translating Homer for a publisher and he told me he was being paid a penny a word.'

coda to his first mysterious self-portrait. In his depiction of himself in *Seven Pillars of Wisdom* and to a lesser degree in *The Mint*, Lawrence created one of the most complex and intriguing characters in all literature.

In Conclusion

In 1817, John Keats wrote that the essential quality of genius was 'Negative Capability' the ability to hold contradictory ideas in the mind at once, to live with doubt and mystery, and not to need certainties. Like few others, T.E. Lawrence possessed this capacity: he subscribed to few orthodoxies of his day and embraced the unusual. He could befriend both Arab and Jew, respect bedouin nomads as much as British lords, serve equally well as a colonel and as a private, ride motorcycles and camels, and design books as well as boats. He was not afraid of following his own logic wherever it took him. He feared only his own sexual desires.

Such a life put him into conflict with some of the major forces of his period. Like more than one genius, he was in constant tension with conventional ideas of how he should think and behave, whether posited by regular officers, politicians or other writers. The problem was not his but theirs, for they needed the narrow certainty that he could do without. Many of Lawrence's biographers, too, have been limited to one perspective which they have attempted to impose upon a man who had several: for them he had to be either a superhero or an antihero. In this hundredth year since his birth it appears that he was both. He was also extremely talented in many fields, which is why his life can be continually reinterpreted in terms that each period and individual onlooker can understand.

By the time of the next centenary, many more Lawrence biographies will have been published. Yet as each biography supersedes the last, as each interpretation of his character illuminates it for a few moments and then joins its predecessors in the shadows of greater or lesser obscurity, Lawrence's achievements and his self-portrait in letters and books — witty, brilliant, and ever ambiguous — will remain permanently in the limelight.

End: Portrait of Lawrence by R.G. Sims, Hornsea, Yorkshire, February 1935.

Chronological List of Photographs

Notes

For a full description of the books and dissertations listed below see the Bibliography

1 20 March 1920 to E.L. Greenhill; in the Harry Ransom Humanities Research Center, University of Texas
2 See Charles Grosvenor, in *T.E. Lawrence Puzzle*, ed. Tabachnick (hereafter *TELP*), pp.159-84; see also J.M. Wilson, 'T.E. Lawrence and the Printing of *Seven Pillars of Wisdom*', *Matrix*, 5,5 (Winter 1985), pp.55-69; and A.J. Plotke, 'Eric Kennington and *Seven Pillars of Wisdom*: A Reassessment', *Biography*, 7,2 (Spring 1984), pp.169-81
3 Philip O'Brien, in *TELP*, p.294
4 Ronald Blythe, *The Age of Illusion*, p.63
5 R.P. Graves, *Robert Graves*, p.223
6 Lawrence, in *T.E. Lawrence to His Biographers*, pp.1:138-39
7 Published in America as *Colonel Lawrence: The Man Behind the Legend* (New York: Dodd, Mead, 1934)
8 (London) *Evening Standard*, 16 January 1937
9 Philip Knightley, 'Aldington's Enquiry Concerning T.E. Lawrence', *Texas Quarterly*, 16,4 (Winter 1973), pp.98-105
10 Stephen Spender, 'Interview', *Paris Review* (Winter-Spring 1980), p.50
11 Knightley and Simpson, *Secret Lives*, p.102
12 Gera, in *TELP*, p.213
13 Ibid., pp.213-14
14 Fedden and Thomson, *Crusader Castles*, p.94. See also M.Allen, in *TELP*, pp.57-58
15 Fedden and Thomson, p.41
16 Smail, *Crusading Warfare*, pp.226, 240

17 Boase, *Castles and Churches*, p.49
18 Kedar and Pringle, 'La Fève: A Crusader Castle in the Jezreel Valley', *Israel Exploration Journal*, 35 (1985), pp.175-76
19 Garstang, *Hittite Empire*, p.282
20 Gurney, *The Hittites*, p.8
21 Güterbock, 'Carchemish', *Journal of Near Eastern Studies*, 13 (1954), p.114
22 Barnett, letter to the *Times Literary Supplement*, 16 October 1969, pp.1210-11
23 Moorey, *Cemeteries*, pp.3-4
24 Silberman, *Digging for God and Country*, pp.119-23
25 Ibid., p.191
26 Benjamin Isaac, 'Bandits in Judaea and Arabia', *Harvard Studies in Classical Philology*, 88 (1984), p.197.
27 Cohen, 'Did I Excavate Kadesh-Barnea?', *Biblical Archaeology Review* (May/June 1971), p.23
28 Woolley, 'The Desert of the Wanderings', *Palestine Exploration Fund Quarterly Statement* (1914), pp.65-66
29 Cohen, 'The Iron Age Fortresses in the Central Negev', *American Schools of Oriental Research Bulletin*, 236 (Fall 1979), p.61
30 Cohen, 'New Light on the Date of the Petra-Gaza Road', *Biblical Archaeology*, 45, 4 (Fall 1982), p.245
31 Glueck, *Rivers in the Desert*, pp.33-35
32 Cohen, 'Iron Age Fortresses', p.75
33 Negev, in the *Encyclopedia of Archaeological Excavations in the Holy Land*, ed. Avi-Yonah and Stern, p.4:1117; see also Baruch Brimer, 'Shivta — An Aerial Photographic Interpretation', *Israel Exploration Journal*, 31,3-4 (1981), p. 227
34 Kenyon, intro. to Woolley and Lawrence, *Wilderness of Zin* (1936 ed.), p.13
35 trans. S.E. Tabachnick from Segal, *Shivta*, p.9 [in Hebrew]
36 Kenyon, intro., pp.12-13
37 Glueck, *Rivers in the Desert*, p.12
38 Gera, in *TELP*, p.206
39 Bidwell, intro. in *Arab Bulletin*, p.1:ix
40 Woolley, *As I Seem to Remember*, p.93
41 Kimche, *Jerusalem Post*, 22 December 1984
42 Scoville, 'British Logistical Support to the Hashemites', pp.262-63
43 Quoted in Ibid., p. 155
44 Winstone, *Illicit Adventure*, p.180
45 Hogarth, *Life of Charles M. Doughty*, p.184
46 Tabachnick, ed. *Explorations in Doughty's 'Arabia Deserta'*, pp.38-39 (n. 39), 137
47 *San Diego Union* (California), 21 August 1986, p.D-9
48 Mousa, 'Arab Sources on Lawrence of Arabia: New Evidence', *Army Quarterly and Defence Journal*, 136 (April 1986), p.159
49 Gera, in *TELP*, pp.213-14
50 Quoted by Morsey, in *TELP*, p.199
51 Lawrence, in *Arab Bulletin*, 60 (August 20, 1917), pp.2:347-53

52 Gera, in *TELP*, p.209
53 Sykes, *Wassmuss*, p.13
54 Gera, in *TELP*, p.216
55 Seth, *Spies at Work*, p.154
56 Kiernan, *The Unveiling of Arabia*, p.303
57 von Sanders, *Five Years in Turkey*, p.145
58 Ibid., p.292
59 Scoville, 'British Logistical Support to the Hashemites', p.208
60 Kedourie, *The Chatham House Version*, pp.33-51
61 Kirkbride, *An Awakening*, p.6
62 Ibid., p.40
63 Ibid., p.49
64 Ibid., pp.95, 119, 118
65 Asprey, *War in the Shadows*, p.1:266
66 Gardner, *Allenby of Arabia*, p.203
67 Orgill, *Lawrence*, p.155
68 Collected in Weintraub and Weintraub, eds., *Evolution of a Revolt*
69 Wilkins, in *Modern Guerrilla Warfare*, ed. Osanka, pp.5-7
70 Hahlweg, *Guerrilla*, p.202 [in German]; quoted in Morsey, *TELP*, p.199
71 Bidwell, *Modern Warfare*, p.197
72 Reid, 'T.E. Lawrence and Liddell Hart', *History*, 70 (June 1985), pp.218-31
73 Gardner, *Allenby*, pp.269-70
74 Singh and Mei, *Theory and Practice of Modern Guerrilla Warfare*, pp.3-4
75 English, 'Kindergarten Soldier: The Military Thought of Lawrence of Arabia', *Military Affairs*, 51,1 (Jan. 1987), p.10
76 Cited by Morsey, in *TELP*, p.199
77 Fairbairn, *Revolutionary Warfare*, pp.152, 153
78 *Encylopaedia Brittanica* (1986), p.29:685

79 Kagramanov, 'Fact and Fiction about Lawrence of Arabia', *Novaia i noveishaia istoriia*, 6 (1971), pp.131-39 [in Russian]
80 Burton, '"Arranging the Minds of Men:" T.E. Lawrence as a Theorist of War', *Army Quarterly and Defence Journal* 106,1 (Jan. 1976), p.58
81 Arendt, *Origins of Totalitarianism*, p.218
82 Presgrove, 'Britain and the Middle East, 1914-1921', p.65
83 Mousa, *T.E. Lawrence*, p.239;'Arab Sources on Lawrence of Arabia', p.167
84 Philip Khoury, *Syria and the French Mandate*, pp. 616-17
85 Ibid., p.46
86 Howarth, *Desert King*, pp.112-13
87 Hogarth, 'Wahabism and British Interests', *Journal of the British Institute of International Affairs*, 4 (March 1925), p.72; see also Gary Troeller, 'Ibn Sa'ud and Sharif Husain: A Comparison in Importance in the Early Years of the First World War', *Historical Journal*, 14 (September 1971), pp.627-33 and Aaron S. Klieman, 'Britain's War Aims in the Middle East in 1915', *Journal of Contemporary History*, 3,3 (1968), pp.237-51
88 Sieff, *Memoirs*, p.113
89 Quoted in Klieman, in *TELP*, p.259
90 Uriel Dann, 'T.E. Lawrence in Amman, 1921', *Abr-Nahrain*, 13 (1972), p.40
91 Hogarth, 'Wahabism and British Interests', p. 72
92 Presgrove, 'Britain and the Middle East, 1914-1921', pp.278, 81
93 Klieman, in *TELP*, p.264

94 Mousa, in *Arabian Studies VII*, ed. Serjeant and Bidwell, p.20
95 Mousa, 'Arab Sources on Lawrence of Arabia', p.169
96 S. King, 'The British Successor States in the Post-War Middle East', p.432
97 Lawrence, in *The Essential T.E. Lawrence*, ed. Garnett, pp.300-301
98 Quoted in Mack, *A Prince of Our Disorder*, p.519 (n.33)
99 H. King, 'Another Lawrence', *Flight International Supplement* (24 Feb. 1966), pp.19-23
100 Desmond and Villa, *World Water Speed Record*, p.114
101 Ibid., p. 115
102 Letter of 24 June 1987 from C.C. Pearson, present Registrar of the Arab Horse Society, to the author
103 Bowra, intro. to Lawrence, *The Odyssey*, p.xvi
104 Notopoulos, 'The Tragic and the Epic in T.E. Lawrence', *Yale Review* (Spring 1965), pp.331-45
105 trans. S.E. Tabachnick from Larès, *T.E. Lawrence, la France et les Français*, p.334; for Lawrence and French writers, see also Louis Allen, 'French Intellectuals and T.E. Lawrence', *Durham University Journal*, 69,1 (1976), pp.52-66; and Virginia Cunningham, 'T.E. Lawrence and Malraux: 1929-46', *Mélanges Malraux Miscellany*, 16,1 (May 1984), 2-30
106 Michael Howard, *Jonathan Cape, Publisher*, p.88
107 See Tabachnick, *T.E. Lawrence*, pp.70-72, 102-103, 107-10
108 S. Weintraub, in *TELP*, p.291. See this article for an illuminating discussion of the fictional biographies of Lawrence across our century.
109 Meyers, *Wounded Spirit*, p.11
110 Hull, in *TELP*, p.110

Bibliography

Bibliography of Books and Dissertations
Articles are referenced in the Notes only

Adam, Colin Forbes. *The Life of Lord Lloyd*. London: Macmillan, 1948
Adelson, Roger. *Mark Sykes: Portrait of an Amateur*. London: Jonathan Cape, 1975
Aldington, Richard. *Lawrence of Arabia: A Biographical Enquiry*. New York: Henry Regnery, 1955; London: Collins, 1969
Antonius, George. *The Arab Awakening*. London: Hamish Hamilton, 1938
Archer, Sir Geoffrey. *Personal and Historical Memoirs of an East African Administrator*. Edinburgh: Oliver & Boyd, 1963
Arendt, Hannah. *The Origins of Totalitarianism*. Cleveland: World, 1962
Armitage, Flora. *The Desert and the Stars*. New York: Holt, 1955; London: Faber, 1956
Asprey, Robert. *War in the Shadows: The Guerrilla in History*. 2 vols. Garden City: Doubleday, 1975
Avi-Yonah, Michael and Ephraim Stern, eds. *The Encyclopedia of Archaeology in the Holy Land*. 4 vols. Englewood Cliffs: Prentice-Hall, 1978
Baker, Randall. *King Husain and the Kingdom of Hejaz*. Cambridge: Oleander, 1979
Benoist-Méchin, Jacques. *Lawrence d'Arabie, ou le rêve fracassé*. Paris: Perrin, 1979
Béraud-Villars, Jean. *T.E. Lawrence, or the Search for the Absolute*. First pub. 1955. London: Sidgwick and Jackson, 1958
Bidwell, Robin, ed. *The Arab Bulletin*. 4 vols. Gerrards Cross: Archive Editions, 1986
Bidwell, Shelford. *Modern Warfare*. London: Allen Lane, 1973
Blackmore, Charles. *In the Footsteps of Lawrence of Arabia*. London: Harrap, 1986
Blythe, Ronald. *The Age of Illusion: England in the Twenties and Thirties 1919-1940*. London: Hamish Hamilton, 1963
Boase, T.S.R. *Castles and Churches of the Crusading Kingdom*. London and New York: Oxford University Press, 1967
Booker, Christopher. *The Neophiliacs*. Boston: Gambit, 1970
Boussard, Léon. *Le Secret du colonel Lawrence*. Clement-Ferrand: Mont-Louis, 1941
Bray, N.N.E. *A Paladin of Arabia*. London: John Heritage, 1936
Brémond, Édouard. *Le Hedjaz dans la guerre mondiale*. Paris: Payot, 1931
Broderick, Houghton. *Near to Greatness*. London: Hutchison, 1965
Desmond, Kevin and Leo Villa. *The World Water Speed Record*. London: Batsford, 1976
Eden, Matthew. *The Murder of Lawrence of Arabia*. London: New English Library, 1980
Edmonds, Charles [C.E. Carrington]. *T.E. Lawrence*. London: Peter Davies, 1935.
Fairbairn, Geoffrey. *Revolutionary Warfare and Communist Strategy*. London: Faber and Faber, 1968
Fedden, Robin and John Thomson. *Crusader Castles*. London: Murray, 1957
Finlay, John. *A Pilgrim in Arabia*. New York: Scribner's, 1919
Flecker, James Elroy. *Some Letters from Abroad of James Elroy Flecker*. London: Heinemann, 1930.
Gardner, Brian. *Allenby of Arabia: Lawrence's General*. New York: Coward-McCann, 1966
Garstang, John. *The Hittite Empire*. London: Constable, 1929
Gilbert, Martin. *Winston S. Churchill*. Volume 3; Volume 4; Companion Volume IV, Part 3. Boston: Houghton-Mifflin, 1971, 1975, 1978
Glueck, Nelson. *Rivers in the Desert*. New York: Farrar, Straus, 1959
Graves, Richard Perceval. *Lawrence of Arabia and His World*. London: Thames and Hudson, 1976
Graves, Richard Perceval. *Robert Graves, 1895-1926*. London: Weidenfeld and Nicolson, 1986
Graves, Robert. *Lawrence and the Arabs*. London: Cape, 1927
Graves, Robert. *T.E. Lawrence to His Biographers Robert Graves and Liddell Hart*. First pub. 1938. New York:

Doubleday, 1963

Gurney, O.R. *The Hittites*. First pub. 1952. Baltimore: Pelican, 1966

Hahlweg, Werner. *Guerrilla: War Without Fronts*. Stuttgart: Kohlhammer, 1968 [in German]

Hammond, Philip C. *The Nabataeans — Their History, Culture and Archaeology*. Lund: Paul Astrom, 1973

Hewison, Robert. *In Anger: British Culture in the Cold War 1945–60*. New York: Oxford University Press, 1981

Hogarth, D.G. *The Life of Charles M. Doughty*. London Oxford University Press, 1928

Howard, Michael S. *Jonathan Cape, Publisher*. London: Jonathan Cape, 1971

Howarth, David. *The Desert King*. New York: McGraw-Hill, 1964

Jarché, James. *People I Have Shot*. London: Methuen, 1934

Kedourie, Elie. *The Chatham House Version*. New York: Holt, Rinehart and Winston, 1981

Khoury, Philip. *Syria and the French Mandate*. Princeton: Princeton University Press, 1987

Khoury, Philip. *Urban Notables and Arab Nationalism: The Politics of Damascus 1860–1920*. Cambridge: Cambridge University Press, 1983

Kiernan, R.H. *Lawrence of Arabia*. London: Harrap, 1935

Kiernan, R.H. *The Unveiling of Arabia*. London: Harrap, 1937

King, Stephen H. 'The British Successor States in the Post-War Middle East.' Ph.D. dissertation. Claremont Graduate School, 1978

Kirkbride, Alec. *An Awakening: The Arab Campaign 1917–1918*. London: University Press of Arabia, 1971

Knightley, Phillip and Colin Simpson. *The Secret Lives of Lawrence of Arabia*. London: Nelson, 1969

Larès, Maurice. *T.E. Lawrence, la France et les Français*. Paris: Imprimerie Nationale, 1980

Lawrence, A.W., ed. *T.E. Lawrence by His Friends*. London: Cape, 1937

Lawrence, D.H. *Lady Chatterley's Lover*. First pub. 1928. New York: Grove Press, 1962

Lawrence, D.H. *Studies in Classic American Literature*. First pub. 1921. Harmondsworth: Penguin, 1977

Lawrence, T.E. *Crusader Castles*. First pub. 1936. London: Michael Haag, 1986

Lawrence, T.E. *The Diary of T.E. Lawrence MCMXI*. N.p.: Corvinus Press, 1937

Lawrence, T.E. *Evolution of a Revolt: Early Postwar Writings of T.E. Lawrence*. Edited by Stanley and Rodelle Weintraub. University Park: Pennsylvania State University Press, 1968

Lawrence, T.E. translator. *The Forest Giant* by Adrian Le Corbeau. London: Jonathan Cape, 1924

Lawrence, T.E. *The Home Letters of T.E. Lawrence and His Brothers*. Edited by M.R. Lawrence. Oxford: Basil Blackwell, 1954

Lawrence, T.E. *The Letters of T.E. Lawrence*. Edited by David Garnett. London: Jonathan Cape, 1938

Lawrence, T.E. *The Mint*. First pub. 1955. London: Jonathan Cape, 1973

Lawrence, T.E. translator. *The Odyssey of Homer*. First pub. 1932. London: Oxford University Press, 1955

Lawrence, T.E. *Oriental Assembly*. Edited by A.W. Lawrence. London: Williams and Norgate, 1939

Lawrence, T.E. *Secret Despatches from Arabia*. Edited by A.W. Lawrence. London: Golden Cockerell Press, 1939

Lawrence, T.E. *Seven Pillars of Wisdom*. Privately printed 1926. First pub. 1935. London: Jonathan Cape, 1939–73; Harmondsworth: Penguin, 1962-87

Lawrence, T.E. and C. Leonard Woolley. *The Wilderness of Zin*. First pub. 1915. New York: Scribner's, 1936

Lawrence, T.E., D.G. Hogarth, C. Leonard Woolley and P.L.O. Guy. *Carchemish: A Report on the Excavations at Djerabis*. 3 vols. London: British Museum, 1914, 1921, 1952

Levin, Bernard. *The Pendulum Years: Britain and the Sixties*. London: Jonathan Cape, 1971

Liddell Hart, B.H. *'T.E. Lawrence': In Arabia and After*. London: Jonathan Cape, 1934

Liddell Hart, B.H. *T.E. Lawrence to His Biographers Robert Graves and Liddell Hart*. First pub. 1938. Garden City: Doubleday, 1963

Lönnroth, Erik. *Lawrence of Arabia*. First pub. 1943. London: Vallentine, Mitchell, 1956

Mack, John. *A Prince of Our Disorder: The Life of T.E. Lawrence*. London: Weidenfeld and Nicolson, 1976

Macphail, Andrew. *Three Persons*. London: Murray, 1929

Malraux, André. *The Walnut Trees of Altenburg*. London: J. Lehmann, 1952

Marwick, Arthur. *British Society Since 1945*. Harmondsworth: Penguin, 1982

Meinertzhagen, Richard. *Middle East Diary: 1917-1956*. London: Cresset, 1959.

Meulenijzer, Victor. *Le colonel Lawrence, agent de l'Intelligence Service*. Bruxelles: Editions Rex, 1939

Meyers, Jeffrey, ed. *The Craft of Literary Biography*. London: Macmillan, 1985

Meyers, Jeffrey. *The Wounded Spirit: A Study of 'Seven Pillars of Wisdom'*. London: Martin Brian and O'Keeffe, 1973

Montgomery Hyde, H. *Solitary in the Ranks: Lawrence of Arabia as Airman and Private Soldier*. London: Constable, 1977

Monteil, Vincent Mansour. *Le Lévrier fatal*. Paris: Hachette, 1987

Moorey, P.R.S. *Cemeteries of the First Millenium B.C. at Deve Hüyük, near Carchemish, Salvaged by T.E. Lawrence and C.L. Woolley in 1913*. Oxford: British Archaeological Reports, 1980.

Morsey, Konrad. *T.E. Lawrence und der arabische Aufstand 1916/18*. Osnabrück: Biblio, 1976.

Mousa, Suleiman. *T.E. Lawrence: An Arab View*. First pub. 1962. London and New York: Oxford University Press, 1966

Mrazek, James A. *The Art of Winning Wars*. New York: Walker, 1968

Nutting, Anthony. *Lawrence of Arabia: The Man and the Motive*. London: Hollis and Carter, 1961

O'Brien, Philip. *T.E. Lawrence: A Bibliography*. Winchester: St. Paul's, 1988

Ocampo, Victoria. *338171 T.E.*. First pub. 1942. London: Gollancz, 1963

O'Donnell, Thomas. *The Confessions of T.E. Lawrence*. Athens: Ohio University Press, 1979

Orgill, Douglas. *Lawrence*. New York: Ballantine, 1973

Osanka, Franklin, ed. *Modern Guerrilla Warfare*. New York: Free Press of Glencoe, 1962

Presgrove, Barbara Ann. 'Britain and the Middle East, 1914-1921: A Study in Personal Policy-Making.' Ph.D. dissertation. Florida State University, 1979

Rattigan, Terence. *Ross*. London: Hamish Hamilton, 1960

Read, Herbert. *A Coat of Many Colours*. London: Routledge, 1945

Rich, Barbara. *No Decency Left*. London: Jonathan Cape, 1932

Richards, Jeffrey and Anthony Aldgate. *British Cinema and Society 1930-1970*. Totowa: Barnes & Noble, 1983

Richards, Vyvyan. *Portrait of T.E. Lawrence*. London: Cape, 1936

Richards, Vyvyan. *T.E. Lawrence*. London: Duckworth, 1939

Robinson, Edward. *Lawrence: The Story of His Life*. London: Oxford University Press, 1935.

Robinson, Edward. *Lawrence the Rebel*. London: Lincolns-Praeger, 1946

Scheyer, Amram. *Lawrence: The Revolt in the Desert and Afterward*. Tel Aviv: Workers' Library, 1972 [in Hebrew]

Scoville, Sheila Ann. 'British Logistical Support to the Hashemites of Hejaz: Ta'if to Ma'an 1916-1918.' Ph.D. dissertation. University of California, Los Angeles, 1982

Segal, Arthur. *Shivta: Portrait of a Byzantine City in the Negev Desert*. Haifa: University of Haifa Press, 1986 [in Hebrew]

Serjeant, R.B. and R.L. Bidwell, eds. *Arabian Studies VII*. London: Scorpion, 1985

Seth, Ronald. *Spies at Work: A History of Espionage*. New York: Philosophical Library, 1954

Sherwood, John. *No Golden Road*. London: Heinemann, 1973

Shotwell, James T. *At the Peace Conference*. New York: Macmillan, 1937

Sieff, Israel. *Memoirs*. London: Weidenfeld and Nicolson, 1970

Silberman, Neil Asher. *Digging for God and Country: Exploration, Archeology, and the Secret Struggle for the Holy Land, 1799-1917*. New York: Knopf, 1982

Singh, Baljit and Ko-Wang Mei. *Theory and Practice of Guerrilla Warfare*. London: Asia Publishing House, 1971

Sjersted, Georg. *Lawrence og Hans Arabere*. Oslo: Aschehoug, 1936

Smail, R.C. *Crusading Warfare*. Cambridge: Cambridge University Press, 1956

Smith, Clare Sydney. *The Golden Reign*. London: Cassell, 1940

Stéphane, Roger [Roger Worms]. *Portrait de l'Aventurier*. Paris: Le Sagittaire, 1940

Stéphane, Roger. *T.E. Lawrence*. Paris: Gallimard, 1960

Stewart, Desmond. *T.E. Lawrence*. London: Hamish Hamilton, 1977

Stirling, W.F. *Safety Last*. London: Hollis and Carter, 1953

Sykes, Christopher. *Wassmuss: 'The German Lawrence'*. New York and London: Longmans, Green, 1936

Tabachnick, Stephen E. *Charles Doughty*. Boston: Twayne, 1981

Tabachnick, Stephen E., ed. *Explorations in Doughty's 'Arabia Deserta'*. Athens and London: University of Georgia Press, 1987

Tabachnick, Stephen E. *T.E. Lawrence*. Boston: Twayne, 1978

Tabachnick, Stephen E., ed. *The T.E. Lawrence Puzzle*. Athens: University of Georgia Press, 1984

Thomas, Bertram. *Arabia Felix*. London: Jonathan Cape, 1932

Thomas, Lowell. *With Lawrence in Arabia*. New York: Garden City Publishing, 1924; Garden City: Doubleday, 1967

Tibawi, A.L. *Arabic and Islamic Themes*. London: Luzac, 1976

Umari, Subhi al-. *Lawrence As I Knew Him*. Beirut: al-Nahar, 1969 [in Arabic]

von Sanders, Liman. *Five Years in Turkey*. Annapolis: United States Naval Institute, 1927

Weintraub, Stanley. *Private Shaw and Public Shaw*. New York: Braziller, 1963

Weldon, L.B. *"Hard Lying"*. London: Herbert Jenkins, 1925

Wilson, Colin. *The Outsider*. Boston: Houghton Mifflin, 1956

Wilson, Jeremy. *Lawrence of Arabia: The Authorised Biography of T.E. Lawrence*. London: Heinemann, 1988

Winstone, H.V.F., ed. *The Diaries of Parker Pasha*. London: Quartet, 1983

Winstone, H.V.F. *The Illicit Adventure*. London: Jonathan Cape, 1982

Woolley, C. Leonard. *As I Seem to Remember*. London: Allen and Unwin, 1962

Woolley, C. Leonard. *Dead Towns and Living Men*. London: Humphrey Milford, 1920

Yardley, Michael. *Backing into the Limelight*. London: Harrap, 1985

Young, Hubert. *The Independent Arab*. London: Murray, 1933

Index